SINJAR

14 Days that Saved the Yazidis from Islamic State

SUSAN SHAND

Guilford, Connecticut

An imprint of The Rowman & Littlefield Publishing Group, Inc.
4501 Forbes Blvd., Ste. 200
Lanham, MD 20706

Distributed by NATIONAL BOOK NETWORK

British Library Cataloguing in Publication Information available

Library of Congress Cataloging-in-Publication Data available

ISBN 978-1-4930-3365-2 (hardcover)
ISBN 978-1-4930-3366-9 (e-book)

∞™ The paper used in this publication meets the minimum requirements of American National Standard for Information Sciences—Permanence of Paper for Printed Library Materials, ANSI/ NISO Z39.48-1992.

Printed in the United States of America

[Yazidis] devotion to their religion is no less than that of the Jews; and I know of no instance of a person of full age renouncing his faith. They invariably prefer death, and submit with resignation to the tortures inflicted on them.

AUSTEN HENRY LAYARD
NINEVEH AND ITS REMAINS: WITH AN ACCOUNT OF A VISIT TO THE CHALDEAN CHRISTIANS OF KURDISTAN, AND THE YEZIDIS, OR DEVIL-WORSHIPPERS; AND AN ENQUIRY INTO THE MANNERS AND ARTS OF THE ANCIENT ASSYRIANS. LONDON 1848

CONTENTS

INTRODUCTION

In August of 2014, I was working as a television producer in the Kurdish Service of the Voice of America when the events outlined in this book unfolded. During those emotional days, I had the privilege of observing my colleague, now friend, Dakhil Shammo, balance the demands of his profession with his heartfelt responsibility to advocate on behalf of his people, the Yazidis of Sinjar. Sinjar is a city and mountain in northern Iraq and the ancestral home of the ancient Yazidi people. After an attack by Islamic State, nearly fifty thousand Yazidis fled to the top of the barren mountain without water or food. Reporting on their plight while tracking the whereabouts of his mother, sister, brothers, aunts, uncles, nieces, nephews, hundreds of friends, and former colleagues required an extraordinary dedication and commitment to journalism. Shammo, however, demanded more of himself, taking on the Herculean task of penetrating the Washington, DC, federal bureaucracy to appeal for action to thwart an evident genocide.

Five days after the Islamic State invasion of the Sinjar region, the first American bombs fell around the base of Mount Sinjar. The US airstrikes, ordered by a president who was loath to engage with Iraq, destroyed Islamic State's positions around Mount Sinjar, which allowed the fifty thousand Yazidis to flee into Syria and evade certain death on the mountaintop. As a civil servant and a longtime Washingtonian, who well understands that nothing happens quickly in this town, I was stunned by the rapid American response to both the military threat and the unfolding humanitarian disaster. How was it possible that the greatest military might in the world could rally so quickly on behalf of an obscure people without influence or power?

The story I have recounted in this book answers that question: by the actions of average, determined Americans, some in government, some not, who demanded the Obama Administration abide by its stated principle that the prevention of mass atrocities and genocide is in the "core national security interest" and is a "core moral responsibility" of the United States.

Furthermore, the efforts of Dakhil Shammo and the other Yazidi immigrants, some of whom had been translators for the US Army during the Iraq War, to galvanize the US government to save their people emerged from their profound belief in American exceptionalism. Their sincere appeal, seemingly naïve now as the United States retreats from its global leadership position, stirred every politician, civil servant, Foreign Service officer, and military officer they contacted. "If not America, then who?" they asked.

In 2015 and 2016, I made several trips to Kurdistan to record the stories of the Yazidis who survived the Islamic State incursion. More than 360,000 lived in heavy cotton tents or small metal caravans in mud-laden camps for Internally Displaced People (IDP) on the outskirts of Erbil, the Kurdistan capital, or Dohuk, a city to the north. Those flimsy and weather-beaten structures were customized with rugs, portable air conditioners, and small washing machines, the household goods that represent permanence. The men were all unemployed, and the women, many recovering from sexual assault or other traumas, needed mental health services that were unavailable. There were four children for every adult, and education was haphazard. The despair was acute.

About ninety thousand Yazidis have emigrated since the autumn of 2014 for Australia, the United States, Germany, Canada, and other democracies. Nearly every Yazidi I interviewed said they wanted to leave Iraq, citing safety as the primary reason.

Within Iraq, the Yazidis have nowhere to go. Sinjar is in Ninewah Province, a disputed territory claimed by both Iraq and Kurdistan. Islamic State reduced Yazidi towns and cities to rubble, and neither the Iraqi government nor the Kurdistan government is making any effort to rebuild those communities.

During my time in Kurdistan, I had planned to interview Kurdish politicians and civil servants to piece together a narrative that might explain the failure of the Peshmerga, the Kurdish fighters, to protect the Yazidis from Islamic State, but I encountered myriad conspiracy theories presented as facts as well as impenetrable political spin from nearly every corner. In the end, I decided to present the betrayal of the Yazidis as just that—a betrayal, perhaps one of indifference, or perhaps one of bigotry. I tend to believe more in pervasive incompetence than conspiracy. I also decided to end my story just as the evidence of the kidnapping and brutal rapes of the Yazidi women was emerging, as other western journalists and several outspoken Yazidi women have begun to document this outrage.

In the course of reporting this book, I interviewed men and women from the US State Department, the US Agency for International Development, the US Army, the US House of Representatives, and the Voice of America as well as those who had put their lives at risk working for American forces in Iraq—all American citizens or on the road to citizenship. Each played a small, but crucial role in the actions that prevented the eradication of a people.

Genocide is a legal term as defined by the Convention on the Prevention and Punishment of the Crime of Genocide adopted by the United Nations in 1948. According to Article 2 of the Convention, it is "acts committed with the intent to destroy in whole or in part, a national, ethnical, racial or religious group."

These acts are defined as: (1) Killing members of a group; (2) Causing serious bodily harm or mental harm to members of the group; (3) Deliberately inflicting on the group conditions of life calculated to bring about its physical destruction, in whole or in part; (4) Imposing measures intended to prevent births within the group and; (5) Forcibly transferring children of the group to another group.

The crime of genocide is defined by the intent of the perpetrators, not by number of people killed.

On June 15, 2016, the Human Rights Council of the United Nations charged Islamic State with committing genocide against the Yazidi people.

"The public statements and conduct of ISIS and its fighters clearly demonstrate that ISIS intended to destroy the Yazidis of Sinjar, composing the majority of the world's Yazidi population, in whole or in part. While noting States' obligations under the Genocide Convention, the Commission repeated its call for the Security Council to refer urgently the situation in Syria to the International Criminal Court, or to establish an ad hoc tribunal with relevant geographic and temporal jurisdiction."

It is the first genocide charge from the United Nations in the twenty-first century.

Susan Shand
Washington, DC
December 2017

List of Participants

Haider al-Abadi—Prime Minister of Iraq since September 2014

Gen. Lloyd J. Austin III—US Army General, Commander, US Central Command

Masoud Barzani—President of the Iraqi Kurdistan Region (2005–2017)

Lt. Gen. John Michael Bednarek—Chief of the US Office of Security Cooperation in Iraq

Leanne Cannon—Foreign Service Officer, US Department of State, Office of International Religious Freedom (Washington, DC)

Hillary Clinton—Former Secretary of State, presidential candidate

Vian Dakhil—Yazidi Member of Parliament, Iraq

Alan Dwyer—Foreign Disaster Assistance Principal Regional Advisor for East Asia Pacific, United States Agency for International Development (USAID)

Haider Elias—Yazidi living in Houston. Former US Army translator, founding member of the Sinjar Crisis Management Team

Congressman Jeff Fortenberry—Republican representing Nebraska's First District, including Lincoln

Col. Charles "Chuck" Freeman—Senior Advisor, Northern Affairs, Office of Security Cooperation—Iraq

Chuck Hagel—Secretary of Defense

Ahmed Jaso—Kocho village leader or mayor

John Kerry—Secretary of State

Hussein Khalaf—Yazidi living in Virginia, Dakhil Shammo's life-long friend

Abu Hamza al-Khatuni— Iraqi Islamic State leader

Rear Adm. John Kirby—Pentagon Press Secretary

Nouri al-Maliki—Prime Minister of Iraq (2006–August 2014)

Fouad Massoum—Iraqi President (2014–)

Thomas Melia—Deputy Assistant Secretary of State in the Bureau of Democracy, Human Rights and Labor, US Department of State

Alifa Murad—Yazidi grandmother from village of Wardiyeh, Survivor of Mount Sinjar

    Daoud—her older son

    Nadira—Daoud's wife

    Jamil—her younger son

    Haval—her grandson

    Vian—her granddaughter

Abdullah Öcalan—Kurdish nationalist leader and one of the founding members of the Kurdistan Workers' Party. Imprisoned in Turkey since 1999.

Douglas Padgett, PhD, Department of State's Office of International Religious Freedom

Joseph Pennington—Consul General at the US Consulate General in Erbil, in the Iraqi Kurdistan Region 2013–2015, Deputy Assistant Secretary of State for Iraq

Hadi Pir—Yazidi living in Lincoln, Nebraska, former US Army translator, founding member of Sinjar Crisis Management Team

Ben Rhodes—Deputy National Security Advisor for Strategic Communications for President Barack Obama

Alissa Rubin—Reporter, the *New York Times*

Sarah Sewall—Under Secretary for Civilian Security, Democracy, and Human Rights, US Department of State

Dakhil Shammo—Yazidi living in Virginia, Reporter and Anchor, Voice of America

Morbad Shammo—Dakhil Shammo's wife

Hakim Shammo—Dakhil Shammo's son.

Abbas Kheder Silo—Yazidi survivor of the Siba massacre

Ali Abbas Smail—Yazidi survivor of the Kocho massacre

Khalaf Smoqi—Yazidi living in Lincoln, Nebraska, former US Army translator, founding member of Sinjar Crisis Management Team

William "Spence" Spencer—Executive Director of the Institute for International Law and Human Rights

Barakat Sulu—Yazidi from village of Tal Banat, survivor of Mount Sinjar

Nassir Sulu—wife of Barakat

CHAPTER ONE

Cries for Help

EARLY AUGUST EVENINGS IN 2014 WERE ODDLY COOL. IN THE WASH-ington, DC, suburb of Centreville, Virginia, the usual oppressive humidity had lifted abruptly at July's end. The pleasant night air flooded Hussein Khalaf with memories of childhood in the ancient Yazidi city of Sinjar. He had immigrated to the United States ten years earlier with his wife, and they reminisced about the sounds of summer evenings that rang through open windows on dusty streets as households prepared to sleep a half a century earlier. They lay in bed with the windows open, and fell asleep to the sound of the swaying leaves of the maple trees around their house. At three o'clock, Hussein's cellphone rang, and he fumbled for it on his bed stand.

"Daesh is attacking Sinjar," cried a voice.

"The Peshmerga have run. All are under attack. They are killing everyone!" his son said from his home in Germany.

"What do you mean? What is happening?" Hussein shouted. His wife jumped out of bed and stood beside him. "Daesh is in Sinjar," he shrieked at her, clutching the phone with his left hand and banging on the wall with his right. His wife cried out with anguish.

Hussein waited as his son sobbed into the phone. "I will call Qassim. He will know what is happening," he said and hung up. He called his cousin, Qassim Shesho, a renowned Peshmerga soldier who lived near Sinjar city.

"Daesh is in Sinjar," Qassim shouted, out of breath. "We are running to the mountain. Our brothers in the Peshmerga abandoned us."

By now Hussein's eight other grown children, who all lived in his house, were awake and stood holding each other in their parents' bedroom. Hussein called a cousin, Suliman, in Sinjar.

"They are coming. We are in our cars. We are trying to get to the mountain," Suliman said. In the background children screamed—Hussein's grandnieces and grandnephews. He pictured his extended family jammed into two cars. "Stay on the phone with me, Suliman," he begged. The screams heightened, and terror gripped Hussein by the throat.

"It's them. Daesh. They are coming for us," Suliman cried. The car engine cut off.

There was silence. Hussein's terror grew. The phone was still connected. Harsh male voices barked "Where are you going? Where did you get this car? Where are you from?" Suliman responded. "Don't hurt us. We are poor. We stole this car from the street near our house. We are nobody." Silence.

"Daesh has them," Hussein shrieked at his family.

Hussein recognized the sounds of children whimpering and their mothers' shushing. He looked around his bedroom and saw his own children frozen, clinging to each other, and his wife kneeling, unable to bear the weight of the scene borne over cell towers and satellites. Was it possible they were about to hear, from thousands of miles away, the murder of their family in Iraq?

"Get out of the cars. Out. Get out!" the Daesh soldier ordered.

Hussein heard Suliman scream. The phone went dead.

———

The destruction of a community of nearly a half million people by a mere several hundred, albeit well-armed, terrorist fighters, was underway. The unforeseen threat of Islamic State, lurking at its base in Raqqa, Syria, had emerged and moved in a direction no one had suspected.

In a multipronged invasion, they swooped down on the Sinjar district of Ninewah Province in northwestern Iraq, killing and abducting thousands of Yazidi men, women, and children. Nearly four hundred thousand Yazidis, members of a minority faith, lived in the region. They either fled or died.

The attack came from Mosul to the east, an Iraqi city Islamic State had taken two months earlier, from Tal Afar to the southeast, an Islamic State base, and west from Syria. With little resistance, Islamic State seized towns and villages on a rampage north to Sinjar, a city of ninety thousand that huddled at the bottom of the southeastern side of Mount Sinjar.

The few who owned cars or tractors drove north just ahead of the advancing Islamic State. The majority fled, running, walking, or hobbling through the desert plain. Tens of thousands of Yazidis sought refuge on Mount Sinjar, an arid, sixty-mile-long range that forms the heart of the region. Temperatures reached 120 degrees. Most of the Yazidis had little food or water. Hundreds died of dehydration and exhaustion.

Islamic State trapped thousands of others at makeshift checkpoints, where many men and older women were executed and young women and children were kidnapped.

It was, officially, the first genocide of the twenty-first century.

The annihilation of a community is rarely accomplished without the complicity of members of the community in which the victims live as well as the incompetence of their designated defenders. Yazidis say they were betrayed twice on that hot August day.

After hearing that Islamic State was on its way, more than eighteen thousand Peshmerga soldiers, members of the Kurdish defense forces assigned to protect the Yazidis, vanished. They abandoned their defensive posts throughout Ninewah in the predawn hours of August 3. Most of the defenders withdrew in organized convoys, taking their weapons. They did not engage the enemy. They did not organize an evacuation of civilians. They did not tell the sleeping Yazidis they were leaving. The Kurdish government denies this was a coordinated withdrawal. It blames this behavior on panic. For the Yazidis, it was an unprecedented betrayal.

The second betrayal occurred throughout the day. As Islamic State fighters massacred their way north, their ranks, which had started in the hundreds before dawn, multiplied into thousands. Those who toiled peacefully in the farmlands for decades along with the Yazidis, Sunni Muslim Arabs, donned the black clothing of Islamic State, and murdered and raped their neighbors.

—◆—

While Hussein and his family stood in their nightclothes, shattered by the merciless and unexpected imposition of violence, at exactly the same hour, more than twelve hundred miles away in the East Texas city of Houston, Haider Elias was awakened by a neighbor. He told the thirty-two-year old Yazidi refugee to go online immediately. "Your hometown is under attack," he said.

Elias called his sister in Sinjar. The line connected; screams filled his ear and he heard gunshots, but no voice. He called his younger brother, Falah, who lived near his sister. Falah shouted into the phone "I am helping two infants" and hung up.

He called his father. To his terror, an Islamic State soldier answered the phone. "Where is my father?" Elias asked. A callous, sneering voice replied that his father would soon face judgment in a holy court. Shaking with fear in the ever-present air-conditioning of a Texan home, Elias called his brother again.

"He did not answer the phone," Elias said. "Later, I learned from my sister that he was shot in the head, right in front of her eyes. She said that his phone was ringing when you were calling and he was dying. He was dying trying to hear your voice for the last time."

His sister had hidden a cellphone in the deep pockets of her skirt. Elias recalled her quavering voice as she explained Islamic State, also called Daesh in Iraq, had seized her while she fled and locked her into a closet-sized room with other young women in an unfamiliar building. She described the murders of their brother, Falah, and two cousins, who were randomly shot in the head as they fled from the advancing jihadists. Each word she spoke clubbed Elias like a pummel to the chest.

When the telephone line broke off, Elias stared at his phone as intolerable grief settled over him.

———

The chaos and brutality unleashed by Islamic State on the unsuspecting Yazidis was not random. It was, in fact, predetermined and precisely coordinated. Whether from a young mother, an elderly man or a child, the stories relayed by survivors to health workers and human rights activists are chillingly similar.

After corralling the panicked Yazidis into controllable groups, Islamic State fighters ordered the separation of males and females, with the exception of boys who appeared to be under ten. Since many of the Islamic State fighters were from Europe or Central Asia and did not speak Arabic or one of the Kurdish dialects, the men issuing the commands were usually local actors, former neighbors or friends of the Yazidis, which added to their demoralization and sense of helplessness.

Following the separation, Islamic State fighters drove or marched the men away from the women and children to a site where the men received an ultimatum: convert to Islam or die. Most chose death, although some did convert and were transferred to Mosul to perform manual labor.

Individual executions consisted of a bullet to the head. Islamic State made groups of men line up and stand while multiple fighters with automatic weapons gunned them down. This allowed a few men to survive by pretending to be dead. There were also random reports of beheadings. The executions occurred while Yazidis were fleeing on roadsides and as they were forcibly assembled in towns and villages, at checkpoints and, on the first day, at the base of Mount Sinjar.

Using trucks and buses brought from Mosul, Islamic State brought the women and children to holding sites in Tal Afar or Mosul, two Islamic State strongholds in Iraq. Within a few days, the fighters began methodically creating subsets of Yazidi captives. They separated married women from unmarried women. Girls over eight joined the unmarried women. Girls under eight stayed with their mothers. They singled out boys between seven and ten whom they eventually sent to a child soldier training camp in Raqqa, Syria. These specific selections happened at every initial holding facility.

Realizing virginity was their greatest vulnerability, unmarried women attempted to pretend their siblings, nieces, and nephews were their own children. For the most part this strategy failed when members of the local Arab community, working with Islamic State, entered the holding facilities to identify the unmarried women.

At the three main holding facilities—schools in Tal Afar, Badush prison in Mosul, and the Galaxy wedding hall in Mosul—Islamic State put together a registry of the women, recording their name, age, village, and marital status. These facilities at various times held hundreds or thousands of women and children, and were guarded by Islamic State fighters. The captives received little food or water. Infants and young children grew ill and died. The only medical attention Islamic State provided came from an Arab female doctor who examined the women for intact hymens.

Within a few days, the selections began. Yazidi women cowered in the corners of locked rooms as the fighters entered to select the woman or girl they wished to take. Islamic State sold 80 percent of the women and girls captured in Ninewah—called *sabaya* or slaves—to their fellow soldiers.

It was now dawn in the Virginia town of Centreville. Dakhil Shammo, a journalist with the Voice of America and a naturalized American citizen, awoke to the shouts of his family. Hunched over his computer scrolling through his Facebook newsfeed, Shammo's son Hakim yelled "Sinjar has been attacked by Islamic State." Shammo ran down the steps to the living room and looked over his son's shoulder as story after story popped up of the Islamic State's invasion of the land of his birth.

Stunned, Dakhil struggled to absorb the implausible information that the Peshmerga had withdrawn from its defensive positions throughout Ninewah Province, including the Yazidi city of Sinjar.

Dakhil called his brother Aziz, an employee of the Kurdish Regional Government, which administered northern Iraq's Kurdish region. Aziz was on his way to the Kurdish city of Erbil, driving southeast to join his wife and his son for dinner. His two daughters and another son were at home at their modest house in the tiny Yazidi village of Baadre Shekan, about one hundred miles east of Sinjar. Dakhil and Aziz's mother lived in an adjacent, crumbling villa, along with their disabled sister.

Aziz contradicted Dakhil and tried to assure him that the family was safe. "The Peshmerga are there. When I left, I told them to stay in their houses in Baadre. They will be fine."

"No," shouted Dakhil. "The Peshmerga have left. They have abandoned their stations. Mama and the others have to get out now."

Aziz slowed his car. Dakhil heard the gears shift as his brother turned his vehicle around and sensed the panic in his voice as he said, "I am going back to Baadre Shekan to get them. I will call you back."

Using his wife's cellphone to keep his own line open for calls from family, Dakhil called his longtime friend Hussein Khalaf a few miles away in Centreville, Virginia. Khalaf sobbed, heaving gasps of air, and recounted his own early morning phone call. "All of my family, gone, gone," he cried. "Daesh has them."

Tears flowed uncontrollably from Dakhil's eyes as the scope of the tragedy became clear. A heaviness settled over him, and he steeled himself for the suffering he knew from experience was coming. He comforted his friend until his own cellphone chimed again. Aziz was calling back.

"I am stuck at a checkpoint with thousands of cars. They won't let me through, Dakhil," he sobbed, "Mama isn't answering her phone. I can't get anyone on the phone."

His words were distorted, each one reverberating twice, and Dakhil could not make out where Aziz was trapped.

As images of Islamic State militants entering his mother's home flitted through his imagination, Dakhil alternated between rage and panic. He felt nauseated.

He hung up and began dialing his niece's phone while his wife and son tried calling the other family members in danger. Miraculously, his call connected.

"Get the car ready. Get food, water and blankets. Take all the money you have in the house. You have to run."

"No, we are safe," his sister responded.

"You must go. The Peshmerga have left," he screamed. "Go north. Go north to Zakho. When you get there, call me. I will arrange for a place. Get everyone in the car now."

Only after his niece promised to pack the car, find his mother and sister, and head north with them did Dakhil hang up. For the next few hours, all the cell towers in Sinjar were overloaded with calls, and he could not get through to anyone.

CHAPTER TWO

Before the Invasion

Iraq

Thousands of scholars and journalists have studied, analyzed, and published accounts of the recent history of Iraq, specifically the years following the invasion by the United States in 2003. In Washington, they claim a professional title among the political and media elite, Iraq Expert, a title that implies a command of even the most arcane details.

That expertise is not needed to understand the events of August 2014, and to appreciate the extraordinary actions of the key protagonists in this story. A compact review of a few crucial elements sets the scene.

In a simple way, Iraq is two ethnicities, Arab and Kurdish, mashed together by history into one country. The lower three-quarters of the country is ethnically Arab and Muslim, with the majority consisting of the more mainstream Shia branch of the Muslim faith. The conservative Sunni Muslims, despite being the minority, held all political and military power for decades as members of Saddam Hussein's Ba'ath party. They enjoyed power, privilege, and wealth; entitlements they lorded over their Shia brothers. Following the US invasion, the American occupiers fired Ba'ath party members from the government and military, leaving tens of thousands of young Sunni Muslim men unemployed and armed. Shia Muslims took control and pledged to share their newfound power.

But the first elected government of Prime Minister Nouri al-Maliki swiftly abandoned that pledge, and Sunni Muslims felt the boot of vengeful oppression. By 2006, Iraq fell into a cycle of violence based on religious persecution and revenge, Shia versus Sunni.

The Kurds, a separate ethnic group, predominate in the northern quarter of Iraq. Kurdistan, a quasi-independent state, is multireligious and includes Muslims, Christians, Yazidis and several other small faiths. Saddam Hussein despised the independent nature of the Kurdish people, who dreamed of their own state. In Iraq, he attacked them with chemical weapons and massacred tens of thousands. He bulldozed their villages and forced them into collective housing, while confiscating large tracts of the richest farmland that he handed over to Arab Sunni Muslims from the south who were living uneasily among the Kurds. Each community eyed the other with resentment, if not hatred.

Kurdistan welcomed the American invasion of 2003 and desired a long-term American presence in their region. Americans, they felt, guaranteed their security. However, as the war dragged on, the American public and the Iraqi government in Baghdad grew weary and said "enough," each demanding the pullout of American troops in 2011.

With the Americans gone, Iraq's security now depended on its national army, a body of men who were untested and galvanized primarily by the notion of a monthly salary. They would prove an unworthy opponent of Daesh, as Islamic State is referred to in Iraq.

Islamic State most likely knew of the national army's ineptitude. Its Lightning Offensive, begun June 6, 2014, was its initial large-scale movement on Iraq resulting in an effortless capture of the nation's second largest city, Mosul. From their base in Syria, Islamic State fighters pushed into central Iraq; the Iraqi army abandoned their posts and ran, leaving behind massive arsenals of American-supplied heavy weapons that were scooped up by the Islamic State conquerors.

In Baghdad, Prime Minister al-Maliki appeared stunned by the collapse of the army and the capture of Mosul. He had held on to the power he had obtained by an inconclusive election just a few months earlier. Isolated, arrogant, if not delusional, al-Maliki rejected calls from the United States, opposition parties, and many within his own party, to step down. He clung to power, paralyzing the government. Iraq teetered on the verge of collapse.

Islamic State was a mere two hundred miles from Baghdad and armed with millions of dollars of American weapons and technology.

A week into Islamic State's Lightning Offensive, US president Barack Obama ordered dozens of American forces to be dispatched to the region. A month later, he sent eight hundred additional troops to secure the US embassy in Baghdad and the US consulate in Erbil, the capital of Kurdistan. This was a painful decision for the Obama Administration, whose members were loath to commit more troops, believing the president had been elected with a mandate to end the war in Iraq.

However, the administration was aware of the furor they would face at home if Iraq collapsed and the American effort in the country had proved to be a pointless fiasco. The reintroduction of American forces continued to rise in the months and years ahead and eventually was named Operation Inherent Resolve.

The American troops' initial mission was to protect American diplomats and oil workers from the threat of an Islamic State march toward Iraq's largest cities. Sinjar city, in the middle of the Ninewah Province, was not a factor. No one in the Iraqi government or American government, or even in the city itself, imagined Sinjar could be considered an alluring target.

Ninewah Province lay just west of Mosul and was a disputed territory. Both the Kurdish government and Baghdad claimed ownership, each wanting to exploit the vast petroleum fields that lay beneath its rich agricultural lands. They squabbled over the protection of Ninewah, each wanting a larger military presence. When the Iraqi army collapsed in June, the Peshmerga, the collective name for the various and disparate Kurdish militias, filled the void. Deploying thousands of men into Ninewah, it established itself as the sole defense force for the region's population of three million.

Despite occasional shelling of villages in Ninewah, Islamic State appeared to be either uninterested in the area or deterred by the Peshmerga. The Yazidis and other Kurdish residents were not concerned about a possible invasion by Islamic State. They had an unquestioned faith in the guarantee of protection the Peshmerga provided as did the Yazidi-Kurdish diaspora in Europe and the United States. This faith was misplaced.

DAKHIL

As a young man, Dakhil Shammo grew accustomed to people calling him "devil-worshipper." He is a Yazidi whose religion worships a Peacock Angel called Melek Taus, a deity that the dominating Abrahamic faiths equate with the fallen angel Satan.

Yazidism is an ancient faith linked to Mesopotamian religions. It is not an ethnicity as Yazidis, like Christians in the region, are considered

Kurdish by Iraq's federal government. Yazidis have long been eyed with suspicion and fear, derided as purveyors of evil, enduring persecution and discrimination from their fellow Kurds, both Muslim and Christian.

Yet, Yazidism has thrived for centuries in the Kurdistan region of northern Iraq, secluded and protected from oppression in the remote mountainous region in and around Sinjar, their traditional capital city.

Like most of the world's three hundred thousand Yazidis, Dakhil's roots are there.

Yazidism is an oral religion and its followers believe their faith once dominated all life in the region before the Muslim invasion. Yazidis consider themselves God's original creation, but they did not chafe under the name Kurd.

When he found himself the only Yazidi among twenty Muslims in his small Washington, DC, office at the Voice of America, Dakhil was comfortable.

"My colleagues, for the most part, respect my faith," he said. "There have been a few jokes, but never anything cruel. Those days are over. Kurds now care about politics much more than religion. That is why we have not slaughtered each other like so many Muslim countries have done. We are all Kurds here at Voice of America."

From 1992 until 2012 the Kurdish Service of the Voice of America (VOA) broadcast three hours daily of international news via shortwave and medium-wave radio to Iraqi Kurds in their two dissimilar dialects, Kurmanji and Sorani. Dakhil and his colleagues translated reams of wire service copy, talked to stringers in the region, and, finally, broadcast the news live from one of the old radio studios that lined the interior walls of VOA.

The Voice of America, once the anti-Nazi and anti-Japanese radio propaganda machine of the 1940s War Department, reinvented itself during the postwar Cold War era. Broadcasting on radio waves behind the Iron Curtain, VOA flourished as a semi-legitimate news organization that often repelled attempts by successive US administrations to sway its reporting for political gain. But the collapse of the Soviet Union brought an abrupt end to its relevance. Ignored by Congress and hampered by ever-diminishing budgets, VOA struggled to adapt to the twenty-first century media environment. Consequently, when Facebook was leaping to the forefront of news distribution, VOA was still primarily a radio broadcaster. In this archaic setting, Dakhil Shammo saw an opportunity.

"It was so obvious. We were broadcasting on radio. Meanwhile everyone is watching the BBC and other news networks. We had to make the move to television," he said.

In 2012, Dakhil and two American colleagues crafted a fifteen-minute, weekly television program that presented international and Kurdish news in the two Kurdish dialects. Dakhil was anchor writer and producer of the program, called *Kurdish Connection*. Kurdish broadcaster NRT agreed to air the show and, within two years, Dakhil Shammo was a hometown celebrity. He interviewed prominent politicians, analysts, and Kurds from the Washington community, about issues of the region, including the aftermath of the American troop pullout, as well as the extraordinary economic growth in the Kurdish north of Iraq. He cultivated friendships and professional relationships among the think-tank policy wonks who hold court in restaurants and universities frequented by the DC political class. He learned to reach out to the Foreign Service officers at the State Department and to other civil servants in Homeland Security and the United States Agency for International Development (USAID).

Relentlessly charming on and off the air, Dakhil favors tailored suits and crisp white shirts on his compact body. Facing the camera with thinning hair and a distinct and well-groomed goatee, he has the alert and engaging eyes of a man born to the demands of television. Like a teenager, he clings to his smartphone, referring to it as a "holy relic." That phone, he says, holds thousands of important contact names and numbers. He claims to personally know every Yazidi in the world, or at the least to be related to him. This claim is quite possible. Yazidis have four tribes or castes and every man has designated "uncles" from the other castes, so it is common for large families with many sons to have forty or fifty "uncles."

Often while conversing, he politely lifts his hand to his mouth and raises one finger, smiling confidently, then says "just let me make one more point," or "but let me say why I disagree." He banters with passion with friends and relatives, debating the minutiae of Kurdish history, rarely mentioning his religion. Although his name clearly identifies him as a member of the ancient faith, Yazidis do not discuss it with nonbelievers. The tenets of the faith, along with its strict caste system and its rules for marriage and rituals, are private.

As a young writer for the Yazidi journal *Lalish Magazine* in the 1980s, he waited for the look of suspicion or fear of his Iraqi countrymen upon introducing himself as a Yazidi journalist. Even the more liberal-minded Kurdish Muslims of the region recoiled, less at the journalist part of the introduction than at the Yazidi one. Not only were Yazidis tainted by rumors of devil-worship, they were also targets of Saddam Hussein's hatred. Seeing little to be gained from association with Yazidis, merchants, cab drivers, and civil servants in Kurdistan and throughout Iraq avoided them. To compensate, Dakhil developed what seemed to be an effortless charm.

He spoke his native Kurmanji dialect at a clipped and quickened pace as if used to forestalling interruption. Early in conversation, he referenced his father, called only Shammo, a renowned fighter in the Kurdish Peshmerga. The reference, he hoped, would dispel the anxiety many Muslims feel in the presence of a Yazidi.

Like most of those who belong to small minority faiths and live among the millions of Muslims in Kurdistan, Yazidis are a rural people. Farmers and shepherds, they participate in the politics of their region with the same fervor as Muslim and Christian Kurds. Shammo's family were followers of the Kurdish leader Mustafa Barzani, a notoriously tough Peshmerga commander who defied the Ba'athists of Baghdad by turning to the Shah of Iran for weapons and financial support in his quest for independence from Iraq.

In 1974, however, Barzani's attempted revolt against Saddam Hussein collapsed and, under pressure, he fled to Iran with one hundred thousand followers. Shammo refused to flee. Instead, he took his wife and five children, including twelve-year-old Dakhil, up into Gara Mountain in the neighboring province of Dohuk where they hid in the caves and tunnels that snake through the craggy landscape.

"My older brother Shawaqi and I hiked around that mountain every day. We ran through its tunnels, suddenly blasting like a bullet from a small opening, and then on to a field to gather wild figs to bring home to our parents. For us, it was a grand adventure," he said.

For more than a year, the family evaded vengeful Ba'athists who hunted down Barzani's supporters and tortured and killed those they captured.

On the mountain, Dakhil helped his father slaughter mountain goats for food, and they bartered with some of the other thirty refugee families. They scraped a living out of that harsh landscape, a rocky mountainside covered in scrub. Winter often dropped more than two feet of hard-packed snow that stayed until early spring. In summer, the sun beat down mercilessly on the unprotected, and temperatures rose to triple digits.

On a frigid winter night, Dakhil's youngest sibling, a sister, Aya, was born in the cave. Swaddled too tightly against the cold, the pressure of the cloth binding forced her right eye to bulge from its socket for the rest of her life. His mother wept bitterly for her newborn until late spring when the advent of summer seemed to bring her some comfort.

When calm returned to the region in 1976, the family climbed down the moutain to find that the Yazidis had lost all their land, and that their villages had been bulldozed by Iraq's central government. The Shammos and thousands of Yazidi families were forced into collective communities on some of the undesirable rocky, infertile land in Ninewah. Desperate to support his family, Shammo traveled secretly, lest he be captured by Hussein's men, to Baghdad where he found work kneading bread dough at a bakery. The cash he sent home allowed his family to move to Baadre, a small Yazidi village that was never collectivized by Saddam Hussein. For years, Shammo lived quietly in Baghdad, sending home whatever money he earned, so his family would survive.

Putting aside his interest in writing and reporting, Dakhil studied auto mechanics in school to more easily find a job that would help support his family. In 1983, like all young Iraqi men during that time, he was drafted into the army at the height of the Iran/Iraq War. He was twenty years old.

It is impossible to overstate the impact the Iran/Iraq War had on the two nations. The barbarous conflict, fought from 1980 to 1988, has often been compared to World War I because of its outdated and deadly tactics. Large-scale trench warfare, bayonet charges, manned machine-gun posts, and the use of chemical weapons killed or maimed an entire generation of young men, just as World War I had. Both countries estimated their losses at half a million soldiers and civilians, and both countries were left with crippling debt.

Believing the conflict to be pointless, and knowing that the Yazidis were mere cannon fodder for Saddam's corrupt generals, Dakhil deserted after basic training, once again hiding from Baghdad's central government in the remote mountain range where he had played and lived as a boy.

The war on the Iran/Iraq front dragged on through the late 1980s, mostly as a stalemate that neither side could push through. As if he had not wrought enough death among his own people, the maniacal Saddam Hussein then declared war on the entire Iraqi Kurdish population of twenty-five million. He launched the Anfal Campaign, one of hatred that incited his army to commit genocide. Saddam's soldiers unleashed poison gas and chemical weapons on Kurds. They held mass executions and dropped countless bombs on villages in the Kurdish areas of northern Iraq. Within three years, one hundred thousand Kurds were dead.

During this time, Dakhil moved from one safe house to another along with other young Yazidi deserters, fleeing to the mountains when discovery seemed imminent. While visiting his family during a time of relative calm, he met his sister's friend, Morbad. They married, and, after the war with Iraq and the war against the Kurds ended, they started a family.

By 1993, Dakhil Shammo was in his early thirties and married with five young sons. He worked as a journalist, writing for *Lalish Magazine* and reporting for a small television station owned by one of the Kurdish political parties. Witness to decades of war, he had seen unspeakable cruelty and human suffering. Every relative and friend bore the scars of trauma. Every one had endured the loss of family and homeland, had lived to see Yazidi village life destroyed and its residents herded into collective villages like prisoners.

For many Kurds, including Dakhil Shammo's family, the outbreak of the Kurdish civil war of 1994 was the breaking point that led to emigra-

tion from Iraq. Militias belonging to the two main Kurdish political parties, the Kurdistan Democratic Party, run by the Barzani Family, and the
breakaway Patriotic Union of Kurdistan, run by Jalal Talabani, clashed
throughout the region.

"The Kurdish civil war—that was the end. No more. No more running, hiding, crying. No more suffering. I wanted my sons to have a
chance at life," Dakhil said. "We paid a smuggler. He took me, my wife,
our three toddlers, and two babies across the Tigris River into Syria in
1995. We lived in a house in a camp filled with mud. But here, the United
Nations High Commission for Refugees granted us refugee status. We
asked to go to the United States."

In 1998, Dakhil, Morbad, and his five young sons trooped off a
plane in Louisville, Kentucky, where a Catholic refugee organization
resettled them.

"To go the US was like a dream. In Syria, we had no money, no
future. Life was so hard and miserable. The shock, however, when you get
here, is that you are so small and this world, America, is so big," he said.

In a modest house in a quiet suburb of Louisville, the Shammo family was safe, but isolated. Peering out the living room window, Dakhil saw
no one. After dinner, the family walked together around the neighborhood and was greeted by the stares of their neighbors. They asked their
sponsor "where do people go to gather, to talk?" She sent them on a bus
to the local mall.

"We felt so isolated. Not just from other Yazidis, and Kurds in general, but from people. We were used to living outside and Americans,
well, they live inside," Dakhil said. "I worked nights in a factory that
made filters for air conditioners. Morbad and I took English classes
every morning at the library. My sons went to elementary school. My
oldest son, Ari, was diagnosed with an extreme learning disability. At
the time, they called it 'brain damage.' This devastated me, and, on top
of the strain of living day-after-day with a new language and new rules,
I felt crushed."

Kurdish friends urged them to move to Northern Virginia, where
there was a large Kurdish immigrant community and the chance to find
better jobs. Settling in Centreville, Dakhil found work cleaning the inte-

rior of used cars at an auto dealership, but quickly became a mechanic, using his school training.

Several months after the move, an acquaintance mentioned that the US government was hiring Kurdish speakers for its international radio broadcasting operation in Washington, DC. Dakhil applied, was accepted, and within a few years was a star radio broadcaster whose low, smooth voice and friendly style was heard via shortwave radio throughout the Kurdistan region of northern Iraq.

By 2014, he was a well-known television anchor and reporter. His visibility and his contacts in Washington, particularly at the State Department's office of International Religious Freedom (IRF), would be crucial to his efforts to save the lives of thousands as Islamic State swept down on Kurdistan.

IRF OFFICE

During the Yazidi crisis, the normally placid Office of International Religious Freedom sprang to life in a scramble to provide the government with accurate information about the status of the refugees trapped on the mountain. Civil servant Douglas Padgett and Foreign Service officer Leanne Cannon, the backbones of the office, had developed strong relationships with diaspora religious communities throughout the United States. Every week small associations of religious minorities, including Yazidis, gathered in a State Department conference room with Padgett and Cannon to lay out their case for a strong American response to religious persecution in their respective homelands. During that cool August week of 2014, the familiarity between Yazidis and the Office of International Religious Freedom galvanized the American response and, ultimately, saved thousands of lives with an efficacy no one could have predicted. The outsized role played by the IRF office during the events of 2014 could not have been predicted. Both the origins and the early actions of the office were manipulated by political ideology rather than a respect for human rights.

The office fell under the human rights mandate of the State Department. In the late 90s, several members of Congress grew concerned about reports of Christian persecution in China and Sudan. Led by these elected representatives and pressed by Evangelical groups, such as

Christian Solidarity International and International Christian Concern, Congress passed the International Religious Freedom Act in May 1998, which allowed the imposition of penalties to combat religious persecution as part of American foreign policy. Congress subsequently modified the law to allow the president to exercise flexibility in dealing with violators that had high value for US national security interests.

The bill landed on the desk of President Bill Clinton, who was mired in the Monica Lewinsky scandal. Distracted, he signed it days after his infamous news conference during which he stated: "I did not have sexual relations with that woman, Monica Lewinsky." At the same time, special prosecutor Ken Starr argued that Secret Service agents should be hauled before a federal grand jury to testify against the president they guarded.

The backlash to the bill slammed Clinton. Critics responded immediately, most saying the act reflected a Christian or a Judeo-Christian bias. The National Council of Churches warned that the new law might "promote the cause of Christians to the exclusion of persecuted believers of other religions." Human rights advocates wondered aloud if the measure would apply to non-Christians, pointing to nations such as Saudi Arabia where Shia Muslims faced severe discrimination. The furor relented after independent academics maintained, however, there was more than enough data to justify the law, pointing to many nations where the absence of religious freedom correlated strongly with low female literacy rates, unstable democracies, and terrorism.

To monitor religious persecution and recommend policies that promoted religious freedom, the small office of International Religious Freedom opened within the Bureau of Democracy, Human Rights and Labor at the State Department. Headed by an ambassador-at-large appointed by the president, its mission was to promote religious freedom as a core objective of US foreign policy. It was required to produce an annual report on religious freedom in 195 countries, a public document it would present to Congress.

The office and the commission created by the legislation, however, were not above politics. In 2001, President George W. Bush appointed Evangelical leader Richard Land, author of the book *A God Blessed America: What It Would Look Like and How It Could Happen*, in which he asserted that Hindu culture and tradition were "superstitious" and "cruel." Also the president of the public policy arm of the Southern Baptist Convention, Land was the primary author of the so-called "Land Letter," an open-letter document written by religious right leaders that argued the "just war" theory in support of the 2003 invasion of Iraq. It referred to "criteria of just war theory as developed by Christian theologians in the late fourth and early fifth centuries A.D." The justification derived from the writings of St. Augustine of Hippo, who said in essence that the pursuit of peace must include the option of fighting for its long-term preservation. "God has given the sword to government for good reason," the letter quoted from scripture.

Land served ten years, and went on to head the Southern Baptists' Ethics and Religious Liberty Commission. He later stepped down amid charges of plagiarism and racism following a controversial radio commentary in which he accused President Barack Obama of trying to "gin up the black vote."

Already straining under criticism from human rights advocates, the new Commission on International Religious Freedom took the opportunity to demonstrate that it sought to protect all religions, not just Christians. In 2005, it held a public hearing on Capitol Hill about the violent 2002 anti-Muslim riots in a rural part of India. During the hearing, eyewitnesses gave vivid testimony, recounting the slaughter of more than a thousand Muslims. This testimony led to the full power of the act being exercised—the only time it has happened—when the State Department banned Hindu nationalist Narenda Modi from visiting the United States. This small-time politician from the Indian state of Gujarat was believed to have tolerated, if not encouraged, the violence. After the hearing, the State Department immediately revoked his tourist visa, and denied him all entry into the United States. For the Bush Administration this was an easy win; Modi was a nobody. Who could have predicted that a few years later he would become the country's prime minister?

By 2010, the Obama Administration had rescinded the ban, and Modi toured the United States several times, including a visit to Menlo

Park, California, where, in front of cameras, he hugged Facebook CEO Mark Zuckerberg during a town hall meeting.

By the second term of the Obama Administration, IRF had settled into a small cubbyhole of offices on the third floor of the vast State Department building on C Street in northwest DC's Foggy Bottom neighborhood. Its staff of about thirteen included interns, a small administrative arm, and its two primary workers, Leanne Cannon and Douglas Padgett.

Before joining the US State Department, Douglas Padgett, PhD was a nontenured professor at Virginia's George Mason University in the religious studies department. He had come to the Washington, DC, area when his wife, an attorney, accepted a government position with the Securities and Exchange Commission. They rented a nineteenth-century row house in the District's Dupont Circle area and began adapting to Washington's frenetic lifestyle, a distinct change from their tranquil Southern roots.

Doug Padgett speaks precisely, in the tone of a teacher, occasionally raising his eyes upward while searching through his prodigious memory for a phrase or fact to demonstrate his point. He is tall, fair-haired, and imposing. Born in suburban Atlanta, he has a pale, boyish face and the demeanor of a southern gentleman. A bit out of place in the nation's sea of gray suits, one can easily imagine him dressed in a white linen suit and straw fedora, sitting on a shaded porch in the shimmering summer heat.

His parents were raised evangelical Southern Baptists in North Carolina, but joined a Methodist congregation in Atlanta after settling there. Padgett attended the Westminster Schools, a prestigious Christian-based academy whose fine academic curriculum attracted a large number of Jewish and Catholic students from the South.

"When I was in the seventh grade I was in a class called Ethics. Half of the class was about ethical situations, but the second part was about cults, sort of a look at 'the evil that is out there for an unsuspecting young man,'" he said. "The teacher was talking about Hare Krishna and reading about the Swami Prabhuphada and everyone was horrified and I am thinking to myself 'Wow this is cool.' So, I went and bought a copy of The *Bhagavad Gita* and some books about Buddhism. I was just fascinated."

At Duke University, Padgett majored in English and religious studies. He joined ROTC and received his commission in the Navy after graduation, becoming a surface warfare officer, but found the long deployments difficult.

"I was in for four years and two months and spent at least half of it floating on the water," he said. "In retrospect I often think I would have enjoyed a career in the Navy, but at the time I had other things I wanted to do."

He considered law school, picked up a master's degree from the University of Florida, and eventually decided to pursue a doctorate at Indiana University in religious studies. He became interested in the politics of memory, the way traumatized refugees recall their history and manifest it in public celebration and ritual. In Orange County, California, he studied the Vietnamese "Boat People," the eight hundred thousand refugees who fled Vietnam and resettled in the United States in the two decades following the end of the Vietnam War.

"We like to think that remembering is a good thing, but remembering is also a way of ensuring that your suffering continues. Many of them didn't want to let go of their loss, and the public ritual of remembering bonded them to anger and sadness. It was not bad or good, it was just what it was," he said.

After years of academic life, Padgett embraced a late-bloomer's ambition. He cast his eye at the State Department where he believed his expertise would be valued. In 2011, he was appointed the ninety-third Franklin Fellow, a midcareer change appointment generally used to bring high-value private sector professionals to the government temporarily. Intrigued by the growing twenty-first century intersection of diplomacy and religion, Padgett hounded his superiors for a full-time civil service position. After completing his fellowship, the Bureau of Democracy, Human Rights and Labor hired him. In March 2014, the forty-nine-year-old became the International Religious Freedom team leader. The job was the culmination of a lifetime of fascination with the tenets of diverse faiths.

Padgett brought a remarkable viewpoint to the IRF office; he understood that in many parts of the world, especially the East and Middle East, faith is often interchangeable with cultural identity. This concept is mostly lost in the West where so-called western Christian values of kindness, charity, and humility are culturally lauded, but the observation of Christian faith is waning.

"Faith demands that you experience the world as more than just what is material or observable. We are all tempered and shaped by the religious experiences of our youths and mine was very well defined," Padgett said. "I don't subscribe to the religiosity of that time of my life, but my family, we come together around that shared Christian experience. That doesn't mean we are particularly religious people, but we are not unreligious. I guess we are postmodern Christians, those that see humanitarian values as more important than dogma or doctrine."

Thirty-four-year-old Leanne Cannon, Padgett's Foreign Service counterpart in IRF, is not a postmodern Christian. The daughter of a military chaplain, she studied at tiny Abilene Christian University in the western part of the Texas. The university is affiliated with Churches of Christ, autonomous Christian congregations that associate with one another through common beliefs and practices. Churches of Christ seek the unification of all Christians in a single body predicated on the teachings of the New Testament.

Within this environment, Cannon excelled academically, studying political science and looking beyond Texas to build her career. In 2005, she was appointed a Presidential Management Fellow, joining a prestigious US government recruitment program for well-educated and ambitious young Americans. Her first position was at the Federal Bureau of Investigation where she trained foreign law enforcement organizations to investigate terrorist financing and money laundering.

She received her master's degree in international communications at Washington's American University, then passed the notoriously difficult Foreign Service exam. As a junior diplomat, she completed postings in Monterrey, Mexico, and Bamako, Mali. She joined IRF in the late summer of 2013.

By August 2014, Padgett and Cannon had met Dakhil several times, inviting him to their office to discuss the plight of the Yazidi in Iraq. So it is not surprising that Sunday night, August 3, just before going to bed, he sent each of them an email marked "urgent, a massacre."

ISLAMIC STATE

Islamic State considers itself a theological empire, otherwise called the Islamic Caliphate. The boundaries of this theoretical caliphate extend to the borders of the Muslim world. But in early 2014, it consisted only of parts of eastern Syria and a few small cities and villages scattered in the desert lands of western Iraq.

In the lands it conquered, Islamic State established a government ruled by religion, and enforced with terror, crucifying, decapitating and burning alive non-adherents. Leaders *institutionalized* slavery and rape and justified those as a weapon of war through a twisted interpretation of Islam.

Islamic State pierced the consciousness of the West through aggressive use of social media. Glorifying violence in deliberately seductive videos that went viral, the group seduced sympathizers with horrific recordings of beheadings and other inhuman forms of execution devised to maximize the suffering of the victims. Citing Sharia law rooted in eighth-century Islam, the bloodthirsty media campaign cemented Islamic State's reputation for terrorism without restraint.

The mastermind and founding father of Islamic State was not a cleric but rather a petty thief and semi-illiterate thug born in 1966 in a slum in Amman, Jordan. Abu Musab al-Zarqawi was a compact and muscular man known in his youth for an uncontrollable temper that often erupted in acts of extreme brutality. In 1989, at twenty-three, inspired by stories of heroic jihad, he left Jordan to fight the remnants of the pro-Soviet government in Afghanistan.

After four years, he returned to Jordan with a well-earned reputation for bravery on the battlefield, but was soon imprisoned by the Jordanian government for suspicion of terrorist sympathies. He would have languished in a cell for years had Jordan's King Abdullah not freed thousands of prisoners with a royal amnesty in 1999. Zarqawi returned to Afghanistan and began jihadi training with the tepid support of Osama bin Laden, who viewed him as little more than a thug.

It now seems ironic that Zarqawi became a household name on February 5, 2003, thanks to Secretary of State Colin Powell, who catapulted him onto the world stage. Powell cited Zarqawi twenty-one times in a United Nations speech attempting to link him to the September 11 attacks. In fact, Osama bin Laden despised Zarqawi, describing him as a man of little intellect, and banishing him to a remote camp. Relying on intelligence that later proved mistaken, Powell inadvertently bestowed on Zarqawi the gravitas bin Laden had long denied him.

Within months, the newly infamous Zarqawi was in Iraq, building the structure that would become Islamic State. Called al-Qaida in Iraq, and loosely tied to bin Laden, Zarqawi's group easily and rapidly recruited embittered Ba'athists who had been banned from the government and army by the United States.

Within a year of his move to Iraq, al-Qaida in Iraq horrified the world with its release of videos of beheadings of two Americans and one British citizen. The United States slapped a $25 million bounty on Zarqawi's head and he became one of the most wanted men in the world. Despite being hunted by Americans and disliked by bin Laden and his lieutenants, Zarqawi grew al-Qaida in Iraq's core membership to more than one thousand, according to State Department estimates.

As with all egomaniacal leaders, Zarqawi eventually overplayed his hand. He not only wanted non-Muslims converted or executed, he essentially decreed the only worthy Muslims were the ones who agreed with his fundamentalist views. Any Muslim who disagreed, whether Sunni or Shia, was an infidel who could be justifiably slaughtered.

On this crucial point, he eventually severed all ties with bin Laden, who had begun a belated "hearts and minds" campaign. Zarqawi targeted Shia mosques and civilians as well as Iraqi government institutions for violent attacks. In pursuing his dream of turning Iraq into a fundamentalist Sunni Muslim state, the Muslim death toll grew.

By early 2006, even the Arab tribal leaders in Zarqawi's western stronghold rankled at the carnage and were revulsed at the rising body count. In what came to be called "the Anbar Awakening," these leaders cooperated with American occupiers by passing along intelligence that eventually pinpointed Zarqawi's location. A US airstrike on a house in Baquba, thirty miles northeast of Baghdad, killed Abu Musab al-Zarqawi in June. Within months, the Islamic State structure he had built was close to collapse.

For a few years, the jihadist group floundered, losing funders and popular support. In the American troop surge of 2007 most of the second-rate leaders who succeeded Zarqawi were arrested or killed. Iraq seemed on the path to rebuilding. In 2011, after spending more than one trillion dollars, and with the American people squarely against the war, President Barack Obama ordered the withdrawal of the last US combat troops. The Iraqi state would now have to stand on its own.

Al-Qaida in Iraq needed to reconstitute itself under the new leadership of Abu Bakr al-Baghdadi. An opportunity presented itself in March 2011 when the Syrian civil war broke out. Syria's nearly unhinged President Bashar al-Assad began gassing and killing his own people in order to remain in power. Al-Qaida in Iraq took advantage of the chaos and moved into Syria, officially renaming itself The Islamic State of Iraq and Syria (ISIS). It became the first anti-Assad rebel group to capture a major city, Raqqa, not far from the Iraqi border. There ISIS set up its headquarters and, once again, began a highly successful social media recruiting campaign, using the same bloody tactics.

In June 2014, a strong ISIS re-emerged in the headlines. ISIS captures Mosul. ISIS is mere miles from Baghdad. ISIS announces a caliphate. ISIS demands that all Muslims acknowledge allegiance.

ERBIL

On Sunday, Consul General Joseph Pennington at the US Consulate General in Erbil learned of the unexpected decision by the Islamic State to move into Ninewah Province. He assumed they would head from there to Erbil.

Pennington had been in Erbil less than a year. He enjoyed the posting, invigorated by the warmth of the Kurdish people and growing optimism of the Kurdistan region. The threat of Islamic State concerned him and his staff, but they considered it to be a problem for the embassy in Baghdad, not this outpost. In Erbil, the consulate sought to cement its relationship with the Kurdish Regional Government and to maintain its military ties with the Peshmerga, the most effective fighting force in the region.

Without doubt, the US consulate had been on alert since the fall of Mosul in June. To be safe, nonessential personnel and families had left Iraq a few weeks earlier. But no one had seriously considered Erbil in danger. The city was full with thousands of Americans and other western consultants for the big oil companies, and several foreign consulates had recently opened. Despite a recent influx of Christian refugees, summer tourists strolled around the citadel that had just been added to the list of UNESCO World Heritage Sites and bargained at the downtown souk. Until that day, an assault on the city would have been considered preposterous.

If Islamic State decided to attack Erbil, Pennington knew the American consulate would be a primary target. He couldn't help but think of the 2012 attack on the American diplomatic compound in Benghazi, Libya. The terrorist group Ansar al-Sharia had killed four Americans, including US Ambassador to Libya J. Christopher Stevens, and had wounded ten other compound employees. Benghazi was the nightmare that kept Pennington on the alert. As he waited for instructions from Washington and Baghdad, with Islamic State a mere thirty miles away, he felt the first signs of panic overshadow Erbil, a hysteria that, if let loose, could erupt in a chaotic, massive stampede out of the city. Pennington knew that the next day, Monday, the consulate had to prepare for a possible abandonment.

In the years following the American withdrawal from Iraq, Erbil was a city poised to benefit from the burgeoning tourism explosion in the Middle East. For the adventurous traveler, it offered a delightful climate, a pro-western population, archaeological sites, and, most importantly, civil order. The Kurdish Regional Government administered services for the city's more than one million population competently, despite near legendary levels of corruption, and the region had none of the violent Sunni versus Shia conflict that plagued postwar southern Iraq.

The government in Erbil also had rights to exploit the one commodity with the power to alter its economy permanently: oil. While southern Iraq had developed an oil industry in the 1920s, Kurdistan's vast oil fields were plundered by Saddam Hussein, who milked hydrocarbon wealth to wage war. Determined to build up their own oil industry, the Kurdish government began wooing international oil companies. In 2011, experts calculated Kurdistan's oil wealth to be the fourth largest in the world with an estimated forty-five billion barrels of reserves. ExxonMobil and Chevron were among the many oil and gas firms that negotiated startlingly favorable contracts with the regional government in exchange for the high-risk commitment to drill. They brought with them contractors as well as service and transportation companies that created thousands of jobs.

The Kurdistan Regional Government built a new oil pipeline to Turkey with the target of transporting one million barrels a day. Crucially, they disregarded the disapproval of Baghdad. Rapidly, the two governments became locked in a nasty dispute over the terms of the Iraqi Constitution that called for revenue sharing. The Kurds believed that ownership of the land that held the oil gave them the autonomy to act.

The city burst with confidence. Construction cranes rose among white, two-story houses like green shoots poking through a spring snow. Construction companies rushed to build luxury hotels, shopping malls, and housing. A shiny new airport opened. Expatriates flocked to the city in a classic gold rush mentality. The city's tourism office released a stunning fifteen-minute high-definition promotional video on the Dis coverErbil.com website, touting the area's seven hundred archaeological sites as well as luxury western-style hotels with sunken bathtubs and fine dining. It proudly proclaimed "law prevails" in Erbil.

The US Consulate General opened on a hot July day in 2011 in Ankawa, the old Christian section of the city, home to several churches and nunneries, including St. Joseph's Cathedral, the seat of the Chaldean Catholic Archdiocese. A two-story, plain, white building, the new consulate sat on land donated by the Kurdistan Regional Government. At an outdoor barbecue on the street in front of the building, Masoud Barzani, the Kurdish Regional Government president since 2005, officially greeted the first consul general, Alexander Laskaris, as well as the US ambassador to Iraq, James Jeffrey. Hundreds of prominent Kurdish officials, members of the international diplomatic corps, and American businessmen sipped soft drinks and discussed Kurdistan's growing economic might. Marriott representatives announced that a five-star, two-hundred-room Erbil Marriott, seventy-five deluxe Marriott apartments, and several restaurants would soon open as part of the Empire Iraq development project in the city's downtown.

In an extraordinary choice, the Arab Council of Tourism tapped Erbil to be its 2014 tourism capital—extraordinary because the city is not Arabic. But the private sector had committed to spending up to $1 billion to build luxury hotels. Estimates of up to three million tourists annually were projected.

The dominoes tumbled quickly in the spring of 2014. Angry over the Kurdish decision to sell oil via the new pipeline without the central government's permission, Baghdad cut off federal money to the region, leaving the Kurdish Regional Government struggling to meet a bloated public payroll. In June 2014, oil prices, which had peaked at $115 a barrel, began to decline. In the midst of this financial panic, Islamic State captured the city of Mosul, and the Iraqi army collapsed. The central government in Baghdad began to fray. Finally, on Sunday, August 3, 2014, Islamic State invaded Sinjar city and the surrounding villages in Ninewah.

From the front window of the consulate building, Pennington saw Christian refugees sleeping on sidewalks and streets. Blankets hung from every building and every cornice or wire to shield refugees from the relentless sun. Mothers and children gathered on the lawns of the city's poshest houses. The area's churches were overflowing and set up communal dining.

A few days earlier, Islamic State had attacked a Peshmerga post in Zumar, thirty miles northwest of Mosul. The Peshmerga fought them off, killing one hundred Islamic State fighters, but a panic set in among the Christian Kurds in the town and thousands fled to Erbil, seeking refuge in the city's old Christian District, Ankawa. Local television stations appealed to Erbil residents for help. Restaurants distributed free food. Housewives gave away extra rice and meat. Thousands opened their homes to their fellow Kurds. Construction sites sheltered hundreds of the displaced.

The Kurdish Regional Government was scrambling to find the money to organize more permanent housing, already thinking about caring for the Christian refugees during the winter. St. Joseph's Cathedral opened its doors to the refugees, who spilled out onto the stairs of the modern fortress-like structure. Many were Assyrian Christians, descendants of the very first Christians, who still speak Aramaic, the language of Jesus Christ.

Now, Pennington realized, thousands of Yazidis had begun to arrive, walking along the highways in groups of ten or twelve, holding plastic bags containing their few possessions. Thirsty, sunburnt children, unaccustomed to city traffic, wandered in front of cars as they begged for help. Most had left their small villages at three or four in the morning and were exhausted. Many were in shock. Pennington heard a low moan, a continuous wail coming from the street as if every woman and child in Ankawa were crying out simultaneously.

Inside the consulate, US Army colonel Chuck Freeman was working the phones, calling senior Peshmerga officials to get an accurate description of events in Sinjar. Freeman, the consulate's senior advisor for Northern Affairs, was Pennington's liaison with the Peshmerga. As each official spun him a different tale, Freeman realized the Peshmerga had lost control of the region and could not give him accurate information. Kurdish workers in the consulate told him the Yazidis were claiming the Peshmerga had run, abandoning them to Islamic State, but senior Peshmerga leaders firmly denied it, saying their troops had fought, but been overwhelmed. He thought about the few cryptic remarks he had heard from Kurdish workers in the consulate, warnings that the people in Sinjar were scared. In retrospect, he wished he had questioned them for specifics.

Texas-born Freeman had arrived in Erbil just eleven days earlier to begin his transition as the new consular liaison, leaving his wife and five children in Texas for a one-year posting. Freeman had completed two tours of Iraq with the 101st Airborne Division, and he had developed a strong affinity for the Iraqi people and their culture. As a career officer, the tall, slender colonel, in his early fifties, had done stints in Germany, South Korea, and Haiti and then studied at the NATO Defense College in Rome and the US Army War College in Pennsylvania. Because he liked the Kurdish people and respected the fighting force, he was pleased with his posting. His primary focus was to interact with the Ministry of Peshmerga Affairs, to build relationships with senior Peshmerga officers, and to organize training for Peshmerga troops. His predecessor had told him in a briefing to "bring lots of books and be ready to hit the gym because you will have loads of free time."

While still trying to learn the names of the consular employees and understand the rules of the motor pool, "the new guy," Freeman, was thrust into the crisis. Pennington was asking for an overview of the situation to report to Washington, so Freeman had to quickly cultivate personal relationships with contacts at the Ministry of Peshmerga, as well as the Ministry of Interior. It rapidly became a crash course in understanding operations in Erbil.

Freeman was also bewildered by his colleagues' surprise at the incursion by Islamic State because it was obvious to a military man that Sinjar was a strategic target. A straight line heading east from Islamic State's headquarters in Raqqa, Syria, connects it to the newly captured city of Mosul in Iraq. Sinjar lies smack in the middle. As a base after crossing the border, an Islamic State stronghold there was invaluable.

From observation, Freeman knew Islamic State fought with combined maneuvers, meaning they used overwhelming firepower with mortar and artillery that had a devastating shock effect on civilians. Villages surrendered almost immediately and Islamic State, always in need of money, looted, destroyed, and took hostages. The region would be ravaged, he knew. But Freeman had little knowledge of the Yazidi people, and, in appraising the immediate military situation, he never considered, on that first day, the massive humanitarian efforts that would be needed to contain Islamic State's genocidal intent.

WASHINGTON

On Sunday evening August 3, 2014, President Obama returned to the White House after a weekend of playing golf at Camp David. The following day, Monday, was his fifty-third birthday, and the first of what he hoped to be a signature event of his presidency.

Washington was in a frenzy. Federal and local government officials were preparing to welcome leaders from fifty African countries for a three-day international summit in the nation's capital. The US-Africa Leaders' Summit was unprecedented. Thirty-seven of the attending leaders were heads of state, the largest gathering of its kind in Washington's history, and it required the highest-level security. The Secret Service planned to escort presidents and prime ministers from the summit's venues across town several times a day, and city officials warned residents of confounding gridlock.

More than three hundred CEOs from some of the nation's largest corporations had also been invited to engage in business and trade discussion with the African leaders. While the press was scornful, deriding the event as "a summit in search of an agenda," the White House hoped the meetings would generate investment on the continent. To add gravitas to its lineup, President Obama prevailed upon business titan Michael Bloomberg to participate as a co-convener. That helped to convince additional corporate luminaries to accept the White House's invitation.

Yet, a pall hung over the event. The White House had invited the leaders to the summit months earlier, and as the event neared an outbreak of Ebola had run amok in West Africa. More than nine hundred died in Liberia, Guinea, Sierra Leone, and Nigeria. It isn't hard to imagine the conversations that took place in the offices of the Centers for Disease Control and Homeland Security. The virus had recently spread via international flights, and the United States was worried about an outbreak domestically. Leaders of the two hardest hit nations, Sierra Leone and Liberia, declined their invitations.

Never before had the leaders of an entire continent gathered in Washington, and the possibility of a political gaffe was uppermost on the minds of the planners. Among the logistical problems was how to avoid one-on-one meetings between Obama and the dictators and despots among the African leaders. Those with the worst human rights records had been excluded, but the lineup included General Mohamed Ould Abdel Aziz of Mauritania, whose nation still practiced slavery; Joseph Kabila, president of the Democratic Republic of Congo, who once commanded an army of kidnapped child soldiers and who institutionalized rape as a weapon of war; and Teodor Obiang Nguema Mbasogo, the president of tiny Equatorial Guinea who overthrew his uncle in a coup and was rumored to have a fortune in the billions from undisclosed oil revenue. Several opposition leaders had also accused him of engaging in cannibalism.

To avoid undesirable photos of Obama shaking hands with those whose names were linked to child armies or cannibalism, the White House decided the president would not meet one-on-one with any of the leaders.

Transportation and traffic, not photo ops, were the greatest concern for Washington residents as the first day of the summit approached. Local television stations went into full crisis mode with nonstop coverage of road closures, parking restrictions, changed public transportation routes, and predictions of commuter Armageddon. As a result, Monday, August 4, the day after the Islamic State invasion, schools, universities, and businesses in the city closed. Federal employees at all branches of the government were encouraged to stay home and telework.

Washington, DC, was in lockdown mode.

CHAPTER THREE

Invasion

Sunday, August 3

When the Iraqi army abandoned their weapons and surrendered Mosul to Islamic State in early June, the residents of Sinjar in Ninewah Province became keenly aware of the threat posed to them by the proximity of the jihadists. Over the next few weeks, they watched as Islamic State extended their land holdings, capturing Tal Afar, a border city of two hundred thousand just thirty miles from Sinjar that separates Kurdish lands from Arab lands to the south. Tal Afar had become a fervently conservative city over the previous decades when Saddam Hussein relocated large numbers of hardline Sunni Arabs to its environs, and its residents welcomed the imposition of Islamic State's Sharia law.

In the Sinjar region, however, most Yazidis were calmed by the general understanding that their location held little strategic value for Islamic State, which had its eyes on Baghdad, they believed. This mistaken understanding was widely shared by the Iraqi government, the Kurdish government, the Peshmerga, American diplomatic staff, and American military advisors. Its consequences would be tragic.

In hindsight, it is obvious that taking Sinjar gave Islamic State a military advantage; it created a direct supply route from their de facto headquarters in the Syrian city of Raqqa to Mosul in eastern Iraq. But, failing to discern the strategic value of their area, and lulled by a belief they were irrelevant, local political leaders neglected to plan for the defense or the evacuation of their communities.

Also, the presence of the Peshmerga, the elite fighters of the Kurdish people, seemed a guarantee to the rural farm communities of Yazidi and Christian Kurds that their safety was secured. The eleven thousand Peshmerga troops had deployed throughout Ninewah when the Iraqi army collapsed. The Kurdish Regional Government and Baghdad had squabbled over control of the province since the American invasion, and now that the Kurds had control, they were determined to keep it. They closed all the roads leading out of Ninewah to eastern Iraq in an effort to contain the population and to cement their ownership of the area. They also acted as an effective buffer between the Kurdish and Arab communities.

It is hard to overstate the level of confidence and trust most Yazidis placed in the Peshmerga's commitment to their defense. It drew not only on the Peshmerga's legendary bravery and military prowess, but on a deeply held belief that the Peshmerga units, consisting of Kurdish Muslims, Kurdish Yazidis, and Kurdish Christians, would stand together as Kurds. Most of the soldiers came from within the province and the population knew them. Few observers understood that the deployment into Ninewah had stretched the Peshmerga to the point of weakness. They had recruited hundreds of new and untested soldiers, sprinkling them among the checkpoints near the rural villages and towns that represented the first line of defense against Islamic State.

Months after the August invasion, many Yazidis recalled some of the warning signs they had disregarded earlier in the summer. Young Muslim men in nearby Arab communities had begun to grow long beards, and they exhibited a newfound religious devotion. Others recalled the exuberant celebrations thrown by Arab communities when Islamic State captured Mosul. And every Yazidi that survived that summer's genocide later related with tears and rage the precise moment of his realization that his Arab neighbors were Islamic State collaborators who were eager to participate in mass murder.

Abbas's Story

Abbas Kheder Silo worked as a part-time driver in the village of Siba, the southernmost Yazidi city in the Sinjar region. He had recently married and planned to start a family. To supplement his income, he had joined the Kurdish army, the Peshmerga. They issued him a Russian Kalashnikov. Having the weapon made him feel safer in his own village. Five years earlier, Siba had been the site of a fatal car bombing that killed four hundred of his friends and neighbors and went unsolved. Like most of Siba's residents, he was suspicious of the Arab Muslims who lived on appropriated land surrounding Siba. With his weapon, he believed he could protect his wife, his elderly father, and four younger siblings.

Abbas knew that Islamic State was staged around Siba, and he sensed a rising anxiety among the villagers. Despite his unwavering belief in the bravery and dedication of the Peshmerga, he sent his wife out of the city with an uncle who was driving to the Syrian border. His own militia unit was not assigned with defending the Sinjar area, and he had not been given a defensive position.

During the dark morning hours of August 3, 2014, Islamic State moved north from their base in Ba'aj and staged its first assault on the three towns of Siba, Tal Azayr, and Ger Zerik. Nearly sixty-nine thousand people, mostly Yazidis, lived in these three collective communities that had been forcibly relocated in 1975 after Saddam Hussein had their villages razed.

Abbas awoke at 2:00 a.m. to the sound of artillery fire that pummeled the town for hours, killing dozens of people. Repeatedly, he heard the low moaning whistle of approaching mortars followed by the screams of his neighbors as the weapon found its mark. He understood Islamic State had attacked, but not yet entered his village. While his sisters cowered in the main room, staying close to the floor under pillows and blankets to protect their heads from falling debris, Abbas grabbed his weapon and ran to find his fellow active-duty Peshmerga fighters, eager to join the battle. The Peshmerga, he discovered with shock, had abandoned the community hours earlier, withdrawing in the dark of night without warning. Siba was exposed and defenseless.

Abbas and a few other armed Yazidis gathered on the rooftops where they could see the Islamic State soldiers' staging point to the west of the village. From that vantage, they waited for their advance. Using cellphones, they called Yazidi men from Tal Azayr and Ger Zerik to join them in battle until they numbered several hundred.

At 6:00 a.m., as Islamic State began their forward movement, Abbas and his fellow Yazidi militiamen met them at the berms that surrounded the outskirts of town. It was a suicide mission. Islamic State fighters had American heavy artillery captured in Mosul. They attacked with automatic weapons and artillery until the Yazidi lines collapsed. Around Abbas, three hundred men he had known all his life lay dead.

Defeated and panicked, he ran to the east side of town to meet his family as they had planned. Sixty or more Yazidi villagers were there, hoping to run away on the single road out of Siba. His family was not among them. Islamic State fighters had surrounded the town and taken over the checkpoints on the road that led northeast to Sinjar, trapping Abbas and other civilians who had not already fled inside the town.

The jihadists rolled in just before 7:00 a.m., and the killing of unarmed civilians began immediately. Abbas saw five trucks with Islamic State fighters driving wildly along the dusty road that led to the entrance of the village. Their trucks, one with a mounted machine gun, barricaded the road, and, as they came to a full stop, the two sides, the terrorists and the terrified, looked upon each other with reckoning. A few women began to scream. Abbas felt his courage shatter. He gazed up at the brilliant sun in the sky as if he might find understanding. Why would he die this way?

"Quiet, Aunties," he whispered to the women. "This is our end."

The Islamic State soldiers ordered them to lie face down on the ground. The soldiers spread out and surrounded them, then sat cross-legged and pointed their weapons at those who lay closest. The commander, a young man dressed all in black, the lower part of his face covered in a black scarf, sat at the head of the group.

"There is only one way," he said. "Only one way for you to go. You must convert, here, now. If you do not we will kill you."

A few of the villagers rose to answer. Abbas immediately recognized his Arab neighbor, Talal Hamid Ali Kassim, sitting beside the commander. Kassim had lived uneasily alongside the Kurds for forty-three years. He was rumored to have masterminded the massive car bomb attack in Siba whose blast used more than two tons of explosives, crumbling buildings, trapping families beneath mud bricks and other wreckage as whole blocks of houses were flattened.

Now Kassim stood with the killers, poised to massacre those who had been his neighbors for decades. He appeared thrilled by his power, his face was alight, his lower lips curled with a sneering savagery.

An old Yazidi man spoke, looking at Kassim, whom he recognized. "We will not convert," he said.

Abbas listened to the silence and then heard the arrival of death. He wondered if the jihadists heard its emergence as distinctly as he, or if that merciless sound was always with them, a musical accompaniment to their perversity.

The young commander ordered the five women removed from the group. The standing men again lay on the ground. No one spoke. Abbas heard the wind as he had never heard it before, like a rushing stream, as if it were pulling time past him and surging him into the future. The sour stench of urine hit his nose as many of the men lost control of their bodies from terror.

About thirty Islamic State fighters opened fire, moving their rifles from left to right and back again. Abbas, shot twice, lay on his stomach and closed his eyes. He wondered if the dark silence around him was death, but then he heard the fighters shouting to each other. The machine-gunner opened fire again on the corpses, and Abbas clenched his eyes, bracing for his inevitable death. Yet he remained conscious. The fighters moved in among the dead, kicking the bodies hard and laughing, checking to be certain all were dead. Abbas lay still. The voices of the soldiers grew faint. He heard the truck engines start up and, after a few minutes, the sound of their humming motors disappeared. He lay still, his heart beating. He could feel moisture around his body, and he knew it was his own blood. He lay still, waiting for the courage to rise.

It was afternoon when he rose and surveyed the mass of dead before him. He stepped gingerly over the bodies. Men's faces collapsed into the dirt and their backs were crimson red. He staggered into the center of the village and thought of calling out for help, but, by the silence and stillness, he knew there was no one alive.

Throughout the day, men and women had been shot and their bodies burned. He walked among smoking, charred corpses. The stench caused him to retch until his dry mouth filled with blood.

In shock, he entered his father-in-law's house and went to the bathroom to look for a bandage or rag to stop the bleeding, but the house had been ransacked. In the living room, he picked up a dirty black sock and went outside. Near the door, he found a rock the size of his fist and put it into the toe of the sock, wrapping the cloth around it to make a ball. He pulled off his bloody shirt, strained his left arm around his neck and stuffed the ball into the hole on the right side of his upper back where the bullet had entered. The bleeding stopped. He slumped on the living room floor, exhausted, and stared out the window looking at the sun until dusk.

"I had a feeling of craziness. I could not believe I had seen all my friends killed before my eyes. I thought, what is this world? But I hoped my family had escaped and were waiting for me, so I did not kill myself," he said.

That night, at sunset, he left the house and walked again through town toward the east entrance and down into the valley several miles from Mount Sinjar, the Yazidi holy place of refuge. Dogs barked and howled around him, and he wondered if they were hungry or mourning their masters. He stayed off the main road, cutting through farmers' fields and avoiding lights. Once, he heard the motors of two cars and dove under some hay until they passed.

He passed the nearby collective town of Tal Azayr, a community of fifteen thousand Yazidis that was now deserted. Most of Tal Azayr's men had fought at the Siba defense line, leaving the women, children, and elderly alone in the town.

When cellphone calls alerted them that defense lines in Siba had collapsed, thousands of the remaining women and children fled on foot, leaving behind most of the elderly who could not walk or run. There was no battle in Tal Azayr. Islamic State walked directly into town and immediately killed the elderly. They drove their trucks to the road leading north and shot at fleeing women as they hurried along, desperately trying to shield their children and grandchildren. It is estimated that nearly seven hundred people were killed in Tal Azayr.

Farther east, beyond Abbas's path to the mountain, lay the third collective village of the region, Ger Zerik, a poor community of four thousand Yazidis and Muslim Kurds. The 150 Peshmerga soldiers at the outskirts of this village initially fought and destroyed most of the first column of Islamic State vehicles that approached the city, but fled at the realization they were vastly outnumbered. When Islamic State entered the town in the late morning, most of the families, Yazidi and Muslim, had left, aided by neighbors from the nearby wealthy farming community of Rambusi. Rambusi Yazidis, alerted early by cellphone calls, drove into Ger Zerik, filled their farm trucks with the terrified Yazidi and Muslim Kurds, and brought them to the foot of Mount Sinjar, where they climbed to safety.

However, Ger Zerik, like Tal Azayr, had a large elderly population. Despite the presence of vehicles that could have carried them to safety, many living alone refused to leave. Their remains lie in a mass grave in the center of town.

From these three collective communities, tens of thousands escaped the noose by fleeing north. Most ran from where they stood, unable to go home for supplies. They had no water or food. Many had no shoes as walking barefoot was common in the summer. Girls as young as ten held the hands of toddlers they had been watching for mothers who were fetching water or hanging laundry at the moment the panic struck. With the only roads controlled by Islamic State, the refugees cut across the flat, desert plain in the burning August sun walking to their holy place, the only refuge they could rely on: Mount Sinjar. Witness testimony makes clear that scores if not hundreds of civilians died from dehydration, and other deprivations, while trying to walk north without water.

As he trod on, Abbas hit upon a mantra. "Life is sweet," he mumbled aloud to himself. Wearing only sandals and his blood-soaked jeans, he staggered east until dawn when he reached the house of an uncle in a deserted village. He slept for an hour then rose and continued his journey to the mountain.

By 11:00 a.m., he reached Mount Sinjar and started his ascent. His wounds had begun to throb and every step sent shudders of pain through his body. He staggered, falling every few steps or so, but rose again and repeated his mantra, "Life is sweet." He heard the sound of a crowd and pulled himself toward it. Hundreds of people gathered on the mountainside in a small clearing. All were crying. Most had the unfocused stare of those in shock. Some old women were shouting to God, while children lay on their backs with their arms across their eyes to shield them from the broiling sun. No one noticed him.

GENOCIDE

The second prong of the attack struck the southwestern villages of Skaniyah and Hayali, which lay at the far western foothills of the mountain. Islamic State came from their base in Syria in the west, and from Siba in the south, moving closer to Sinjar. Skaniyah and Hayali learned of the threat when thousands of fleeing Yazidis arrived in the early morning hours and recounted stories of indiscriminate shooting and the blood-bath in Siba. Residents called friends and relatives to the north and warned them of the oncoming siege before fleeing.

Skaniyah, a poor, rural and isolated village, was home to five hundred Yazidi families, mostly farmers and shepherds.

Enclaves of Arab farms surrounded the village, built on ancient Yazidi lands that Saddam Hussein had confiscated years earlier and given to Ba'athists. The area, however, had a reputation for being remarkably peaceful. Arabs and Yazidi farmers cooperated during harvest times as they struggled to grow crops in the arid soil, and men from both faiths had established long-term friendships.

Most of the Yazidis of Skaniyah escaped, running north directly from their pastures, too terrified to return to the village to aid the elderly who were not at work in the fields. By midmorning, ten carloads of Islamic State fighters held the elderly and disabled Yazidis at the center of the village. "Your safety is guaranteed," one fighter said, laughing when he was asked about the massacres in Siba and whether the same fate lay in store for these villagers. "Just stay in your house and fly a white flag to show you are friendly," he suggested. They were held captive for two days, and then murdered.

Survivors of the murders in Skaniyah provided the first evidence that Islamic State's attack on Sinjar and its outer regions was not solely a strategic ploy, but, in fact, was a well-executed plan to commit ethnic cleansing by exploiting the resentment of minority Arabs. Most of the Islamic State fighters who came to Skaniyah were not foreign fighters from Syria, or Iraqi jihadists from other parts of the country. They were Arabs from the adjacent villages who enthusiastically joined Islamic State as they pushed past their lands toward the Yazidis.

Genocides are rarely possible without the support of local actors who collaborate with the planners, whether it be the Hutus hunting down their Tutsi neighbors in Rwanda, or the Polish and French reliably turning in their Jewish compatriots during the Holocaust. Sinjar was no different. The forcible relocation decades earlier of the Yazidis into collective villages and the reallocation of their land to Arabs from Iraq's south had created a province where ethnic rivalries and jealousies ran rife. The collapse of Saddam Hussein's regime had left his previously powerful Arab supporters vulnerable and angry.

Attempts at social integration had once seemed promising. Since Saddam Hussein began his campaign to repopulate the area with Arab Muslims, the Yazidis had extended to their new neighbors the honorary title of Kreef. At the birth of every Yazidi child, a non-Yazidi became the child's godfather or Kreef. It was an attempt to build ties of loyalty between the Yazidi and Arab Muslim communities. Kreefs attended wedding celebrations and birth ceremonies, and they were welcomed into Yazidi homes with great respect.

There were Kreefs who honored their Yazidi ties, yet survivors of the Sinjar genocide uniformly describe the moment of despair when they first spotted their Kreefs among the killers. Following the attack, many Kreefs bought their goddaughters from Islamic State before raping them and then holding them for ransom.

Yet amid the horror of genocide, a few instances of human decency were recorded. The poor village of Bashuk had fewer than one thousand occupants, evenly divided between Yazidis and Mandikan Sunni Muslims, non-Arab Muslims. In this tiny community, where farming and other occupations were interdependent, strong emotional ties had been forged between the two faiths. As word of Islamic State's advance reached the community, the Yazidis fled on foot, leaving behind the sick and elderly who could not run. The Mandikans chose to hide these vulnerable Yazidis inside their own houses. When Islamic State entered the village, believing it emptied of Yazidis, they greeted their fellow Muslims warmly and offered to be of service. The Mandikans, terrified the Yazidis would be found, assured Islamic State they were well off and needed nothing, hoping they would leave to push farther north.

But a few fighters stayed, and the Mandikans were forced to hide the Yazidis for eight days, until they were smuggled out to the foothills of the mountain where they followed a guide to safety. The next day the Mandikans fled themselves, traveling through Islamic State–held territory to the border of Kurdistan, where, as Muslims, they were allowed to cross the border. There does not appear to have been a single murder by Islamic State of a Bashuk Yazidi.

Ninewah Province is a dusty flat open plain with a hundred miles' visibility. As thousands of cars and tens of thousands of people fled north, they kicked up a great confluence of dust. From villages closer to the mountain, the exodus appeared as a massive ball of sand roiling across the plain. As the day's temperature climbed, eventually settling at 115 degrees Fahrenheit, the sun reflected off the ball, making it seem to bounce between the earth and the sky as it swept toward Mount Sinjar. During the morning's three-hour escape window, thousands more joined its chaotic path until noon, by which time Islamic State held the region.

In a mere two hundred minutes, a half a million people had taken flight, abandoning their homes and meager possessions, clinging desperately to their parents or siblings, running for their lives through an unforgiving desert.

BARAKAT'S STORY

Tal Banat was a thriving community of nearly twenty thousand Kurdish Yazidis, Kurdish Muslims, and resettled Arabs just ten miles southeast of Sinjar city. It was guarded by a large Peshmerga unit that occasionally engaged in battle with the nearby Islamic State. For the previous three days, Islamic State gunmen, dressed in trademark black pants and T-shirts, their faces covered by improvised balaclavas, had driven their pickup trucks and American Humvees to the outskirts of the village and launched mortars into its center. Peshmerga fighters had raced to the site of the launch and watched the fighters flee, shooting off rounds as their trucks sped into the dusty countryside. Residents like Barakat Sulu, a Yazidi from the Azawy tribe, were unconcerned. The presence of the Peshmerga provided strong security.

Early Sunday morning, relatives calling from Siba delivered the first warning. Barakat, a tall, muscular man, clean shaven, but for a thin line of a mustache, was at home with his wife, Nassir, and their two young children. Almost simultaneously, the couple heard screams rise around the village. *"They're coming. Daesh. They're coming."* The screams became a chant as every panicked resident shouted the warning into the air while bolting to their homes to gather supplies and belongings. The absence of the Peshmerga, who had left during the night, added to the general confusion. The unit had initially moved to help defend another nearby village, but at 6:00 a.m., it ran out of ammunition. It withdrew from combat and left the area.

Barakat and his wife hoisted containers of water and food to their old car. Their young children helped, throwing blankets and towels onto the back seat. In the midst of frenzied preparations, the son of the family's Kreef called and implored them to come and hide at their house just outside the village.

"You will be safe with us," he guaranteed Barakat.

Barakat pressed the mobile phone to his ear. He thought he heard the man's father, their Kreef, screaming, "Bring those infidels to us." Desperately frightened, Barakat asked the Kreef's son: "Will you help us?" "Yes, yes," came the reply, but as he pressed the telephone harder to his ear, he heard his lifelong Arab friend shout "infidels" in the background. He told his wife he believed they would be killed if they trusted their Kreef. At first stunned into silence, she then replied "Yes, you are right."

They left their house.

Islamic State fighters did not enter the village, but ringed the perimeter and held the main street leading out of town, so that those fleeing could only run directly toward them.

Barakat drove his family to the edge of the village. The children crouched on the floor of the backseat, covered in blankets and packages of food Nassir had arranged around them to provide a protective barrier.

As he pulled out of a side road, he stopped aghast and watched barbarity play out before him. In the scorching heat, extended families ran barefoot, clutching babies, blankets, and packages of food. Islamic State gunmen screamed as they shot and killed old men and women whose families watched their bodies fall while they kept running. Mothers tried to wrap their babies into their blouses as if to shield them from the bullets. One young man was running with his elderly father in his arms when a gunman shot the old man. The son dropped the body, sobbing, and ran on. The gunmen shot him in the back. Fighters were pulling young women and girls away from their relatives, and Barakat heard their high-pitched screams cutting through the chaos. Men were being pushed against a wooden fence and stripped of their weapons and supplies. Bodies lay on both sides of the road. Abandoned cars blocked the road, some with the engines still running.

Barakat recognized the fighters. They had not come from Syria or other parts of Iraq; in fact, they had not belonged to Islamic State until a few days earlier. They were his neighbors from the Arab Khatouniyah tribe of the Ba'aj district. This confirmed his earlier hunch that his Kreef had been setting a trap. The monstrous situation became clear: Islamic State had recruited their Arab neighbors to cleanse the land of the Kurds. No Kurd was safe, not Shia, Christian, or Yazidi. Islamic State had reanimated an old hatred between Kurds and Arabs and now their former neighbors were madmen, driven by ethnic revulsion and true or imaginary grudges, released among the innocent to slaughter for their pleasure.

Panic surged through his body. "Get away from this horror," was his only thought.

While his children screamed, he veered his car forcefully to the right and slammed his foot onto the gas pedal as his wife wrapped her arms around her head, screeching in terror. He did not hear bullets, but braced himself to be shot. He stayed off the road, clutching the steering wheel, and the car lurched on every rut and crack in the dried, desert soil, and once even seemed to take flight. He drove madly and courageously. His eyes focused on the terrain directly before the car. He did not slow.

His wife looked to the west to the road and watched the massacre proceed. Islamic State had positioned small convoys along the main highway to await the arrival of fleeing Yazidis. From their trucks, the jihadists shot their automatic weapons indiscriminately, causing cars to spin off the road or crash into each other. Emerging from their immobilized vehicles, families scattered, running blindly, in sheer terror. Nassir saw each parent and child crumble, their knees buckling slowly while their arms jerked up to the heavens, their mouths agape as they fell, cut down by the machine guns mounted on the backs of captured American Fords.

Barakat reached the sharp curve of the main highway and looked in both directions before driving onto the tarmac. The road was clear. He continued to Mount Sinjar. Barakat was simply lucky that day.

Several minutes after Barakat's escape, Islamic State soldiers set up a blockade in that curve so that it was visible only after a driver rounded the corner. As a result, cars came around the bend and crashed at full speed. The drivers who were still alive stumbled from the wreckage and ran off through the fields. They were shot before they got far. The estimated death toll from this region was two thousand.

Inside the town, the jihadists immediately began looting. As they had before, they killed the elderly and disabled who were not able to run away. The few survivors later identified the Islamic State members as residents of the Arab town of Ain Ghazal that lay a few miles away. Only the military leaders of the invaders were actual Islamic State fighters; the rest were Arab farmers who lived nearby.

The residents of the Tal Banat region, now a swarm of twenty thousand people in flight, overtaken by a delirium of fear and driven by the urge to stay alive, moved over the desert sand in a slow stampede toward Mount Sinjar.

They walked through the August heat, scattering into small groups of extended families or neighbors as morning turned into afternoon. Several hundred walked toward the village of Solagh, north of the highway controlled by Islamic State. On the outskirts of that village, they stopped at abandoned farmhouses in the agricultural area of Tel Wusifka to rest and look for water. Islamic State arrived suddenly. They separated families, rounding up the young women, herding them onto the back of pickup trucks, and then moved south of the highway. The fate of these women is unknown.

The men, held at gunpoint, were marched deeper into the fields and shot. In 2016, the scene of this massacre was marked by investigators who noted that the main burial pit was surrounded by additional smaller killing sites, perhaps of those who fell dead while trying to run.

Barakat and his family finally reached the foothills of the mountain where three small villages held thousands of Yazidis. Many sat on the ground in shock, their minds unable to process the debauchery they had just witnessed. Small groups of men pointed toward the mountain, debating the wisdom of the climb. Could this sacred land protect them from Islamic State? The Yazidis venerate Mount Sinjar. They believe its highest peak to be where Noah's Ark rested after the biblical floodwaters receded. Since the twelfth century, they have sought refuge in the mountains during periods of conflict. Many of the older men had ascended the mountain alone in their youths, seeking spiritual comfort or guidance, and they were acquainted with its harsh landscape. The sun beats down all day onto the hard rock until it becomes as hot as a wood stove. There are few trees to throw shade, only thin shrubs that jet up from the dirt between the crevices. Without enough water, life cannot be sustained.

Curiously, a group of Arabs, who had been relocated to the nearby village of Ghillo an Gasser by Saddam Hussein years earlier, appeared among the thousands of Yazidis. Three were dressed in black and had Kalashnikov assault rifles. One stood on his truck.

"We are your friends, and we will not allow anyone to hurt you," he assured the Yazidis. "Fly a white flag and we will tell Islamic State that you want to return to your village."

They told the Yazidis to give up their weapons and to await the arrival of the Islamic State fighters who would give them food. They drove off. There was a brief silence. Barakat, thinking of his Kreef, doubted their assurances, as did most of the other Yazidis. They drove their cars up the mountain before the soldiers returned, leaving about forty men behind. After ascending less than half a mile, gunshots rang out. From his vantage point on the mountain, Barakat watched the brutal execution of the forty men, murdered for refusing to convert to Islam.

The family stayed with their car, rather than walk on foot, knowing it offered some nighttime shelter. Despite daytime temperatures of 120 degrees Fahrenheit, nights could drop to the low 50s. Barakat also knew that with his car, he could recharge his mobile phone and stay in touch with other family members and friends who were on the run, too. He drove as high as he could maneuver his vehicle until he stopped, and the family walked from their car to a small fleck of shade where two hundred other refugees had gathered, in shock. Their reactions were delayed, their conversations were repetitive, and their emotions pivoted from numbness to distress. The wailing never ceased, even late in the night, and Barakat's children joined in, crying almost constantly, worsening their dehydration and exhaustion. At nighttime, he lay with his wife and cuddled their children. They stayed for four days.

FINAL ASSAULT

The city of Sinjar lay at the foot of Mount Sinjar. A north–south road ran directly through the city and connected to the mountain switch-back road at the point of ascension. This main intersection included the checkpoint for the ring road that encircled Mount Sinjar. By holding this checkpoint, Islamic State controlled vehicular access to the north side of the mountain, forcing Yazidis to flee up its southern side along the switchback road.

Islamic State never attempted to drive up the switchback into the interior of the valley at Mount Sinjar's highest elevation, as the route is easy to defend from higher ground. Armed Yazidi fighters from the mountains remained on the heights above the city, and it was an active front line between local fighters and Islamic State until the final liberation of the city in November 2015.

Even under normal circumstances, the tension between Kurds (Muslims, Yazidis, and Christians) and Arabs (Sunni and Shia Muslims) in Sinjar city was palpable. Decades earlier, the city's population was mostly Yazidi and Christian, and they lived amid the ancient structures as they had lived throughout history, in small stone houses with attached lean-tos for shade. But Arabs began to arrive under the Ba'athist Arabization and new neighborhoods with larger, sturdier houses were built. The local marketplace grew as the city became a center for commerce, and Yazidis began to feel they were losing their homeland to the new majority population, the Arabs. After the US invasion of Iraq, the Peshmerga assumed control of Sinjar city and civic power returned to the Yazidis. The local Arab community that had dominated the city suddenly found itself disenfranchised and belittled. Resentment and jealousy simmered beneath every social interaction, at the markets, the schools, and sporting events.

After the fall of Mosul, Kurdish Muslims, Yazidis, and Christians were anxious about the appearance of Islamic State in small Arab communities around Sinjar. On the streets of their own city, they overheard their Arab neighbors whisper words of praise for Islamic State's violence and imposition of Sharia law. The neighbors seemed to exhibit a growing religiosity evidenced by increased attendance at the mosque. When Mosul fell, they were gleeful.

For the previous few weeks, Peshmerga leaders had worried they were containing a tinderbox that could catch fire at the slightest provocation. Individual soldiers worked hard to reassure the population that the defensive forces were committed to the protection of the city while senior commanders cultivated relationships with Yazidi and Christian elders to allay their doubts.

That is why the withdrawal of the Peshmerga and the ease with which Islamic State conquered the city on that Sunday morning are seen by Yazidis worldwide as an unforgivable act of cowardice and betrayal.

At 3:00 a.m., cellphones began to ring. Reports from the frontline towns of Ger Zerik and Siba were first unbelievable and then terrifying. Within a few hours, the Peshmerga soldiers guarding Sinjar began their withdrawal, quickly followed by the city's political leadership. Those residents who had been awakened early also began to flee, but, because it was the morning after a major holiday celebration in the city, many slept late or were at the homes of relatives and did not have their own vehicles.

At 9:00 a.m., an explosion rocked Sinjar when the Sitee Zaynab Mosque, frequented by Kurdish Muslims, blew up. But Islamic State had not yet entered the city. Survivors later reported there had been a cell of Islamic State sympathizers inside the city waiting for the invasion. These collaborators appeared on the streets just before dawn with automatic weapons, dressed in black and wearing balaclavas. They screamed insults at the fleeing Yazidis and, on several occasions, pulled young women out of cars to hold as prisoners before telling their families to run. They, it is believed, bombed the mosque to heighten the sense of chaos and siege.

Islamic State entered the city at 10:00 a.m. At this hour, nearly half the city's ninety thousand population had left. The Yazidis and Christians who delayed began to run on foot along the only road up to the mountain, but groups of local Arab men drove pickup trucks into the crowd, corralling them like cattle, and forcing them back into the town.

As Islamic State fighters dispersed throughout the city, local Arab collaborators pointed out the homes of prominent or wealthy Yazidis and they were spray painted with marks to indicate they were to be bulldozed. At the hospital, established by Ba'athists years earlier and staffed with southern Arabs, doctors welcomed Islamic State and escorted them through the wards pointing out Yazidi and Christian patients. The doctors loitered in the hallway outside each ward as the jihadists executed Yazidis and Christians as they lay sick and defenseless in their beds.

Writing in the August 6, 2014, edition of the *New Yorker*, reporter George Packer described events in Sinjar as reported by his friend Karim: "Later, ISIS posted triumphant photos on Twitter: bullet-riddled corpses in the streets and dirt fields; an ISIS fighter aiming his pistol at the heads of five men lying face down on the ground; Arab locals who stayed in Sinjar jubilantly greeting the new occupiers."

Those who made it to safety appear to be either the ones who fled early, or those who left on foot and stayed off the main road up the mountain. It is still unclear how many Yazidis died in Sinjar. The kidnapped women were taken to Tal Afar, the Islamic State stronghold, and, later, brought to Raqqa in Syria where Islamic State sold them on the sex slave market. Many of the arrested were boys as young as five, who were transferred to Mosul and placed into child army training units. Many of these children survived and are in dire need of psychiatric care that is unavailable at the IDP camps.

In April 2016, the US Army released a Threat Action Report called "Battle for Sinjar, Iraq" that describes Islamic State's subterranean command and control center in Sinjar. After taking the city, the jihadists dug a series of thirty to forty tunnels that linked significant buildings used as military posts. "The sandbagged tunnels, about the height of a person, contained ammunition, prescription drugs, blankets, electrical wires leading to fans, and lights and other supplies." Living mostly underground allowed Islamic State to destroy the city, to ensure that the Yazidi homeland would be nearly impossible to rebuild and that a three-thousand-year-old community would vanish.

During the fifteen months that Islamic State held Sinjar, neighborhoods were destroyed with explosives and anything of value was looted. When the Peshmerga retook the city in November 2015, not a single building was intact except for a few structures in a small section of the Arab quarter. The city was an uninhabitable ruin. According to Agence France-Presse, groups of armed Yazidi men returned to Sinjar city immediately after its liberation to engage in reprisal killings, targeting the Arabs who had aided Islamic State, forcing the city's remaining inhabitants to flee as well.

In 2016, two large mass gravesites near Sinjar had yet to be excavated. West of the city, in 2015, in the agricultural area of Zumani, Peshmerga fighters found a mass grave containing hundreds of bodies. Only a few houses were scattered about a vast area so it is believed that the victims were either killed in Sinjar and their bodies dumped or that captured Yazidis were driven here to be more efficiently despatched after execution. Islamic State used earth-moving equipment to cover the bodies, but the dirt layer was shallow. When the first Peshmerga came across the site, bones and the remnants of clothing were scattered about: The dead had been disturbed by animals, most likely street dogs.

PESHMERGA

The first western news reports of the pre-dawn attack on the Yazidis were erroneous. "Militants with the Islamic State extremist group on Sunday seized two small towns in northern Iraq after driving out Kurdish Security Forces," The Associated Press reported. But Kurdish security forces, the Peshmerga, had not been routed by Islamic State. In the majority of villages, they had left before, upon learning of Islamic State's approach. In almost every case, they failed to notify village elders of their departure, delaying by several hours an evacuation that could have saved thousands.

It is hard to overstate how traumatic the Peshmerga withdrawal was for the Yazidis. For all Kurds, Yazidi and non-Yazidi, the Peshmerga warrior tradition reaches near mythic levels. It has existed for thousands of years, linked to Kurdish wars fought against the Persian, the Ottoman, and the British Empire. Deep pride and allegiance to the Peshmerga was evident in Kurdish homes, including Yazidi ones, with large framed photographs of grandfathers, fathers, husbands, and sons in full Peshmerga uniforms displayed prominently in the living room.

In Dakhil Shammo's family home in Baadre, a large oil painting of his late father, Shammo, hangs on the wall in the entrance hall of the stone house. It is a full body portrait. Shammo is standing slightly at an angle, a wide red sash covering the tuck where baggy khaki green pants and shirt of the same fabric meet. He stares fiercely at those who enter.

Peshmerga in translation means "those who face death." These warriors are responsible for defending the people, land, and government of Kurdistan. It is not an army in the usual sense, meaning it does not report to one central command with a top-down command structure. Rather it is a series of militias, all ethnically Kurd, that belong to one of the two main political parties: the Democratic Party of Kurdistan (KDP) or the Patriotic Union of Kurdistan (PUK). Members of all Kurdish faiths join the militias, many coming from poor villages with few job prospects. Almost all things in Kurdistan—including cellphone companies, radio and TV stations, and newspaper and taxicab companies—are owned by one of these two political parties. The Peshmerga is no different. Volunteers typically join one of the units loyal to their or their family's political party.

The exact size of the Peshmerga is unclear. There are estimates ranging from 80,000 to 250,000. These forces are organized into roughly thirty-six military brigades, controlled separately with little or no coordination, by the two political parties or by the Ministry of Peshmerga Affairs in Erbil. The Ministry has a quasi-authority. Their arsenal is limited, confined by international restrictions that prevent Kurdistan from buying arms since it is not an independent state. Baghdad, the federal capital, had cut off the flow of arms years before, fearing Kurdish aspirations for independence. Peshmerga forces largely rely on old Soviet weapons captured from Saddam Hussein's Iraqi army during the American invasion of 2003 as well as Soviet weapons purchased from Iran.

When the Yazidis understood that the estimated eighteen thousand Peshmerga troops in Ninewah had abandoned them, they were incapable of believing it was due to cowardice or incompetent leadership. For the Yazidis, the withdrawal, or "the betrayal" as Yazidis now refer to it, must have resulted from an order from high above, where it was determined that Yazidis would become human pawns or sacrifices to the Kurdish cause. Someone in the Kurdish government must have ordered the withdrawal calculating that a massacre would follow and garner international attention, so that the West would finally agree to give or sell arms to the Kurds.

Indeed, certain facts and certain behaviors of troops in the withdrawal are so similar that it is hard to believe they were spontaneous. As news of the advance spread, the men of each unit in disparate locations north of Siba changed into civilian clothes and drove their military vehicles, laden with weapons and supplies, toward Erbil. The Yazidis in the unit were not informed of the departure. The others left without warning, in the dark of early morning, abandoning three hundred thousand Yazidis, nearly half of them children, unprotected.

Video taken by a local television station showed lines of military vehicles that could only belong to Peshmerga forces driving before sunup on the roads leaving the area.

Anonymous Kurdish sources later told news agencies the Peshmerga had made a "tactical retreat" from Sinjar. Individual Kurdish soldiers told others they had run out of bullets and fled for their lives.

Senior Kurdish officials continue to deny that any authority had ordered or coordinated the withdrawal. "There was categorically no order to withdraw from any front. There was negligence," Peshmerga Ministry spokesman Holgard Hekmat has insisted. In 2015, in a howler of an understatement, he told the German website Spiegel Online, "Our soldiers just ran away. It's a shame."

It is possible that some inexperienced unit commanders closest to Islamic State encampments panicked, pulling their men from the front lines and alerting other units as they fled. However, while there may be some truth in that scenario, it seems implausible that it would replay the same way in nearly every Yazidi community.

In the weeks that followed the genocide, conspiracy theories began to make their way into local newspapers. One of them is the cannon fodder theory. Yazidi survivors in the Internally Displaced People camps that grew around Dohuk almost to a person believe that they were sacrificed for Kurdish benefit.

Kurdistan's President Barzani addressed the failure of Peshmerga, opening a high-profile investigation during which he stated: "What happened in Sinjar did not happen to the Yazidis alone; it is an injury that has hurt us all. Those officials should not have withdrawn; they should have sacrificed themselves in defense of the region." Despite the rhetoric, not a single military leader was relieved of command and the investigation quietly slipped from the headlines.

In an extraordinary reversal of blame and pointing of fingers, mainstream Kurdish news outlets openly alleged Yazidi leaders had been arguing with the Peshmerga just before the invasion and that they had ignored Peshmerga warnings to leave. The victims were at fault, they wrote.

Conspiracy theories arise and are often believed when the truth reflects incompetence and feckless behavior on a massive, destructive scale. It can be easier to believe in nefarious conspiracy than gross incompetence that seems too random to be possible.

Whatever the cause of the Peshmerga withdrawal on that day, and it is doubtful the truth will be known, it created an irreparable breach between the Kurdish people and the Yazidi people. The hostility and blame is so strong that Yazidis stopped considering themselves Kurdish, rejecting their traditional ethnicity to claim Yazidism as both a faith and an ethnicity for the first time in history.

The failure of the Barzani government to undertake a rebuilding of Sinjar and the villages scattered around the region since the Islamic State invasion gives credence to the Yazidi claim that they are a dispensable people.

All of which leads to the current division among the Yazidi people themselves: those who want to stay and rebuild their homeland and those who see no future there save additional massacres or the meaningless day-to-day existence in camps for Internally Displaced People. The latter apply to leave. They hope to go to Germany, Australia, Canada, and the United States, even if it means breaking apart their tightly knit culture, and, in a way, allowing Islamic State to succeed in its desire to eradicate the Yazidi people from the region.

Abbas's Story Part II

Still resting on a low plateau on Mount Sinjar, the gaping wound in his back stuffed with a dirty sock, Abbas lay among hundreds of traumatized Yazidis in the brutal sun.

Abbas saw an acquaintance and waved for his attention. He used the man's mobile phone to call a cousin. His father and siblings were alive and with him, his cousin said. Abbas described his surroundings to the cousin, who left his hiding place on the mountainside and searched until they reunited. Hoisting Abbas's bloodstained body on his back, his cousin carried him to an abandoned village cut into the mountain where he met his father and siblings.

His two sisters tended his bullet wounds by wiping the edges with a household cleaner they had found in a deserted house. The stinging pain caused him to faint several times. They wrapped the wounds in torn sheets from the same house. His brothers scavenged food for the family, finding old bread and canned goods in other houses. They hid for five days and four nights while Abbas rested to regain his strength.

His odyssey was not over.

On August 9, six days after Abbas was shot, the family set out at night, walking around the mountain to where they hoped to reach the border with Syria. His father, brothers, and sisters took turns holding him up as they picked their way along the craggy cliffs. The sun, high in the cloudless sky, burned their faces and ears until their skin split. Finally, after seven hours, they reached Karsi, a small town on the north side of the mountain where villagers gave them water. From Karsi, they joined the Yazidi exodus from Iraq as thousands of refugees, walking past the ravaged villages of Duguri and Sinuni, headed toward Syria.

The next day Abbas was unable to walk. The pain was unbearable. He fainted constantly. His sister flagged down a Syrian Kurdish military vehicle whose occupant agreed to take him alone across the border to a Syrian refugee camp. He does not recall leaving his family. He remembers only hearing himself groaning as the car lurched forward through desert sand, and he remembers once noting the bodies of the dead that had been left roadside.

The car brought an unconscious Abbas to a makeshift aid camp set up by Syrian Kurds who lived along the border. Syrian Kurdish fighters, known as the YPG, had gone into Iraq to fight Islamic State on August 3, the day of the invasion, and opened a safe corridor from Mount Sinjar into Syria. As the refugees fled, Syrian Kurds greeted them with food, water, and basic medical assistance before bringing them north to Fish-kilbur, a bridge crossing into the safety of Dohuk Province in Iraq.

Knowing Abbas was near death, YPG soldiers did not stop at the camp, but drove him immediately to the crossing where an uncle, alerted by cellphone, was waiting to bring him to the Dohuk hospital in Kurdistan.

Eight days after two bullets tore through his body and the main bullet hole was stuffed with a dirty sock, Abbas Kheder Silo finally received medical attention. The doctor who tended him said, "You are a living miracle."

CHAPTER FOUR

First Reactions

Monday, August 4

THE SINJAR MOUNTAINS FORM A SIXTY-TWO-MILE MOUNTAIN RANGE that rises boldly out of the alluvial steppe plains of northwestern Iraq. It is a spectacular example of a breached anticline wherein the crest that once topped the peak is so eroded that it forms a valley within the mountain, with inward-facing cliffs, the way a baker punches a loaf of bread before putting it in the oven. Mount Sinjar, its highest elevation at just under a mile, rests in Ninewah Governorate. Set between the Tigris and the Euphrates Rivers, the area has the characteristic climate of steppes: semi-arid and continental. Seasons are marked by extreme temperature changes as are winter and summer days. The ridge is barren, devoid of most plant life, water, or shade.

Since the twelfth century, Mount Sinjar and the eponymous city to its south have been the center of the Yazidi culture. They lie in the heart of Mesopotamia, from which the human race bounded forward during the Neolithic Revolution of 10,000 BC, inventing the wheel, cursive script, mathematics, and astronomy. Often referred to as the cradle of civilization, the region still echoes with the ancient prayers that formed the religious absolute of the Abrahamic faiths. The Yazidis believe they are the world's oldest people, claiming they are descended from Adam alone and not from the lineage of Adam and Eve. They don't see good and evil as opposites personified in particular gods, but as qualities that are integral parts of creation—they exist throughout the world, within the mind and spirit of human beings.

The origins of the Yazidi faith remain unclear. It is not, as commonly explained, derivative of other faiths, although it has some elements of Christian, Jewish, Sufi Muslim, Zoroastrian, and Manichaean traditions. It is an oral religion, without a holy book of defining protocols, and most likely adopted rituals of other faiths as they spread into the region.

The supreme being of this monotheistic faith is known as Yasdan. He is the creator of the world and watches it passively. Seven great spirits emanate from him, the greatest being the Peacock Angel known as Melek Taus. Melek Taus is considered God's alter ego.

Yazidis pray to Malak Taus five times a day. He is also called Shaytan, which is Arabic for devil, and this has led to the Yazidis being mislabeled as "devil-worshippers." That misconception has been reinforced by the lack of the concept of a hell in Yazidism. The Yazidis believe in transmigration of the soul, which leads to its purification through continual rebirth, so death cannot lead to a final location, heaven or hell.

The worst possible fate for a Yazidi is to be expelled from his community, as this means the soul of the expelled can never progress. Conversion to another religion is, therefore, out of the question. Only those born into the Yazidi community can belong to the religion. The Yazidis do not appear to accept converts. Within the faith, the Yazidis live in a caste system. The highest caste consists of the Baba Sheik, the highest holy man, and his family. The second and third of the four castes are reserved for holy men, or those who assist in religious ceremonies, and their families. The majority of Yazidis belong to the fourth caste, called Murid, or commoners. The castes cannot intermarry.

After centuries of obscurity, the Yazidis leapt onto the world stage in the mid-nineteenth century when intrepid British explorer Austen Henry Layard returned from the Ninewah plains after several years of participating in archaeological digs. Frustrated by the British government's failure to fund additional exploration, Layard decided to ratchet up public interest in the region, and hopefully, government funding, by publishing his two-volume memoir, the generously titled *Nineveh and Its Remains: With an Account of a Visit to the Chaldean Christians of Kurdistan, and the Yezidis, or Devil-Worshippers; and an Enquiry into the Manners and Arts of the Ancient Assyrians* (2 vols., 1848–1849). Cleverly, and with publicity in mind, Layard wrote of his interest in the Yazidis and gave much ink to exploring rumors of "worshipping the devil" and of a people whose "ancient ceremonies, midnight orgies, a worship that led to every excess of debauchery." In the latter part of his book, however, he debunked those notions, describing his attendance at a religious ceremony at Lalish Temple, and writing there were "no indecent gestures or unseemly ceremonies." Layard became almost enamored with the Yazidis, writing of their living quarters, "I never before saw so much assembled cleanliness in the East." His publicity stunt worked, however, for the prurient Victorian reader made his book a bestseller and the Yazidis were now marked in the West as well as the East as the devil-worshippers of Iraq.

More than one hundred years later, an explorer with a different purpose also went to Mount Sinjar. Canadian-American rocket scientist and artillery expert Gerald Bull was hired by Iraq's then defense secretary and soon-to-be dictator Saddam Hussein to build a "supergun" in a scheme that later came to be called "Project Babylon." Dr. Bull began in March 1988 to develop the prototype for his supergun, a .350-caliber gun with a barrel length of thirty to fifty-two meters that could shoot a 1.5-meter projectile of about four hundred kilograms to a range of more than one hundred miles. Despite Hussein's assurances that the gun would be used for shooting satellites into the sky, Israel was not pleased. The CIA was confused, as documents declassified in 2012 show:

"The most frequently asked question about the Supergun is why anyone would want to develop such an expensive system to accomplish what surface-to-surface missiles (SSMs) already do quite effectively," one analyst mused.

The prototype, named Baby Babylon, was eventually assembled and mounted on Mount Sinjar for testing. A few months later, Dr. Bull was assassinated in his Brussels apartment, most likely by a western intelligence agency, although his murder remains unsolved, and the project collapsed. Components for the actual supergun, Big Babylon, were confiscated by British customs as they were leaving Britain for delivery to Iraq and are now on display at the Royal Armouries in Portsmouth, England.

Yazidis to this day lower their voices when they speak of Saddam Hussein's Secret Project or else they refuse to discuss it, just as they did thirty years ago when United Nations Weapons Inspector Scott Ritter tried unsuccessfully to track down the rumors of "a supergun." They believe Saddam Hussein's decision to test his potentially devastating weapon on sacred Mount Sinjar was an affront to God.

Yazidis have always believed Mount Sinjar was holy. Throughout centuries of violent persecution, they have taken refuge on its craggy mountainside, hiding in caves, or small valleys, or at the site of their eight-hundred-year-old sacred temple, Sharfadeen.

As Islamic State swept through their towns and villages in 2014, fifty thousand Yazidis instinctively fled to their traditional protector: Mount Sinjar. At the time, it was difficult to obtain an accurate count of the stranded. Some reports said there were more than two hundred thousand—others said fewer than fifty thousand. Today, with hindsight, most researchers have accepted the fifty thousand estimate.

It is important to remember that the number arose solely from the estimates of officials from nongovernmental charities in the region who were desperate to call attention to the humanitarian crisis. No one on the mountain was counting and crowd estimates are notoriously difficult to ascertain.

Whatever the number, those seeking refuge on the mountain had little to eat or drink. A few men had weapons. But every single Yazidi man and woman had a cellphone.

BARAKAT'S STORY PART II

During the first two days on Mount Sinjar, Barakat shared as much of his family's food and water with other refugees as he dared. Later he recognized that he had been overly generous when his own children began crying for water. After the fourth day, he decided to return to the village at the foothills to scout for supplies.

As he neared the base of the mountain, he spotted five or six Islamic State trucks. Nearby, gunmen were screaming at a line of twenty or so men, berating them as "devil worshippers and infidels." The men stood with their arms dangling, shoulders slumped, and eyes vacant. Their bodies quaked. One fighter faced them as the others walked behind them.

"Will you convert?" demanded the fighter in the front. Groaning, the prisoners shook their heads. Someone called out "No." The soldiers behind them opened fire. Barakat watched the Yazidis go limp and fall like dolls dropped in the dirt. Without looking further for water, he climbed back up the mountain.

The plight of people on the mountain had become calamitous. Children wandered the crags, dazed with thirst, begging for water. Old women cried out to end their suffering and beseeched their families to leave them to die when they went in search of food. The shrieking never let up. Hundreds of voices of men and women wailed around him. Barakat learned he could tell who was near death by the sound of their lament, by its desperation and futility. His family's situation was no less dire. He administered drops of water to his wife and children every few hours. They lay on their backs in their small patch of shade, not speaking, their skin covered with dirt and sweat, preserving their energy for breathing.

Islamic State controlled the road ringing the mountain and patrols ascended a few hundred yards to search for Yazidis, but they never climbed farther. The refugees speculated ceaselessly about the possibility of an attack on their camp and the younger ones began to climb higher, believing an extra buffer of two or three hundred yards of rock provided greater security. On the fifth day, Barakat went to search for wild figs and saw an Islamic State fighter disassembling a water wheel at a narrow stream near the mountain's base. That is when he realized that Islamic State would not attack, but instead would wait at the foothills until the thousands of Yazidis hiding on Mount Sinjar died of dehydration and starvation.

"I picked herbs and took rotten bread from an abandoned house. There were still thousands of people at the foothills. I saw one man try to go to a water wheel at another village. They shot him. There were bodies all around. Near me, I saw the bodies of a man and two children. I took their water bottle and I used that water and rotten bread and shared it with my family and others near us," he said.

By the seventh or eighth day, he had lost his sense of time but on one of those days, Barakat's two children screamed, pointing at a young woman who had sheltered near them for days. She had stayed close to Barakat's wife, looking to her for guidance, if not hope. A shy, frightened woman, married less than a year, she had an infant in her arms. She had lost her husband in the chaos and had not found him again. Barakat saw that she had fallen, her face pale, her eyes fluttering, nearly unconscious, her baby still in her arms and a dirty blue cloth around her head. He shouted for food and someone handed him a piece of stale bread that he spat on, and worked through his fingers until it softened. He fed it to her in tiny pieces until she was stronger.

Smoke curled up from among the trees, and he knew someone was baking bread. He followed the smoke until he came upon an encampment. He asked for some bread. When they shooed him away, he lunged at the loaves, grabbing one and running. He returned to his family and they shared the bread with the refugees sheltering near them. Some of the women were able to coax the wild goats to stay still for milking. They fed each other goat milk that they cupped in their palms.

On about his tenth day on the mountain, Barakat returned to the foothills to search again for food. Though he no longer cared if he lived or died, he was driven by the crying of his children. He saw an Iraqi helicopter in the sky, but Islamic State gunmen from the ring road opened fire and it flew away. After searching for hours, and dodging Islamic State along the base of the mountain, he returned empty-handed to his camp midway up the mountain. His family and most of the refugees were gone.

He lay down on the ground. Heat and hunger made his head thump with pain. His feet and hands were swollen. Burned skin peeled from his forehead and cheeks. He could not comprehend the disappearance of the others. He did not recognize anyone nearby. Then he heard the swishing rotor of a helicopter and saw one hovering high above his encampment. It dropped a small cache of supplies that floated downward and scattered around the camp. Two cans hit the rocks and split open. Children scurried around the site, rubbing their hands on the rocks and then licking them. Two young mothers crawled on the hot rocks to scrape food with their fingernails. They put their fingers in their babies' mouths to nourish them. Among the few supplies, they found axes and shovels. One young man asked Barakat, "What are they for?"

"They are for our graves," he answered.

Later that day, Islamic State began shelling the mountain, and their mortars landed close to Barakat's encampment. He knew he had to go farther up the mountain and enter the valley, but his location required him to first descend several hundred yards before he could hike up. As he went down, cautiously watching for the gunmen, he saw a middle-aged woman with eight young children near the ring road. They were being held up by two Islamic State fighters and the woman was pleading with them to spare the children. Crouching down, hiding, he heard eight shots and the hysterical screams of the woman. He raised his head slightly and watched her run from one dead child to another, screaming "Kill me, kill me." The soldiers laughed and left. Barakat was too numb to feel rage, but he was grateful that he hadn't been seen.

He ascended the mountain, stumbling frequently. A flock of birds flew above him and he marveled at their flight, feeling their weightlessness as they soared away from the suffering on that mountain. He arrived at the highest point, surrounded by thousands of other refugees. It was quiet. No one had the strength to cry out. Men, women, and children lay in dirty rags on the ground, listless and defeated. He sprawled out under a shrub, exhausted, dehydrated, and thought of his mother, the caress of her gentle hands. He pulled leaves from the shrub and ate them. Within minutes, his body responded with an allergic reaction. His throat and neck swelled and his gums began to throb. He lost sight in his right eye. "This is my death," he thought as his head rolled back and he fell unconscious.

Barakat Sulu awoke on a cot, lying beneath white sheets. Syrian women in military uniforms, armed with Kalashnikovs, were distributing water to the hundreds of refugees around him. He was unable to formulate questions or comprehend his situation. A woman approached and stood near him.

"The YPG (Syrian Kurdish troops) got you off the mountain," she said. "You are in Syria. You are safe."

"Have you seen my family?" he asked, shouting their names to those around him. No one answered.

"Thousands have come off the mountain," the woman told him. "I am sure your family is among them."

He lay in his cot and sobbed.

After four days of treatment for his allergic reaction, his feet wrapped in bandages, and his facial burns treated, Barakat was driven by Syrian Kurdish troops to the border with Iraqi Kurdistan. As he shuffled across the bridge that divides the two countries, he saw the son of a friend from his village. The boy held his hand, and took him to the house where he was living with his family. After resting there, Barakat used his friend's mobile phone to track down his family, calling everyone he knew, begging for information, until finally, he found them in the nearby village of Khanke where they had found shelter with an old friend after being rescued by the YPG.

WASHINGTON

It was unusually pleasant in Washington, DC, on August 4, 2014. The city's notorious humidity had not yet appeared and the Monday morning was a cool 72 degrees. Sun and clouds battled for control of the sky. Sprinkles of rain fell on Leanne Cannon as she made her way up the stairs from the Metro station to her office at the US Department of State. The thirty-two-year-old Foreign Service officer was not involved in the Africa Summit and was anticipating a quiet day.

She arrived before her civil service counterpart, Douglas Padgett, because today the nearly empty Metro train sailed right along, depositing her in the middle of DC's Foggy Bottom neighborhood without delays. She put down her bag and flicked on the office coffee machine. Doug arrived a few minutes later, along with some of the administrative staff.

Doug and Leanne had worked together for less than a year, but they had developed a solid office partnership, if not a friendship. Their strong mutual respect would become the basis for the extraordinary success and attention they brought to their tiny office over the next two weeks.

"She is absolutely the smartest, most effective policy officer I have worked with in the State Department," Padgett said.

Sitting in her windowless office, sipping coffee and scrolling through emails, she noticed an "urgent" subject line and opened an email from Dakhil Shammo. He asked for an urgent meeting to discuss the situation on the ground in northern Iraq. This was not an unusual request, in fact, it was the normal protocol for the IRF office to invite dissidents, religious leaders, or small religious communities into their small conference room to discuss issues of religious persecution in their home countries. Yet Leanne knew something about this was different. She immediately forwarded the message to Doug and her superior, Tom Melia.

Tom Melia, the deputy assistant secretary of state for democracy, human rights and labor, was fifty-eight, had worked in government since graduating from Johns Hopkins University with a master's degree from the School of Advanced International Studies. As a young man, he once served as a legislative assistant to the revered senator from New York, Daniel Patrick Moynihan, employment he called "life-changing." He had long been interested in policy issues that advance the building of civil societies in the Middle East and South and Central Asia, Melia was briefed by Padgett and Cannon and immediately grasped the acute need for action. "I think most people involved in elevating the story of what was happening couldn't explain to you what a Yazidi is," Melia said, "but the fact that there was this small group of people with no friend around them, surrounded by a people who don't like them, and had their Sunni Arab neighbors turn on them from a Monday to a Tuesday, that was breathtaking to me. You think about these little towns and villages and these guys, Islamic State, with their black flags and pickup trucks coming in, and then all your neighbors suddenly pull out their black flags from the back of the closet, and you say 'I thought you were my neighbor.'"

HARDAN

During the early morning hours of Monday, August 4, Islamic State reached three small villages on the far northeast flank of the mountain. Hardan was a community of 1,917 Yazidis and Gormiz was barely a village, but rather an enclave of 150 Yazidi families living up a slope that offers a clear view of Hardan on the plain below. The third village, Ger Shabak, was home to more than thirty-five hundred Sunni Arabs.

At a highway intersection just outside Hardan, Islamic State committed one of its worst massacres. More than three hundred men were executed, ten by beheading, and hundreds of women and girls were seized. From their perch on the slope above, a few men of Gormiz witnessed these atrocities in Hardan as they peered through binoculars.

Residents of the third village, Arab village elders from Ger Zerik, played a role in the massacre. Survivors told investigators the Arab villagers arrived in Hardan on Sunday afternoon. They, the elders, confirmed that the Peshmerga had left the region and that Sinjar city had fallen. They reassured Hardan's residents that Islamic State was not coming to their community, but instead was sending "tribal revolutionaries" to talk to the Yazidis. If the Yazidis allowed them to advance into town without a struggle, no one would be hurt, but if they resisted, they would all be killed. They left and returned to Ger Zerik.

Surrounded as they were by Sunni Arab farms and outposts of Ger Zerik, the Yazidis of Hardan didn't flee. It was not possible to run secretly. Instead, they waited for the arrival of the "tribal revolutionaries."

"Those Arabs told us that ISIS was coming and they began shouting over the loudspeakers [of the mosque] and wandering through the streets. 'We are not going to kill any Yazidi. We having nothing against the Yazidis,'" a young male survivor of the massacre told investigators.

Monday morning the men of Hardan learned they had been deceived. They allowed Islamic State to enter without resistance. When the convoy drove in, town villagers immediately recognized ten local Arab men accompanying the jihadists. They spoke reassuringly to the Yazidis and said they would be safe. At noon, they abruptly withdrew.

Hardan was then quickly overrun by Arab men from neighboring Ger Shabak and Turkmen from another nearby village. These men visited the homes of the senior Yazidi men, talking to them respectfully and kindly, trying to reassure them they were safe. In retrospect, many survivors believe the purpose of these visits was to observe the village to scout whether people were planning to flee or to defend the town.

By late afternoon, hundreds of phone calls from relatives and friends throughout the Sinjar region related tales of massacres, the kidnapping of the women, and the flight to the mountain. At almost the same moment, panic seized everyone in the village and they began to flee. Multiple families packed into cars and onto tractors, clutching water or a few belongings, and headed out of town.

Islamic State was waiting. They had set up an ambush at the intersection of the highway and the village road. The first few cars were stopped and their occupants were captured. Drivers at the back of the convoy turned around and headed back to Hardan. The captured families began to call them. They said the women were being separated from the men.

A female survivor told investigators, "Everyone who came wrote a list and in his hand was a pen and a copybook. And they say, this one and I want that one. They would take her and beat her . . . And the one after her, if she says, 'I will not come,' they will drag her by the hair. Whether she wants it or not, her name is recorded on the list . . . Everyone who came took almost 20 girls. Until now, the screaming of girls is in my mind, even if I went to doctors and psychologists, their screaming is in my mind and won't leave."

The women and children were taken to Tal Afar, an Islamic State stronghold, and later brought to Raqqa, Syria, where they were sold on the slave market.

During the next six days, from the high ground above, Yazidi men from Gormiz watched as Islamic State and local Sunni Arabs committed a series of mass murders.

The killings took place at twilight, presumably after a day spent hunting down Yazidi men who were either fleeing or hiding. The militants lined up a group of twenty to thirty handcuffed men in the headlights of a bulldozer and opened fire. The bulldozer then pushed earth over the bodies.

There are six confirmed mass graves around Hardan.

Some residents of Hardan did survive. A convoy of twenty cars left after dark Monday, with their lights off, and drove west to Kharaniya, another small Yazidi village, eluding Islamic State. They continued traveling west through the night until they arrived at Sharfadeen, a Yazidi temple at the northern foothills of Mount Sinjar.

NEBRASKA YAZIDIS

On Monday morning, the Lincoln, Nebraska, police department prepared for a large downtown demonstration of the city's Yazidi population.

The previous day, Sunday, the city had been caught by surprise. Late morning, as many residents were leaving church, about five hundred colorfully dressed Yazidi men, women, and children, many holding large signs, arrived at the Governor's Mansion in downtown Lincoln. It was oppressively hot, and most of the protesters stood under the leafy umbrella of a massive elm adjacent to the metal fence that surrounded the thirty-one-room Georgian colonial home. Forming a circle, they began to chant "We need help" while holding their signs aloft.

"Help the Yazidis."

"They are killing us."

"Stop ISIS."

Lincoln city police showed up within minutes of the start of the gathering, and confused officers waded into the group to determine the reason for their protests. Crying women and children surrounded the officers, and a few men asked them to ask the governor to come out to talk. The police told the demonstrators to disperse because they did not have a permit. A dozen Nebraska state troopers arrived to help maintain order. The marchers grew agitated when Governor Dave Heineman failed to appear, although it was unclear whether he was in the residence at the time. Local television news crews set up their cameras at the perimeter of the mansion's grounds. A neighborhood bike club cycled past, then stopped to watch. The twenty or so city police, once they understood the cause for this spontaneous release of emotion, were sympathetic. They recognized it as a misdirected but sincere plea for help. Nevertheless, the officers pointed out, the gathering was illegal. A few older Yazidi men became overwrought with emotion and acted aggressively toward the police, resulting in two arrests.

On Monday Chief of Police Jim Peschong assigned several officers to meet the protesters at the State Capitol building and escort their protest march to the Cornhusker Marriott Hotel, where Congressman Jeff Fortenberry held an emergency meeting with several Yazidi activists.

"I had a group of young men who were all gathered, called quickly, who came to plead with me, beg me, were on the verge of tears and on the verge of breaking out in anger," Fortenberry recalled.

"There was a tension in the room, I understand it, it was about their families that were about to be killed. These were very dignified young men who had made their way to America who had earned it but at the same time were trying to protect their families back home. So, there was a tension within them to maintain composure and respect for the office and yet at the same time how could anyone maintain composure under that kind of pressure? In that agony?"

Outside the hotel, the protesters chanted and waved their signs until one of Fortenberry's aides came out and asked them to go home. The meeting had ended, he explained to them, and Fortenberry had drafted a letter to President Obama.

As he was leaving the hotel, Fortenberry told local reporters that he hoped the United States would demand the Yazidis be protected and provide humanitarian help for the refugees.

"This is genocide," Fortenberry said, "against the Christians and the Yazidis who are there."

He described Islamic State as "fanatics who fly the black banner of death."

His letter, co-signed by Republican congressman Frank Wolf and Democratic congresswoman Anna Eshoo, expressed "grave concerns about the ongoing genocide against Christians and other religious minorities in Iraq" and called "for a humanitarian intervention by the United Nations Security Council and led by the US to champion basic human rights and religious liberty."

For the young men of the Yazidi community, many of them former US Army translators who had immigrated with their families under a special visa program, this was their first interaction with representative democracy.

"It's one of those piercing moments for you in public service where you don't just say let's call the State Department and try to figure this out. There was a resolution that had been introduced in Congress for another purpose and we were able to pick it up and recraft it, so that the House of Representatives could make a quick statement that I hoped would be in concert with the Obama Administration," Fortenberry said.

The resolution passed by the House reaffirmed US support for religious freedom in the Middle East and called on the US Department of State and the United Nations to work with the Kurdistan Regional Government, the government of Iraq, and neighboring countries to help secure safe havens for Christians and religious minorities being persecuted by Islamic State.

Lincoln

No one can recall exactly how Lincoln, Nebraska, became a destination for Yazidis immigrating to the United States. Presumably one refugee family settled—or was settled—in the small city and liked it. Others followed. The Yazidis came in two waves, the first after the Gulf War ended in 1991, and the second more recently, under an expedited-visa program for military translators. By 2014, more than 150 Yazidi families, nearly five hundred individuals, lived in the Lincoln area, and they were simultaneously tight-knit and loosely organized. Lincoln had no Yazidi community center, house of worship, or commercial district. The Yazidis gathered exclusively at each other's homes to organize support for new arrivals or celebrate religious holidays. They seemed to assimilate easily into American life while maintaining a distinct and strong ancestral bond.

Lincoln was the perfect American city for refugees. It was ninety-two square miles of low-rise urban buildings with a population of just under three hundred thousand. The city included former small towns that had been annexed, giving the neighborhoods a close community feel. It had much less poverty and crime than larger American cities. Housing was inexpensive and plentiful. Because most of the economic activity derived from service and manufacturing industries, jobs were not difficult to get. The public schools were well run, and the main campus of the University of Nebraska and its Cornhusker football stadium sat squarely in the middle of town.

Hadi Pir liked Lincoln almost immediately. He arrived in February 2012 with his young wife, Adula Mato, and baby daughter, Yara. They rented a two-bedroom apartment in a small complex not far from the downtown area. With his near perfect command of English, he quickly found a job as a teacher of English as a second language in one of the many language programs the city ran for refugees.

Hadi Pir appeared much younger than his thirty-eight years. He had the trim athletic body of a former military man, which, in some ways, he was, having worked for the US Army in Sinjar for several years. A fast talker with a sharp mind and alert eyes, his boundless energy and his enthusiasm for life in America made him a natural leader among his fellow Yazidis.

In Lincoln, he was relieved to be free of the relentless politics and ethnic strife of Kurdistan. He had grown up in Sinjar and, after high school, had attended college in Mosul, where he was shocked at the level of hatred for Yazidis. Previously an indifferent student, his Mosul experience instigated an extraordinary amount of reading, much of it in

English, in an attempt to understand the human need to hate. He considered himself apolitical and avoided discussions about Kurdistan's two political parties, the KDP of Barzani and the PUK of Talibani. In the United States, he tended to lean Republican, mostly from the conviction that the United States should continue to intervene in Iraq, but otherwise had little interest in American politics.

Hadi Pir was about to become an American political activist.

Monday afternoon he posted a call to arms on Facebook, inviting other Yazidis to join him on the long drive to Washington to demand action for their fellow Yazidis on Mount Sinjar. Although Adula had given birth to their second daughter just thirty-four days earlier, he rented several vans and took a leave of absence from his job. About sixty Yazidis planned to leave Tuesday to drive all day and night. They would demand action from the politicians in Washington. He learned that other Yazidis from Texas, Michigan, and Canada were planning to head to Washington also.

Before the group set off on their long drive, Pir told a local newspaper "We can't wait. People are dying. We have hours, not days." He and his wife had more than twenty-five close relatives in Sinjar they could not locate.

Yazidis at the State Department

At the Voice of America, Dakhil Shammo was unable to work. He sat at his desk in a small grayish cubicle near a window overlooking southwest DC's 3rd Street and listened to his Kurdish colleagues discuss the news. There were endless discussions about the pullout of the Peshmerga, an event that most of his colleagues dismissed as untrue. The editors called stringers in the Ninewah area continually. They all repeated the same story—the Peshmerga had withdrawn without fighting. The Peshmerga had run.

From Kurdistan's online reporting community and various international news gathering organizations, stunning stories continued to emerge.

Iraq's minister of human rights, Mohammed Shia al-Sudani, told Reuters that Islamic State had killed at least five hundred Yazidis from Sinjar, burying some of them alive. He added that more than three hundred women had been kidnapped and had been brought to the pro–Islamic State city of Tal Afar.

Embattled prime minister Nouri al-Maliki issued an order to the Iraqi air force to provide aerial support to the Peshmerga in the first sign of cooperation between the two sides since Mosul fell.

The United Nations Mission in Iraq said as many as two hundred thousand Yazidis had fled to Mount Sinjar and were surrounded by militants. The United Nations envoy to Iraq, Nickolay Mladenov, added that "a humanitarian tragedy is unfolding in Sinjar . . . the situation is dire, and they are in urgent need of basic items such as food, water and medicine." UNICEF reported more than forty children had already died on the mountain from dehydration.

The State Department spokeswoman, Jan Psaki, said little else besides that the United States continued to support "Iraqi Security Forces and the Peshmerga Forces," as if neither had collapsed.

Reuters reported "Kurdish Forces retreated after putting up little resistance," and added "Kurdish troops loaded their vehicles with belongings, including air conditioners, and fled."

Agence France-Presse wrote, "the losses to the Peshmerga, who have been seen as the only force in Iraq capable of standing up to the Islamic State, have profoundly alarmed the Kurds. Some speculated that the withdrawal of their forces was a ploy to force the United States to supply the Kurdish government with advanced weapons, but reports on the ground suggested they may simply have run out of ammunition," the first iteration of a now-popular conspiracy theory.

A few media outlets including Voice of America noted an additional Agence France-Presse report that stated, "For the first time, fighters from the separate Kurdish forces who operate in neighboring Syria and Turkey also crossed the border to help." Syria and Turkey's Kurdish militias entered Iraq to defend the Yazidis at the urging of their political arm, The Kurdistan Workers' Party. It called for fighters of the party's military arm—the YPG—to go to Iraq in a statement that said: "The treacherous ISIS attacks have been humiliating for the Kurds. Until the Kurds develop a strong resistance, they will not be able to take back their honor." Local news reports claimed these fighters had engaged Islamic State near Mount Sinjar.

No one yet understood that the entrance of the YPG would prove crucial to American military efforts to save the Yazidis on Mount Sinjar.

Dakhil, under normal circumstances an advocate of believing information gathered on the ground by VOA stringers, did not engage in the discussion about the Peshmerga's withdrawal. He could not think about politics—and to him the Peshmerga was mere politics—when he knew his family, friends, and fellow Yazidis were being massacred and that his culture was being destroyed. He called his brother in Erbil and asked for the whereabouts and safety of those trapped in the cruel roundup. The news of missing and murdered old friends left him distraught. His colleagues stepped lightly around him.

At noon, he received an email from Leanne Cannon inviting him to the State Department building for a 3:00 p.m. meeting. She urged him to bring other Yazidis. Dakhil immediately called his wife and two other Yazidi families.

A few hours later, the three Yazidi families of Virginia gathered at a parking lot in Washington's Foggy Bottom neighborhood where the US State Department hulks rise amid concrete barricades and security checkpoints. Road closures from the Africa Summit had made navigating the streets maddening, and they were relieved to enter the lobby with a few minutes to spare.

Leanne Cannon cleared the group of twelve through security and escorted them to a small beige conference room with fluorescent lights. Dakhil sat with his wife, Morbad, and his son, Hakim. Hussein Khalaf sat with his wife and his daughter Nofa. His son, Attallah, acted as his translator. Another Yazidi, Suliman Shammo (no relation to Dakhil), brought his sister and three brothers.

Padgett was quick to grasp the urgency of the situation and he asked Dakhil Shammo, the evident leader of the group, for an overview of the plight of the Yazidis.

"I told them what I knew from talking to VOA's stringers and from my own phone calls with friends and relatives," Dakhil said. "The United Nations said 200,000 Yazidis were heading toward Mount Sinjar where there was a huge humanitarian disaster. I described the massacres at Siba and other villages due to the withdrawal of the Peshmerga. I tried to stay composed, but I could hear my voice cracking. Attallah was translating for his father, Hussein, and his mother. They were weeping as I described the catastrophe."

Staffers in the IRF office were moved by the genuine emotion of the group, but were as yet unaware of the seriousness of the situation. While the events described by Dakhil Shammo were horrible, the IRF office often had meetings with diaspora communities that were concerned about human rights abuses in their home country.

"When you work in human rights, people come to you all the time," said Leanne Cannon. "We weren't expecting to do anything at this point. That the situation was so dire and so dramatic was not clear. That being said, I also knew, maybe in the back of my mind, this was different. Never before did I have to find some tissue for people because they were crying so hard."

Dakhil sensed he had not moved the State Department group to action. "I told them children were dying of dehydration because the mountain had little shade. I tried to impress them with the urgency of the situation, but I could see they thought we were exaggerating. At the end of my description, Doug asked 'How do you know all this?' and I explained we have been talking to them on their cellphones. They sneak at night to the bottom of the mountain where they left their cars and charge their cellphones to call us."

"We explained that we used the VOIP (voice over internet protocol) app WhatsApp and the calls go immediately through. Everyone in Kurdistan uses WhatsApp because it is cheaper than using a phone line," added Dakhil's son Hakim. "So, we use the WhatsApp numbers that we have and ask for other numbers to call other Yazidis and find out their situation."

Doug Padgett unfolded several maps of Iraq on the table that allowed the State Department officials to begin to familiarize themselves with the remote region of Iraq that had been the traditional home of the Yazidis.

The group begged the State Department to pressure the Iraqi and Kurdish government to intervene and help the Yazidis. Dakhil asked for airdrops of water, food, and medical supplies.

Doug, and Leanne discussed efforts that could be made through State Department channels. Then someone in the room, no one remembers who it was, suggested the group reconvene at the end of the week.

"At the end of the week," Hussein Khalaf's daughter Nofa responded, "they will all be dead."

CHAPTER FIVE

Appeals

Tuesday, August 5

THE KURDS

ETHNIC KURDS ARE ONE OF THE INDIGENOUS PEOPLE OF THE MESOPO-tamian plains and the highlands of southwestern Asia. Sumerian clay tablets dated to the third millennium mention "the land of the Karda" and its people as the Qarduchi or the Qurti. To historians, it's not clear if this is the etymology of "Kurd" since the term is not found until the seventh century in Arabic sources. Kurds are generally thought to have descended from an ancient Persian people. During the first millennia AD, Arabs conquered most Kurdish regions and gradually converted the majority of Kurds to Islam. The Yazidis were the holdouts then as they were in 2014 when Islamic State pressured them to convert at gunpoint. Many Kurds, particularly those in Turkey and Syria, consider the Yazidis to be the original or "the pure" Kurds and revere them as their forefathers.

The opposite is true in Iraq, however, where Kurds view the Yazidis through the prism of racism and prejudice. It is nearly impossible, for example, for a Yazidi to work in a restaurant in Iraq due to the common prejudice that they have poor personal hygiene. Many Kurds will refuse to eat food if they know it has been touched by a Yazidi.

Today Kurds comprise the fourth-largest ethnic group in the Middle East, after Arabs, Persians, and Turks. They have never obtained a permanent nation-state. Rather, the approximately thirty to forty-five million Kurds straddle the mountainous borders of Turkey, Iraq, Syria, Iran, and Armenia. They form a distinctive community, united through race, culture, and language, even though they have no standard dialect and they adhere to several different religions and creeds. The majority, though, are Sunni Muslims.

For centuries, the Kurdish people have dreamed of their own state. In the early twentieth century, the possibility of establishing a Kurdish nation-state was quashed by the Sykes-Picot Agreement, the secret 1916 accord between the United Kingdom and France that divided the Arab lands in the Ottoman Empire into separate spheres of influence. Drawing "artificial" borders and installing client rulers, the agreement has come to epitomize the arrogance of colonial rule and its long-lasting aftereffects, namely sectarian and ethnic violence.

Not long after capturing Mosul in 2014, Islamic State leader Abu Bakr al-Baghdadi declared in a speech at the Great Mosque of al-Nuri, "this blessed advance will not stop until we hit the last nail in the coffin of the Sykes-Picot conspiracy."

Kurdish nationalism was a byproduct of the dissolution of the Ottoman Empire after World War I. Somewhat successfully integrated into the Ottoman Empire, the Kurds nevertheless had never assimilated. When the Empire collapsed and Turkey changed dramatically following its defeat—moving toward secularization and centralized authority—the Kurds, still deeply religious and accustomed to a small amount of autonomy, sought self-determination. The 1920 Treaty of Sevres that abolished the Ottoman Empire made provisions for a Kurdish state.

It was short-lived. The great secularist Turkish leader Kemal Ataturk quashed that treaty after defeating its signers in the Turkish War of Independence. The next treaty signed by the allied powers and Turkey, 1923's Treaty of Lausanne, dropped all references to Kurdish autonomy.

For generations, Kurds received harsh treatment at the hands of the Turkish authorities. In response to ethnic uprisings in the 1920s and 1930s, many Kurds were resettled, Kurdish names and costumes were banned, use of the Kurdish language was restricted, and even the existence of a Kurdish ethnic identity was denied, with people designated "Mountain Turks."

In the late 1970s the Kurdistan Workers' Party (PKK), a Marxist-Leninist group, emerged from ethnically oppressed communities and launched an armed struggle against the Turkish government. Its leader, Abdullah Öcalan, called for an independent Kurdish state within Turkey and the Turkish government responded with outrage. Since then the two sides have been in a near constant state of conflict. More than forty thousand people have been killed, many of them Kurds, and hundreds of thousands have been displaced or forcibly moved. In 1997, the United States designated the PKK a terrorist organization because of the extreme violence of its armed struggle, including bombings and assassinations.

In 1999, Öcalan was on the run in Nairobi, Kenya, when he was captured by Turkish intelligence with the support of the CIA. He was taken to Turkey and sentenced to death, a sentence that was commuted to life imprisonment when Turkey abolished the death penalty as a part of its bid to join the European Union. Demonstrating the level of threat Öcalan represented to Turkey, one thousand Turkish military policemen were detailed to guard Öcalan even though he was the sole prisoner on Imrali Island in the Sea of Marmara. In 2009, he was relocated and his solitary confinement ended.

Since his incarceration, Öcalan has significantly changed his ideology. He released a statement in September 2006, calling on the PKK to declare a ceasefire and seek peace with Turkey. Öcalan's statement said, "The PKK should not use weapons unless it is attacked with the aim of annihilation," and added that it is "very important to build a democratic union between Turks and Kurds. With this process, the way to democratic dialogue will be also opened."

Öcalan now argues that Turkey's fourteen million Kurds should work toward a political solution to the question of a Kurdish homeland.

The PKK, meanwhile, has expanded to Syria where the Kurdish region shares a long border with Iraq. In the alphabet soup of Kurdish politics, it is called the PYD and its armed militias, the People's Protection Units, are referred to as the YPG. The PYD effectively runs the Kurdish areas of Syria, granting its 1.6 million people a taste of liberation, ironic given the horrific violence that engulfs the rest of the country.

The YPG has been fighting Islamic State since 2013, not only in Kurdish areas, but in Aleppo and Raqqa Provinces as well.

On Tuesday, August 5, two days after Islamic State invaded Ninewah, Öcalan called on all Kurdish units from his prison cell to come to the aid of the Yazidi people, reminding his followers that he believed the Yazidis were the original Kurds. PKK troops immediately crossed the border into Iraq from Turkey to take on Islamic State. The YPG, Syrian Kurdish militias, moved from northern Syria to Sinjar in the south of Iraq and began to battle Islamic State at the northwestern base of the mountain. Neither group liaised with the Peshmerga as they moved into Iraqi Kurdistan, although the PKK's military leader, the battle-hardened Murat Karayilan, told the local press that all Kurdish troops should now unite.

"Our efforts alone are not enough. Let's form a joint command. Let's make preparations and take IS out of the areas it occupied, including Sinjar," he said in a statement that was heavily quoted in the region's local news media.

The Peshmerga demurred, but thousands of Kurdish militiamen from Turkey and Syria heeded his call and swept into the area. The number of fighters and their movements were either unknown or underestimated by the Americans who still looked to the now-absent Peshmerga for its intelligence. Within twenty-four hours, the Syrian YPG began battling their way up Mount Sinjar and building the escape corridor the Yazidis needed so desperately.

VIRAL APPEAL

On Tuesday morning, forty-three-year-old Iraqi parliamentary representative Vian Dakhil stood up from her chair in the Iraqi Parliament in Baghdad and walked to the designated position for legislators who have been granted permission to address the body. A member since 2010, the petite, auburn-haired Yazidi woman had a reputation as a passionate orator and fierce defender of her people. Facing the chamber's speaker, she waited to be recognized as almost fifty grim-faced and somber fellow parliamentarians gathered around her in a show of support. At their seats, several hundred others carried on with political business, shaking hands, calling out names, and conferring with colleagues. Surrounded by supporters, Dakhil was barely able to contain her fury at the others' lackadaisical attitude.

Dakhil's background was unlike that of most of her Yazidi constituents, who lived as subsistence farmers on government collectives in varying degrees of poverty. Born in 1971, she grew up the eldest of nine children in Mosul, Iraq's second largest city in a wealthy, politically connected family that valued education for daughters as well as sons. Her father,

Saeed Khuder Dakhil, was a surgeon who became an official with the Kurdistan Regional Government. Most of Dakhil's siblings became doctors, another was a lawyer, and one sister was a pharmacist. Her family belonged to Iraq's modern elite, urbane internationalists, yet as Yazidis, their clan identity was pure. They observed the strict guidelines their faith laid out for marriage eligibility. Educated and professional, Dakhil remained single, leaving many to speculate that she had rejected the few acceptable suitors—those available from her bloodline or caste. She lived with her parents in their massive compound in Erbil where they moved after the American invasion. In some ways, Dakhil embodied the modern Middle East and the tension that exists when people try to reconcile traditional and progressive social views.

She became interested in politics while working as a biology lecturer at one of Kurdistan's universities during the aftermath of the fall of Saddam Hussein. In the chaos that followed the US invasion and the collapse of Hussein's Sunni-led government, she witnessed the targeting of minority Yazidis by the newly dispossessed Sunni Arabs at the university. Within a few years, she emerged as a strong advocate for minority rights in Iraq.

She entered Parliament in 2010 on the Kurdistan Democratic Party's ticket. The KDP is the more established and traditional of Kurdistan's two political parties, and party members endorsed her for a second term in early 2014.

In press reports at the time, she was often described as the only Yazidi member of Iraq's representative government, but, in fact, there was one other, an older man on the payroll of Parliament who rarely attended the sessions of Baghdad's notoriously corrupt body. Indeed, a 2016 audit by a British think tank, International Center for Development Studies, rated the government of Nouri al-Maliki, Iraq's first prime minister, the most corrupt in the Middle East and revealed that more than $120 billion disappeared from the treasury in the six years of his term.

On Sunday, August 3, Dakhil's chiming mobile phone had roused her at four in the morning. A hysterical voice called her name and then the line cut. As she turned over to try to fall back asleep, the phone chimed again.

"Vian," cried the voice of a lifelong friend. "Daesh has invaded Sinjar. The Peshmerga abandoned us. I am running to the mountain. Help us, Vian."

The phone cut off again and she sat up in her bed stunned. "My people will be slaughtered," she thought.

While she was aware of the threat Daesh posed to her constituents, she had always believed the Peshmerga would maintain their command of the region. But the Peshmerga's retreat now exposed every Yazidi and Christian to the vicious sectarian hatred promulgated by Islamic State.

There were two options before her: She could go to Sinjar to help with the rescue operation or she could go to Baghdad and use her position as a member of the Iraqi Parliament to raise her voice during the Tuesday parliamentary session and demand the government's attention. She chose to go to Baghdad.

—◦—

Baghdad's Green Zone is a nearly four-square-mile area in the city's center, fenced off with barbed wire and secured with checkpoints, in 2014 officially called the International Zone of Baghdad. Its nickname, the Green Zone, was a decades-old military designation that protected military bases, government ministries, and several of Saddam Hussein's many presidential palaces, including his Republican Palace, where he often sat, enthroned, passing gruesome death sentences on his countrymen.

Following Saddam's overthrow and after some delay, President Bush appointed retired Foreign Service officer Ambassador Paul Bremer to lead Iraq's reconstruction. Bremer, an extraordinarily well-educated managing director at Henry Kissinger's worldwide consulting firm, Kissinger and Associates, ruled Iraq almost by decree. He compared himself not only to Gen. Douglas MacArthur in Japan, but, as well, to Gen. Lucius Clay who led the American Zone in postwar Germany. Despite, or perhaps because of, his supreme confidence, Bremer beat a hasty retreat fourteen months later. He was widely blamed for deteriorating security in the country after he disbanded the army and fired most government officials.

During his tenure, the Republican Palace became the headquarters for the American administration of the country, the Coalition Provisional

Authority. In the Green Zone, other villas were taken over by members of Bremer's team, government officials and private contractors.

During the subsequent years of the Iraq War, the Green Zone represented American power and American powerlessness; at times, it confined senior American officials within its walls out of security concerns. With each attempted attack on it, the eight-mile perimeter boundary hardened and eventually the Americans reinforced it with ten-foot-high concrete blast walls.

The Green Zone protected Iraqi government workers, journalists, and foreign embassy workers, including those in the American embassy's sprawling campus that takes up 104 acres and is nearly as large as Vatican City. Construction on the embassy compound began two years after the invasion and US diplomats began moving in three years later. By its completion in 2012, cost estimates ranged from $700 million to $740 million. Its staff numbered more than sixteen thousand. Later that same year, the State Department announced a re-evaluation of its diplomatic strategy with Iraq and began a huge staff reduction, all due to the pullout of American troops.

The area was officially returned to the government of Iraq in 2009, and most of Iraq's political class took apartments or small villas for their families. To many Iraqis, the Green Zone became a symbol of the disconnect between the country's top officials and ordinary citizens, but for politicians elected from the country's outlying regions like Vian Dakhil, it was a peaceful sanctuary, most appreciated when they went to Baghdad for parliamentary sessions.

———

Standing with her back against the wall of the massive curtained hall of Iraq's Parliament, surrounded by supporters yet hemmed in by rows of elected male representatives, the representative of the Yazidi people contained her rage. Her face was taut and her eyebrows furrowed above her bloodshot eyes. Her nose, upper lip, and chin were red and swollen from crying. The speaker called the body to attention and introduced her. With a gasp, Vian Dakhil realized that she had left her speech, approved by the speaker as protocol requires, on her chair. She had worked on it for six hours the previous evening in her Green Zone apartment. Her mind became a blank.

She took the floor, speaking in Arabic, her second language after the Kurdish dialect, and the official language of the parliament.

"In the name of Allah, the Merciful, the compassionate, honorable Presidential Council, colleagues, representatives of the Iraqi people," she called from the far end of the hall, her shrill voice piercing the mumble of the other, mostly male, lawmakers.

Some legislators continued to chat and mill around, ignoring her, although most stood erect before their chairs looking toward the speaker, a show of professional respect for the speaking parliamentarian. The western press misinterpreted this scene, assuming those looking to the speaker with their backs to Dakhil were ignoring her. In fact, they were showing solidarity. Similarly, reports that fellow parliamentarians had tried to quiet her, saying "shush," were untrue. They were shushing each other so they could better hear her words.

Her voice quavered.

"I am standing here not in order to deliver a speech to the Iraqi people, but in order to convey the bitter reality of the Yazidis currently on Mount Sinjar. Mr. Speaker, we are being slaughtered under the banner of 'There is no god but Allah,'" she said. She wagged her finger at her colleagues for emphasis. At the end of this sentence, the entire body in the chamber was still, frozen in place and the room was silent save for her trembling voice.

She drew in a breath. Her eyes were teary as they flitted around the chamber, looking for someone to acknowledge the scale of the tragedy. She was relieved by the quiet shown by her fellow legislators.

"Over the course of forty-eight hours, thirty thousand families are stranded in the Sinjar Mountains with no water and food. They are dying—seventy kids so far died from thirst and suffocation," she said. "Brothers, let's put our political differences aside and work together as human beings," she pleaded.

As she said "brothers," she paused slightly and extended her hand in a gesture of community. Her colleagues turned to look at the tiny woman.

Surrounded by Kurdish and Iraqi supporters, she seemed to embody the Yazidi women who lay dying on Sinjar Mountain. As her words implored her countrymen to intervene and prevent genocide, they could see only the crown of her auburn hair and two hands held out in desperation.

The speaker interrupted Dakhil, surprised that she had abandoned her approved text. "Madam," he said with annoyance, "please abide by the statement that was agreed on." Knowing he could cut her off for failing to stick to what she had written, she screeched in a panic "This is my statement" and he relented.

"For forty-eight hours, thirty thousand families are besieged in the Sinjar Mountain without water or food. They are dying. Seventy babies have died so far from thirst and dehydration. Fifty old people have died from the deteriorating conditions. Our women are taken as slaves and sold in the slave market. Mr. Speaker, we demand that the Iraqi Parliament intervenes immediately to stop this massacre."

The timbre of her voice revealed a passionate refusal to believe her fellow Iraqis would abandon the Yazidis.

"We are being slaughtered. We are being exterminated. An entire religion is being exterminated from the face of the earth. Brothers I appeal to you in the name of humanity to save us! Mr. Speaker, I want..."

Her words were so charged with pain and her mind was in such torment that her legs buckled and she fell to the ground.

"Vian, Vian," a friend called out as the women and men around her leaned to prevent her body from hitting the floor.

Those fewer than two hundred words, an appeal fraught with the weight of thousands of years of persecution, would soon reach directly into the Oval Office of the White House.

"I didn't realize the impact of the speech at the time," she said. "I thought I had embarrassed myself from my tears. But I knew no one else in the chamber would speak on behalf of my people. Maybe someone would have pointed out the illegal nature of Daesh's actions, but I believe no one else would have expressed outrage, or used the word 'slaughter.' Not because they didn't care ... perhaps we are just too used to death in Iraq."

After regaining her strength, she went to the press room. Inside, she saw several young men, reporters, with tears streaming down their faces. The few women in the room ran toward her and embraced her.

"Then I knew," she said. "I knew I had not failed."

Throughout the remainder of the day, as she sought help at the American and British embassies and several nongovernmental organizations (NGOs), her phone rang constantly.

"Hour and hour my phone rang. It was phone calls from Yazidis on the mountain. Many had my phone number and they were calling and begging for help. They just cried and said 'We are dying,'" Vian said.

That night she returned to her Green Zone apartment.

"Then I saw the speech on TV," she said. "It was on all the channels. I flipped from one to the other. I couldn't stand to listen or watch myself. I turned the TV off and then I sobbed for hours."

Iraq's Parliament voted to start humanitarian airdrops over Mount Sinjar and to launch airstrikes on Islamic State positions in the area. "The first time our government has ever agreed on anything in its history," Dakhil recalled with slight disdain.

The parliamentary in-house video recording of Dakhil's plea was picked up and distributed by The Associated Press TV and Reuters TV. It showed a close-up shot of Dakhil's face, except for the few times the camera cut away to reveal her colleagues as they slowly realized the importance and emotion of the moment. The next day, CNN ran clips that ended with her dramatic collapse. The two and a half minutes quickly spread on YouTube, alerting the world to the plight of the Yazidis on Sinjar Mountain.

Thursday morning, the *Washington Post*'s Terrence McCoy reported on the extermination of minorities in Iraq with the sub-headline "Even Genghis Khan didn't do this." The story opened with quotes from Dakhil's plea. And continued: "Far away from the hotly covered regions of the world, there is an unfolding humanitarian crisis—others say an emerging genocide—occurring on a dust-choked spit of earth called Sinjar Mountain."

Dakhil's dramatic appeal ricocheted around social media, headlined traditional newscasts, and was replayed constantly on twenty-four-hour news outlets around the world. The image of this tiny, tear-stained woman surrounded by hundreds of dark-suited men in a vast political hall, begging for a genocide to be averted, was too compelling to ignore.

Several days after her speech to Parliament, Islamic State released a "kill list," marking its enemies for assassination. Vian Dakhil was the first name.

—⁓—

On Tuesday morning at the US consulate in Erbil, Army colonel Chuck Freeman began to piece together details of the situation in the Ninewah and Erbil regions of Kurdistan. Islamic State was moving almost unchecked toward Erbil, but they had not yet crossed the Great Zab River about twenty-five miles northwest of the city. The Peshmerga had pulled out and were attempting to regroup in Dohuk, northeast of Mosul. More than a quarter of a million people were in flight, mostly Yazidis and Christians. American and other western oil businessman were telephoning the consulate every hour, asking if American personnel were leaving the city.

Freeman met with Consul General Joe Pennington.

"In the first days of August, we were focused on our own security and the call of whether to evacuate or stay. Secondarily was the military side and subsequently the Yazidis," Pennington said.

"We discussed bringing Marines in to defend the consulate. This was not long after the attack on the Benghazi consulate in Libya and, of course, it was on our minds," he said. "But we also considered, what does it say about the future of Iraq if the Americans evacuate from its most peaceful and sophisticated region?"

Later that morning Freeman received a telephone call from Doug Padgett and Leanne Cannon at the IRF office at the State Department. They explained their relationship with the Virginia Yazidis and the information they were passing along. After a brief exchange of emails, they quickly established that both had attended Abilene Christian University in West Texas—although more than a generation apart. They bonded despite the interagency rivalry that often plagues the American government. Knowing very a little about the State Department prior to his arrival, he checked her out with colleagues.

"I was discouraged from talking to Leanne," Freeman said. "I was warned about the DRL and the IRF office. They had a reputation for being too idealistic. Some were also concerned they were being back-doored, or cut out of the normal chain of command because of my relationship with them. That's a regular concern in a large bureaucracy. In the days that followed, Leanne would email or call with information. At one point, she sent a grid of where Yazidis are. I was able to move that information to the appropriate people. I saw Doug and Leanne as the only people I knew in Washington who were really working it, and giving me information that was solid and usable."

During the next two weeks, these two mid-level State Department functionaries redefined the meaning of government employment.

NADIRA'S BABY

Alifa Murad, a fifty-year-old widowed grandmother, had lived in the tiny Yazidi village of Wardiyeh all her life. In this enclave at the southern foothills of Mount Sinjar, she was born, married, raised six children, mourned the premature death of infants and recently, of her husband. Her children grew up surrounded by aunts and uncles, cousins, and second cousins as nearly all Wardiyeh's four hundred residents were related through several generations of bloodlines.

Alifa had a short, round body that was common for middle-aged Yazidi women who had endured many pregnancies. A large bulbous nose emerged from thousands of tiny cracks on her skin, making her face resemble the reflection from a fractured mirror. Each day, she wore the traditional long white dress of the Yazidis, covering it with a brown or green apron that wrapped around her generous figure.

On Sunday, she woke early, rolled up her bed mat, and walked into the sunshine outside her ramshackle, stone house. She had planned to make bread before her grandchildren rose, but she felt unsettled. Walking beyond the dusty dirt road near her house, she saw in the distance, perhaps less than a mile away, a staggered line of people, many of them children, walking toward Wardiyeh. They held containers in their arms and kept their heads bowed down. She waved, but no one looked up. Alifa watched for a few minutes, and beyond them she spotted a second wave of people, a much larger wave. Despite the early morning, the heat distorted their figures and they appeared to be levitating along the plain. As they came closer and settled into view, she realized she was watching a great throng, more than one thousand people in a huge cloud of yellow dust, staggering toward her.

"Daoud," she called to her son while hurrying back to her house. "Come now!"

By 8:00 a.m., thousands of Yazidis from the far southern communities poured into small villages like Wardiyeh or Zumani that sit at the edge of Mount Sinjar. Daoud and the other men of Wardiyeh met the refugees with water at the road at the edge of the village. The refugees told stories of Islamic State's brutality and murder. Many sobbed while they recounted the death of family members or the kidnapping of their young daughters. "Run," they said. "You must run. Daesh is on their way here."

Alifa urged family members to flee as soon as they could organize enough water, food, and other supplies for the extended family. Her own household consisted of her son Daoud, his wife Nadira, and their four-year-old son Haval. Nearby, another son, Ido, lived with his wife and four toddlers. Her unmarried third son, Jamil, and Nadira's mother also lived in small adjacent quarters.

Daoud, a clean-shaven and slight man with sky-blue eyes and an aura of sharp intelligence, was not certain that fleeing was the best plan. Nadira was due to give birth any day to their second child. He doubted she would be able to walk the two miles to the mountain's edge, and he was certain she would not be able to climb Mount Sinjar's steep sides. But Nadira's mother, who lived nearby, thought they should evacuate and pledged that she would watch over Haval, the four-year-old, leaving Daoud free to carry his wife, if necessary. Within an hour of the first warnings, they set out for Mount Sinjar with a group of fifty villagers. More than half were children.

Since it was still early, they walked in the relatively cool morning air. They stuck close to friends, avoiding the traumatized Islamic State victims who had come from farther south and west and talked of gruesome murders. They had plenty of water, and Nadira displayed tremendous strength—walking calmly but steadily, asking to stop for a rest every thirty minutes or so. Alifa and her family were among the earliest arrivals on the mountain, hours before Islamic State arrived in the southwest region. They avoided the hysteria and fear, the desperation and 120-degree heat that led, later in the day, to the dehydration deaths of hundreds, mostly children and the elderly. Safely tucked into the valley, they planned to stay for as long as necessary.

Down below in Wardiyeh, Islamic State drove into the main square at 10:00 a.m. In the moments before their arrival, forty or fifty villagers had panicked and run directly down the north road toward the mountain. The militants blocked that road and sent patrol vehicles to its east and west flank to contain the area. Standing on the back of flatbed trucks, the militants shot in the air, corralling the terrified Yazidis like cattle, forcing them to run back to Wardiyeh to avoid getting run over or shot.

For the next twenty-four hours, the militants held the town without violence but forced residents to stay inside. For an unknown reason, they did not take away the villagers' cellphones as they had done in other communities. Trapped in their homes, the Wardiyeh Yazidis watched the reports of mass murder and rape as they were broadcast on satellite TV. They called relatives from other towns who confirmed the tales of unthinkable brutality, and they grew panicked.

At 7:00 p.m. a senior Islamic State commander knocked on a few doors and said his men had been called to join a battle between armed Yazidis and Islamic State fighters in Baray, on the northwest side of the mountain. He warned the Yazidis to stay in their houses until the fighters returned the next day. Night fell, and the village was silent. Using cellphones to coordinate staggered departures, the two hundred residents crept out of their houses lugging as many containers of water as they could manage. They walked to the mountain.

When Islamic State returned on Wednesday, the commander was enraged to find the village empty except for twelve elderly men who had been too infirm to leave. He demanded phone numbers for the relatives of the men, called them, and demanded they return.

"On the Wednesday one of my brothers still in the village called us and put Islamic State on the phone," said Alifa. "'If you don't come back to Wardiyeh, we will kill everyone here,' he said. This is our family. What could we do? We must return. We went back. The shame would be too great if we abandoned them to die."

She led her family down the mountain and back into her village. Several other families also headed home after being blackmailed over the phone. So Wardiyeh now held fifty to sixty villagers, Alifa's clan gathered in her stone house at the village's edge.

"On the mountain those first few days, we didn't see anything bad. We got there early, and had a good position. We had fled before Islamic State entered our village and we didn't witness the type of massacres that others saw. We had heard of the massacres and atrocities, of course, but they were difficult to believe. Then we put on the TV and saw people talking about genocide and the United Nations and the United States," said Daoud.

As the grave danger of their situation became real, Daoud urged his family to make their second escape, and Alifa, hesitantly, agreed. They had to put the lives of their children before the lives of their relatives.

They left at 3:00 a.m. in darkness. Everyone was dressed in black. They did not use flashlights. They each carried a single bottle of water so they could be swift and unburdened. They walked through the night, staying away from the main road. Alifa's sons lifted their mother by the arms as she tried to scramble over sharp rocks without making a sound. At dawn Thursday, they reached the mountain for the second time with no food and just a few sips of water for each person.

It had been five days since the Daesh invasion, and Daoud was shocked by the state of the refugees. Around him, children were begging for water. It was difficult to tell the living from the dead as both lay with their faces in the dirt, turned away from the brutal sun. Small patches of shade thrown by a scraggly shrub sheltered four or five children who clung to each other and moaned from thirst.

The family sat in a circle. The women ripped pieces of cotton from their long skirts to wrap around the children's faces to prevent sunburn. Haval lay between his grandmother's legs in the front fold of her skirt. She watched his small chest rise and fall beneath the fabric.

They sat for two days. Each person had one sip of water per day.

On Saturday, Nadira gave birth.

"You can't imagine how hard it was. When it was time, I lay down. This was my second child so I knew how it would happen. I don't remember how long I was in labor. My husband and mother took turns holding my hand. I think I moved in and out of consciousness. I knew there was no water or blankets. The pain that I remember came from my lips. They were so dry that with each push they would crack more. It felt like my face was being ripped open, not my womb. I remember thirst. And I remember the panting hurt my throat, like the air was scraping my throat. I tried to keep my eyes closed, not to see her being born. When they were forced open from the pain, the sun hit my eyes. I thought, is this what birth is like for a wild animal? But I am not an animal. Not yet," she said.

The birth took less than an hour.

"She was born. I was covered in dirt and sweat. I really didn't care if she lived. To give birth was an inconvenience you see? She was born. Some others helped. Daoud took off his T-shirt and used it to wipe the blood and embryonic fluid from her eyes and nose. He put his finger in her mouth to make sure she could breathe. A man nearby had a small knife so he came and cut the cord. He got a lot of blood on him. I think the knife was dull. The baby had large splotches of blood on her face, arms, and torso. Her white blonde hair was matted to her head with yellowish goop. I had no rags to clean her. It all eventually dried on her body so that she really didn't resemble a child, more like a creature whose skin was lined with red, brown, and yellowish fur. Like a puppy or a fox. A few days later, it formed a kind of crust that began to flake off. I held her, but felt no love. Just worn down. I felt betrayed. My dying body had given [a] life that would die too. Unimaginable sadness. I was too exhausted to be angry."

Daoud managed to find water by scouting around the base of the mountain at night. For five more days, Nadira sat in blood-covered clothes under the hot sun, giving her infant sips of water from a bottle cap. She could not nurse her child.

"I couldn't make milk. I was too hungry, and my body stopped working. The baby never stopped crying. It seemed to me that I was holding my child as we waited for death."

Rumors spread that Islamic State would soon attack the south side of the mountain. Daoud had heard airstrikes for the past two days, but he didn't know the Americans had intervened, so he assumed it was Islamic State bombing the Yazidis on the mountain. He believed the rumors and told his family they would have to walk to the north.

He went to Nadira and sat beside her. They gazed at their four-year-old son, Haval, and at their mothers. The two elderly women sat close, holding hands, while Haval and his cousins leaned against them to hide their faces from the sun. The trek that lay ahead for them all seemed unbearable. Nadira pressed Daoud's hand onto her stomach. He held her chin with his other hand. They looked at each other without speaking.

Daoud and Nadira decided together to abandon their newborn in a shady crag in the mountainside.

"I looked down at my little girl and I decided to leave her on the mountain," Nadira recalled. "Not kill her, but leave her. Perhaps someone stronger would take her. I could hardly walk myself. I couldn't carry her. I told my husband we must leave her, and he agreed. We believed she would die anyway. We believed we would die also. If we left her, perhaps she would survive if that is what God wanted."

As the family members assembled to begin the walk to the north side, Daoud and Nadira quietly placed their infant in the shady spot and walked toward their family.

"Where is the baby?" demanded Alifa. "Is she dead?"

"No, but she soon will be," Daoud replied.

"Get the baby. Get the baby," Alifa screamed.

She sat down on the ground and refused to move. She said she would carry the baby or die. She screamed meaningless words of anguish until Daoud retrieved his daughter. Alifa stood and grabbed the baby from him. She put the dirty infant in the bodice of her dress and announced, "Now we can go."

"I was worried about my mother, not my daughter," Daoud said. "I was sure she would die anyway. We had five little children—and now a newborn? To make the decision this child will live and that one will die. How can I be that kind of man? But I did. Only my mother stopped it. The situation decided what kind of man you will be."

The group moved slowly on rocky paths to the north side. The sun beat down without mercy. Several times, Nadira collapsed. Eventually,

Daoud lifted her onto his left shoulder, allowing her head, arms, and hair to hang down his back as if he held a corpse. The children were quiet and walked with their eyes fluttering open and closed from exhaustion and dehydration. It took hours to walk a few miles.

"We walked without thinking. I thought how wonderful it would be to die, to lie down and rest before dying. To just give up," Daoud said.

Alifa suddenly sat.

"No more," she said. "I can't. Please just leave me here and save your children."

No one argued or cried. No one had the strength to object. They walked on, leaving Alifa and her newborn granddaughter on some rocks at the very edge of Mount Sinjar's north side.

A few minutes later, a military truck came into view. Uniformed men waved their arms in the air as their truck raced toward them.

Kurdish YPG fighters from Syria gave the family water and helped them onto the covered back of the truck. They drove the two hundred yards to where Alifa had crumpled, gave her water, and helped her stand. She pulled the baby from her bodice and gave it to the young Kurdish soldiers who looked confused at the dirty bundle until the child wailed. They gave the baby water and mashed fruit.

The soldiers drove the family to Camp Nowruz in Syria, the staging point for the thousands of Yazidis the Syrian Kurdish fighters had saved from Mount Sinjar. A nurse rushed to meet them and brought the baby to a clinic. She was released a day later, cleaned and healthy.

Eventually, Nadira and Daoud named their daughter Vian to honor Vian Dakhil, the Yazidi legislator who had worked to rally the world to stop the genocide. The word *vian* in Kurdish means something that is greatly desired.

Alifa and her family are almost the sole survivors of those villagers who returned to Wardiyeh after receiving phone calls from the Islamic State commander ordering them back. The other was a five-year-old girl who was kidnapped by Islamic State and released a year later. When reunited with family, she demanded to pray like a Muslim so she would not be beaten. She no longer spoke Kurdish, just Arabic.

WHITE HOUSE DINNER

While Vian Dakhil was in her Green Zone apartment flipping through the channels to avoid her own image, 1600 Pennsylvania Avenue was aglow for a remarkable social function. Not quite a state dinner, but nevertheless an event fraught with potential social faux pas, President and Mrs. Obama were hosting the Africa Summit Dinner. Held in honor of the dignitaries of more than fifty African nations and their spouses, White House protocol experts contended with such dilemmas as identifying guests whose faith forbade alcohol, determining a seating pattern that avoided placing guests from conflict nations near each other, and making sure leaders with several wives appeared with just one.

The most obvious difference between a formal state function and this event was in the attire of the president and the first lady. President Obama wore a smart suit, rather than a tuxedo, and Michelle, his wife, stunned in a short, bright chartreuse, halter-top dress by Prabal Gurung, the young Nepalese-American designer favored by Oprah Winfrey, the Duchess of Cambridge, and Lady Gaga.

In fashion-challenged Washington, where most women opt for the safe and conservative black dress, it was the brilliantly colored ensembles of the African women that turned the North Portico into a New York–style fashion runway. Chantal Biya, the first lady of Cameroon, captured the night with a Pepto-Bismol-pink mermaid gown and a matching pink floral backless headdress from which her maroon curls seemed to explode. The *Washington Post*'s Style section described her coif as "a beauty school master's thesis in contradictions." Sylvia Valentin, the wife of Gabon's president Ali Bongo, was attired in an elegant and restrained full-length gray gown with bright, embroidered leaves and flowers. The most viral image from the evening belonged to twenty-five-year-old Ange Ingabire Kagame, the 6'8" daughter of Rwandan president Paul Kagame, who accompanied her father draped in a figure-hugging white sleeveless evening gown. She towered over her 6'2" father, who had been recently named by the *New York Times* as one of the continent's most repressive leaders.

The four hundred or more guests posed for photographs with the first couple at the White House before boarding traditional trolley cars that conveyed them to the South Lawn tent for the dinner. On their tables, guests opened an African-inspired menu that included spiced tomato soup and socca crisps, made of chickpeas, and grilled dry-aged Wagyu beef served with chermoula, a marinade used in North African cooking, sweet potatoes, and coconut milk. Chocolate cake made with papaya and scented with Madagascar vanilla topped off the meal.

Celebrities, now a mainstay of White House dinners, included actor Chiwetel Ejiofor, star of the Academy Award–winning drama *12 Years a Slave*, Meb Keflezighi, the Eritrean-born American winner of that year's Boston Marathon, and pop icon Lionel Richie, who entertained with one of his hits from his days with the Commodores, "Easy."

"I stand before you as the president of the United States, a proud American. I also stand before you as the son of a man from Africa," Obama said in his short speech welcoming his guests. "The blood of Africa runs through our family, so for us, the bonds between our countries, our continents are deeply personal."

He recalled family visits to Kenya during his youth and offered a toast to "the new Africa, the Africa that is rising and so full of promise."

Human rights advocates were horrified that some of Africa's most admirable democratic presidents, Tanzania's Jakaya Kikwete and Ghana's John Dramani Mahama, were forced to sit, at least metaphorically, side-by-side with leaders who ruled brutally and oppressively. But the announcement earlier in the day of $14 billion in new US private sector investments in Africa seemed to underscore the administration's belief that democracy often follows economic development.

As National Security Advisor Susan Rice admitted in 2013, "Let's be honest: At times . . . we do business with governments that do not respect the rights we hold most dear." She went on to say, "Still over time we know that our core interests are inseparable for our core values, that our commitment to democracy and human rights roundly enforces our national security."

Her thesis was about to be tested.

KOCHO

Ali Smail was a high school teacher in the farming village of Kocho south of Sinjar. He and the other eighteen hundred inhabitants of the village were accustomed to the feeling of isolation, since they were surrounded by Arab villages and lived the farthest south from the mountain of all the Yazidi communities. Throughout the summer Smail and his townsmen felt uncomfortable knowing Islamic State controlled areas nearby, especially since most of the neighboring Arab villages were said to be infiltrated by the jihadists, and many of their neighbors were thought be sympathetic to Islamic State's radical beliefs. To add to their jitters, three Kocho men had been kidnapped by unknown assailants a month earlier, and the local Peshmerga unit of seventy soldiers stationed at the high school had done nothing to help the families or to locate the men.

About the same time as the kidnappings, Islamic State began launching artillery from their stronghold in Tal Afar in their direction, landing shells to the east of Kocho. Feeling vulnerable, the local men, including Smail, built with shovels a defensive berm around the village and conducted daily defensive drills. The Peshmerga did not participate and mocked the farmers' efforts. Townspeople took this as a sign of the Peshmerga's professionalism rather than a lack of dedication to the protection of the village.

"In the two days before the invasion, there had been rumors that Daesh was preparing an attack, although the Peshmerga laughed at our questions," Smail said. "Nevertheless, the men were up patrolling at night. That is why we knew about Siba almost immediately because we had sentries watching the area."

When Islamic State began its attack on Ninewah—the province containing most of Iraq's Yazidi population—it focused on Siba and roads heading north to Sinjar. On the first day, after hearing mortar explosions ten miles away in Siba, the Peshmerga packed their belongings. Residents standing on their rooftops to watch the battle at Siba saw the convoy of Peshmerga vehicles drive out of their village and head north.

"By God," said Smail. "Our confidence in the Peshmerga was strong. They withdrew without explaining why or what was happening. It doesn't really seem possible, but they just withdrew and left us to die."

By 7:30 a.m., the Yazidis of Kocho were overcome with panic and about four hundred fled, a few in vehicles, but most on foot. They soon discovered that Islamic State had taken all roads heading north with intent to kill. It is unclear how many of the residents of Kocho were captured or murdered along the main roadway by Islamic State on that fatal Sunday. Some returned to Kocho because there was nowhere else to go.

Smail left the village with his wife and two daughters in a vehicle owned by his neighbor, Shamo Khdir Hassan. He was among the first to leave, and that is probably why he survived. He and his family decided that heading to Sinjar was the safest option, because they did not understand that Islamic State was on a military drive to capture Sinjar.

"We decided to drive to Sinjar city for sanctuary," he said.

When they arrived at the south of the city, they saw that Daesh controlled every checkpoint and had already taken the city. Surrounded by the jihadists, they entered the lion's den through a small side road to look for a place to hide.

"We tried to run away, both east side and west side of the town, but Daesh fighters fired at us and we were forced into the town," he said. "While in Sinjar, we were hiding in a building until about 1:30 p.m., hoping to find a way out. We suddenly saw Hassan Hamada coming into the building. He was an Arab and a Kreef (godfather) to one of the families hiding with us. I don't know how he found us, but I think he was watching us in the building. He told us he could rescue us and drive us to outside Sinjar. He said he was not able to fit all of us in his car at one time. He took the first family he knew and promised to come back for us. We were waiting for Hassan Hamada to come back to take us, but it took him too long. We called the family he had driven away to find out why no one was coming to our rescue. One of the children answered the cellphone and said 'Daesh fighters took all of them away.' We became very scared when we heard that and started calling tribal leaders and other people asking for rescue." It is unclear if Hamada was trying to help the Yazidis or whether he betrayed them.

Back in Kocho, the mayor, Ahmed Jaso, waited at the entrance of the village for the inevitable arrival of Islamic State. Jaso was between fifty and sixty years old and had been the village leader since the death in 1979 of his father who had been the headman before him.

Islamic State entered before noon, accompanied by an emir of Islamic State, Abu Hamza al-Khatuni, a young, lean man of about thirty, a Sunni

Arab from a nearby village. He assured the Yazidis they would be safe. He, Khatuni, personally guaranteed their safety, and he urged them to call relatives and neighbors who had fled. Many did. Khatuni announced that Sinjar had fallen to Islamic State and joined the caliphate. Then he left with the jihadists. There were 1,172 villagers in Kocho.

Later that afternoon, another Islamic State delegation arrived at the village once again accompanied by Emir Khatuni. He repeated his reassurances, telling the villagers they were not in danger. They would get "safety passes" that would allow them to move around the area unmolested, Khatuni said. The militants established a command post at the high school and demanded the Yazidis bring all weapons to this new de facto headquarters for safekeeping. The Yazidis complied.

In Sinjar, Smail and his friend hid in a small shed, terrified and unable to decide what to do next.

"Then we got a call from someone called Sleman Taha Psi who told us that a Daesh commander known as Abu Hamza al-Khatuni has met with tribal leader Sheikh Jaso and others at the village," Smail remembered. "He told them to tell all Yazidis who have fled to Sinjar Mountain should return because they are not target(ed) by Daesh and no one will harm them. Sleman Taha Psi also said that the Daesh leader said any Yazidi coming into Sinjar should put up a white cloth on his car and he will be safe. 'We won't harm a single Yazidi,' Psi said the Daesh commander vowed.

"However, we didn't believe what Psi said. After around 15 minutes, he called us again and told us the same thing again—that we will be safe and that there is no reason to hide. He told us to tell Daesh fighters 'We are in the group of Abu Hamza al-Khatuni' if the fighters ask. However, we still did not believe him. He called us again, twice, telling us the exact same thing, but still we did not believe what he said. He and his friend called us several more times until they convinced us. We did not quite believe what they were telling us, but we did not have any other choice."

The men debated whether to return to Kocho or to continue to attempt to go north to Mount Sinjar. Before they could leave the shed where they were hiding, Daesh fighters discovered them.

"Throughout that time Daesh fighters came to us three times and asked us several questions," Smail said. "The first time they asked us what tribe and ethnicity we belonged to. We told them we were Sunnis. The second time they asked us if anyone in our family members held a government position such as Peshmerga, doctor, engineer, or lawyer. The third time they asked us if we were armed. These questions made us worried that the fighters were planning to kill us. At around 5:30 p.m. we decided to run away toward north of Sinjar hoping that Daesh was not present there. However, Daesh had surrounded the entire town by then and we were forced to go back into the city again.

"On the way back, we came across a big Daesh checkpoint on the highway. Daesh fighters asked us who we were and where we were heading. We said we were the group of Abu Hamza al-Khatuni just as we were told. The fighters asked the driver of our car what the white clothes that we tied to the car meant. The driver responded that it was a sign of surrender. The Daesh fighter asked the driver, 'Why? Are we enemies?' The Daesh fighters then said, 'No problem. Come, become Muslims and leave.' The fighters asked the driver, 'What do you say?' The driver responded, 'As you like.'

"Later on, there was an ambulance on the right side of the road and the fighters asked us to follow it. As we were following the ambulance on the right side, four Daesh fighters were driving in front of us and four others were following us. They stopped us at Sinjar's main road intersection that heads toward southern Mosul to Arabic areas. The fighters started talking among each other but we did not know what they were saying. They later drove us back to the same checkpoint where they stopped us at the beginning. Then they told us to go back to our village.

"On the way back to Kocho village, we were stopped by another Daesh checkpoint where they told us not to use the road toward the village because they have planted explosives on it. We took a longer road to go back and by the time we arrived home it was dark. When we arrived home, we asked the villagers what happened and they told us a Daesh commander known as Abu Hamza al-Khatuni came to them and told them they will be safe under the Islamic state. The Daesh fighters also took all weapons from the villagers and told them to put a white cloth on the roof of their houses."

They returned to Kocho Monday and found Islamic State soldiers there, but the armed men stayed mostly at the high school and did not bother the villagers.

"Everyone was tense and afraid, but we had no other choice. We chose to believe they would not kill us as they said," Smail said.

There were around eighteen hundred people living in Kocho village before the invasion. On the day Daesh arrived, some villagers fled to Sinjar Mountain. Some of them were arrested or killed on the way.

"When Daesh came to our village with trucks, there were still 1,172 people in the village who were all gathered in Kocho High School. Of the original 1,888 residents, 845 were women and children and 380 were young men," Smail said.

Smail and the remaining residents of Kocho lay in their beds Tuesday night, most without sleeping, waiting and worrying about the early morning arrival of yet another Islamic State delegation. Since the time the militants had driven into their village Sunday, the Yazidis had tried to carry on with their day-to-day activities. They worked their farms and kitchen gardens, ignoring the jihadists who patrolled their village with automatic weapons. Despite the tales of massacres and brutality that their relatives and friends in Sinjar had related during cellphone conversations, there had been no violence in their village.

But by Tuesday evening, something in the air had changed. The Islamic State fighters seemed agitated and surly. Their commander told the villagers to be ready for the arrival of a high delegation of Islamic State leaders Wednesday morning.

At midnight, the village lay still. One resident, who was awake and on the alert, later recalled that the howls of a newborn infant once pierced the eerie silence and trilled through the streets, reverberating like a siren.

Yazidis pose in front of the White House after meeting with Obama advisor Ben Rhodes, August 8, 2014 (left to right, Atala Hussein Elias, William Spencer, Basim Bebani, Hadi Pir, Hussein Elias Khalaf, Dakhil Shammo, Leila Khoudeida, Mirza Ismail, Khairy Murad Shammo, Haider Elias) (Dakhil Shammo)

First meeting at State Department, August 4, 2014 (Dakhil Shammo and Leanne Cannon at right end of table) (Dakhil Shammo)

Humanitarian airdrop ready to go, August 2014 (US Govt.)

President Obama discusses airstrikes with eighteenth Chairman of the Joint Chiefs of Staff Martin Dempsey, August 7, 2014 (US Govt.)

Left to right, Daoud, Alifa Murad, Vian (crying), Nadira's and local children at IDP camp in Kurdistan, May 2017 (Shand)

Peshmerga troops near Sinjar, 2017 (US Govt.)

Alifa Murad, Nadira's mother-in-law, May 2017 (Shand)

Col. Charles "Chuck" Freeman and Foreign Service Officer Leanne Cannon meeting in Erbil, Kurdistan, February 11, 2015 (Col. Charles Freeman)

Lt. Gen. John M. "Mick" Bednarek, Chief of the Office of Security Cooperation—Iraq, meets Iraqi minister Karim Sinjari at the Kurdistan Regional Government building in Erbil, August 19, 2014 (Col. Charles Freeman)

Map made by the translators for the State Department showing the YPG escape route (Khalaf Smoqi)

Left to right, Alifa, Vian, Nadira and local children inside their tent at IDP camp in Kurdistan, May 2017 (Shand)

Yazidis on Mount Sinjar (Zmnako Ismael)

Yazidis on Mount Sinjar (Zmnako Ismael)

President Barack Obama in the Situation Room during the raid on Osama bin Laden, May 1, 2011. Seated (left to right): Joe Biden, Vice President; Barack Obama, President; Brig. Gen. Marshall B. Webb, Assistant Commanding General of the Joint Special Operations Command; Denis McDonough, Deputy National Security Advisor; Hillary Clinton, Secretary of State; Robert Gates, Secretary of Defense (US Govt.)

YPG soldiers help Yazidi children (Zmnako Ismael)

Yazidi mother holds her child on Mount Sinjar (Zmnako Ismael)

YPG soldiers help Yazidi children (Zmnako Ismael)

Yazidi women and children in a YPG truck (Zmnako Ismael)

CHAPTER SIX

The Red Line

Wednesday, August 6, Thursday, August 7

In 1887 John Emerich Edward Dalberg-Acton, 1st Baron Acton, also known as Lord Acton, wrote a letter to the Archbishop of the Church of England decrying the tendency of religious leaders to gloss over the corruption and abuse of past popes. "Power tends to corrupt and absolute power corrupts absolutely. Great men are almost always bad men," he wrote, a statement that has long outlived him. A decade later, while writing about Oliver Cromwell, the Lord Protector of the Commonwealth of England, Scotland, and Ireland, he penned a less known, but perhaps more relevant, sentence: "There is not a more perilous or immoral habit of mind than the sanctifying of success." Power and success both can lead to madness. For Iraqi prime minister Nouri al-Maliki, a political nonentity in 2006, the journey from normalcy to megalomania took precisely four years.

In the aftermath of the 2003 American invasion of Iraq, ethnic and religious tensions reached a catastrophic point. Iraq's ruling Shiites dreamed up retribution schemes against the deposed Sunni minority that had oppressed them for years under Saddam Hussein. Washington was desperate for a leader who would play the role of unifier, bringing together the Shiite, Sunni, and Kurdish populations under one national Iraqi banner.

Casting about for a leader for this new democracy, the United States hand-picked a hardworking and relatively corruption-free minor politician, Nouri al-Maliki, to be a unifier. He was not ideal but he would do. He became prime minister in May of 2006.

Seven months after becoming prime minister, Maliki signed the death warrant of Saddam Hussein, citing the wishes of Hussein's victims. "Our respect for human rights requires us to execute him," he told his nation. Despite asking to be shot, Saddam was hanged on the first day of the Muslim feast Eid ul-Adha on December 30, 2006, at a joint American-Iraqi army base named Camp Justice.

In the beginning, Maliki hurled himself into the work. Vowing to lead a strong, united Iraq, he met with US ambassador Ryan Crocker and Gen.

David Petraeus every day for several hours, strategizing how to keep the Iraqi state from collapsing. He benefited from the Awakening movement, a time in 2008 when Sunni Arab tribal leaders and Sunni insurgents turned on Zarqawi and his bloodthirsty philosophy of "true" Muslims. As the nation calmed, Maliki presided over negotiations with multinational corporations that bid to modernize Iraq's infrastructure. He held weekly videoconferences with President George W. Bush, who seemed to relish guiding him on the intricacies of leadership. After just two years in office, he took on Shiite leader and rival Moqtada al-Sadr, successfully defeating his Iranian-backed militia, long a thorn in the side of the Americans. His successes led Maliki to believe he was all-powerful. And as soon as power went to his head, he became the divider-in-chief.

At the close of the Bush Administration, a strong Maliki negotiated bilateral agreements with President Bush, whose ability to govern had been damaged by a series of missteps ranging from his handling of Hurricane Katrina to the global economic collapse. With his legacy on the line, Bush was desperate for Iraq to appear stable and asked for little, while Maliki got a guarantee that American tax dollars would continue to flow.

On a ceremonial trip to Iraq to sign the "bilateral accords" at the prime minister's palace in Baghdad in December, Bush and Maliki faced a skeptical international and Iraqi press. Unexpectedly, an outraged Iraqi journalist shouted "This is a farewell kiss from the Iraqi people, you dog," and threw his left shoe at the president. "This is for the widows and orphans and all those killed in Iraq," he yelled as he threw his right shoe. Bush ducked twice and dodged the shoes.

The global economic crisis was the immediate focus of the incoming Obama Administration, which shelved Iraq and its problems. Maliki, free from oversight, went on a campaign to cement his leadership, seeking out loyalists and punishing rivals. Squandering the democratic advances Iraq had made during his first two years in office, Maliki became obsessed with holding onto power. Despite an earlier promise that he would step down after two terms in office, his consolidation of power appeared to have a long-term intent. Rather than curtail their chosen leader's worst impulses, the United States doubled down, certain he would extend the

SOFA, the status of forces agreement that allowed US troops to remain in Iraq until December 2011.

But the United States underestimated Maliki's growing megalomania and overlooked its consequences. He refused to support legal immunity for American troops, a key point of the SOFA, giving the Obama Administration no choice but to observe the deadline and pull out its troops. Internally, he never appointed an interior or defense minister, naming himself to both posts. Both of his sons-in-law worked for his office, and his son Ahmed was head of his security. He began to purge the government of those he suspected of disloyalty. The United States had deposed the dictator Saddam Hussein and replaced him with the tyrant Nouri al-Maliki.

For the next eighteen months, Maliki's relentless divisive politics and growing authoritarianism alienated him from Sunnis, Kurds, and many members of his own party. Despite pledging not to run for a third term, his State of Law coalition party won the most votes in the April 2014 election. Maliki changed his mind, and decided he wanted to stay in power for a third term. The United States, however, preferred parliamentary speaker Haider al-Abadi, a highly educated electrical engineer who had lived in self-imposed exile in Britain before the US invasion. Abadi had a reputation for working well with westerners and appeared committed to ending Maliki's corruption. (Indeed, several months later, as prime minister, Abadi announced the purging of fifty thousand "ghost soldiers" from the Iraqi army payroll. These were enlisted men who did not show up for duty but who split their monthly salary with officers.)

Months of political infighting started, with no central authority in Baghdad. Abadi was unable to form a government within the constitutionally required ninety days, so, as the Iraqi constitution also required, Maliki, the previous government's prime minister, stayed for another three months.

In June, Islamic State moved into Iraq from Syria, took Mosul, and destroyed the Iraqi army. Baghdad was in political paralysis as the military threat from Islamic State grew increasingly perilous. The Kurds took the opportunity to expand their territory and sent the Peshmerga into Ninewah Province, claiming it for Kurdistan.

For American officials in Baghdad, including Lt. Gen. Mick Bednarek, the senior American defense official in Iraq, and the chief of the Office of Security Cooperation, the Maliki situation presented a constitutional quagmire for Iraqis that the United States was loath to interfere with, while, at the same time, it hamstrung American military involvement in the country's response to Islamic State.

"You have an angry, embittered lame duck Maliki who was still technically in charge of the country," Bednarek said. "So, the decision from United States is very clear. The United States was not going to intervene or get involved until it is very clear that Maliki is out and Abadi is in. So all through June and July our phones are ringing off the wall in the embassy, particularly in my Office of Security Cooperation because I'm the key to their military and foreign military sales. (The Iraqis say) you are signatories of the Security Framework Agreement. You're supposed to help us, but we're not because we want to confirm that Maliki is out and Abadi is in."

On Wednesday, August 6, as Yazidis lay dying on Mount Sinjar, Maliki appeared on television for his weekly address and warned his countrymen that an "unconstitutional" attempt to form a new government—meaning without him—would open "the gates of hell." Elegantly dressed in a dark gray suit, a crisp white shirt, and purple silk tie, his demeanor was somber, dignified, if not imperious. Eyebrows furrowed, he warned against a coup, rejecting outside interference in the process, a reference to the United States, and appeared to be directly challenging the wishes of the Obama Administration. Meanwhile, Islamic State stayed on course toward Erbil.

KURDISTAN

After the toppling of Saddam, the Kurds were once again allowed to speak their dialects in public. Schools throughout the Kurdish region designed a Kurdish language curriculum, abandoning the Saddam-era edict to hold classes only in Arabic. Within a decade, the media landscape in Kurdistan leapt from an early twentieth century to an early twenty-first century one.

Large Kurdish companies like Rudaw, a television, web, and newspaper conglomerate, built a twenty-four-hour presence that was embraced by a population unaccustomed to news and information that had not been filtered through the lens of a tyrannical regime. Criticized as a mouthpiece of President Barzani's ruling KDP party, Rudaw nonetheless built a tremendous following from its inception in 2010. It became the default channel for breaking news for many Kurds, just as CNN is for many Americans. It was seen in shops, restaurants, and at the airport. Rudaw's anchors were well-respected media personalities.

Late Wednesday afternoon, hundreds of thousands of Kurds were watching as young anchorman Dildar Herki introduced a live interview with Rudaw reporter Berekat Isa, who had fled along with the Yazidis to Mount Sinjar.

Talking on his cellphone, Isa described his own desperate predicament as well as the circumstances that had befallen the Yazidis on the mountain.

"I can tell you, since yesterday when I had some rice with no bread or water, I have had nothing to eat . . . like everyone else. I haven't seen my child and wife for five days. My situation is like anyone else's in Sinjar," he said. "I am asking the authorities as a person not as a Rudaw reporter. There are thousands of children who need to be rescued. They are all trapped there."

His hoarse voice quavered as he spoke, and Herki, the anchorman, was overcome with emotion. He rested his head in his hands, then placed his thumbs to the inside of his eyes to wipe away tears. For a Kurdish audience, for any audience, the sight of a news presenter breaking down is compelling, and it cements the sense of a national tragedy in the minds of the viewers.

For the next few hours Kurds remained riveted to their televisions. First, Rudaw reported that Islamic State had emptied the Christian town of Qaraqoush, sending more than one-quarter of the country's Christian population fleeing to Erbil. Then it followed that story with the stunning news that Islamic State had crossed the Great Zab River and attacked the nearby town of Mahkmour. That's when panic set in throughout the region, but especially in the Kurdish capital city of Erbil.

At the front, a mere twenty-five miles from Erbil, the Peshmerga and the Iraqi army, under orders from Maliki, scrambled to contain

Islamic State's lightning advance. The jihadists had pushed east, crossing the Tigris until they came to one of its tributaries, the Great Zab
River. Here Kurdish and Iraqi forces attempted a counterattack, but they
were overrun with ease. As they evacuated, they loaded up their military
vehicles with as many refugees as they could carry and headed back to
Erbil. Rudaw reporters and television crews from other networks met the
defeated forces as they unloaded thousands of traumatized refugees at
the Erbil outskirts. Played relentlessly on television and shared on social
media, these images convinced the people of Erbil that their city was
about to fall to Islamic State.

Simultaneously, Islamic State troops pushed north of Mosul, capturing the Mosul Dam, the largest source of drinking water for all of Iraq.
Iraqi and American officials were concerned that Islamic State would
destroy the dam, releasing a sixty-five-foot wave that could engulf the city
of Mosul and rush hundreds of miles south toward Baghdad. The dam was
already unstable, requiring daily shoring up to prevent its collapse from
the results of poor initial engineering. Even a short interruption in the
remedial work needed to keep the dam from bursting raised the possibility
of a catastrophic breach. Earlier that year, Islamic State had seized control
of the Fallujah Dam, in Anbar Province, and flooded a vast area, sending
thousands of refugees fleeing, submerging hundreds of homes and several
schools and interrupting the water supply to southern Iraq.

Late in the evening, broadcasters reported that Islamic State had
successfully taken not only Makhmour, but the city of Gwer as well. They
warned viewers that Islamic State was a mere twenty miles from Erbil.
As residents prepared to flee, Islamic State released a boastful statement
on one of its affiliated websites. Claiming they had captured the dam and
more than seventeen cities and towns, the jihadists vowed to "march in all
directions" to expand its caliphate.

Watching from Baghdad, Lieutenant General Bednarek knew then
that military action was inevitable.

"We are watching this pretty close because we have got pretty good
intelligence, information, surveillance, but as soon as Daesh threatened
the Peshmerga on the east side of the Zab River, and they are thirty miles
from Erbil, that from a United States perspective was the infamous Red

Line. Because our US consulate there in Erbil was potentially threatened," Bednarek said. "At that point it was an easy political decision for the US to enter to make sure that the US interests were protected. You know, there, with Joe Pennington and the consulate there in Erbil. No brainer to enter in, for the US airstrikes to curtail that potential and evolving threat."

At the US consulate in Erbil, Consul General Pennington was inundated with telephone calls from European and other western consulates. The diplomats had only one question: Was the United States evacuating its diplomatic mission in Erbil and and if so, when? Pennington demurred, knowing if he implied the United States was preparing to leave, others would follow and the subsequent panic could unravel the entire diplomatic community.

"We were absolutely preparing to go," Pennington said. "Absolutely, I think that we were on the verge. Obviously, our security was one aspect and the most important thing we looked at. But we were also looking at it from the standpoint of what it would mean if the United States left Erbil."

Within the consulate staff worked furiously, dismantling hard drives from all nonessential computers, shoving documents into shredders, burning sensitive papers, and destroying cables between the consulate and the embassy in Baghdad and Washington.

By late morning, members of the Kurdistan Regional Government called the consulate to warn there were fewer than twenty-four hours to prevent a catastrophe in Erbil.

"I will never forget that day," Pennington said. "I got a call—several—from the minister of the interior, another from Fuad Hussein [Kurdish President Barzani's chief of staff]. Basically, they were saying the same thing—'We know that Washington is going to do something, but you have to understand if they don't do it today it will be too late.' They were extremely alarmed that Erbil would be attacked—if not fall. Because it's a big city, it would be hard for two hundred or a thousand jihadists to take Erbil, but certainly they could have entered the city or started shelling the city. But we were in touch with Washington and they were working toward a decision to start a military response."

WHITE HOUSE DEMONSTRATION

Dakhil Shammo arrived at the Voice of America early to alert his editors to a demonstration by Yazidi-Americans in front of the White House. Within the Kurdish Service, reporters were calling Yazidis still trapped on the mountain to make audio recordings of their ordeal. An uneasy quiet descended on the newsroom when Shammo entered as his colleagues affected an aura of intense concentration. As the scope of the humanitarian disaster became clear and other journalists began to use the term *genocide*, they seemed to have become stricken by shame, as it was now clear to all that the Peshmerga had behaved cowardly and abandoned the Yazidis.

Standing near an edit room, Shammo listened to audio of the desperate pleas of Yazidi men and women who were starving and dehydrated. He heard them describe their listless children who lay still under the hot sun covered with dirt and sweat, inhaling and exhaling, calling for water, then falling silent as they dozed.

"To say I felt grief or rage, is wrong," Shammo said. "I felt desperation. I felt responsibility. I am a Yazidi in the United States government. If not me, then who will demand or beg for action?"

Shammo and his cameraman left to cover the White House demonstration that took place directly in front of the North Portico. About fifty demonstrators were gathered, holding signs that said "Save Us," or "Stop ISIS." There were older women wearing the Yazidi traditional white headscarves and long colorful skirts, young women in professional dress, and men in jeans and T-shirts. Ten men arranged themselves in a circle and lay on the ground to represent the dead. The group began to chant "Stop the Genocide."

"It was one of the hardest days of my professional life," Shammo said. "I wanted to chant along with them. I wanted to stand among them and hold hands with the crying women, but I couldn't. It sounds funny, but it helped that I was wearing a suit. I was the only one dressed that way and it reminded me that I was a journalist. Of course, a Yazidi journalist, but at this moment a journalist. It gave me comfort to know that my report would tell my countrymen that American Yazidis were here, less than four hundred yards from this great American man, telling him only the US could do it. Begging him to save our people."

Several hundred tourists gathered around the demonstration, many curious about the cause that inspired people to lie on the ground. A few moved closer to question demonstrators. Shammo and his cameraman set up among the chanting Yazidis, asking some to step aside with him for an interview. He heard stories of murder and kidnapping. He listened respectfully as they broke off the interviews to cry, then regained their composure to continue the story. After an hour, he returned to the Voice of America to edit his report.

Alone in an edit room, he viewed his video, deciding how to arrange the images and weighing the effectiveness of different lines of script. A few hours later, his two-minute report was on the air in Kurdistan. Sitting in the edit room, he wept.

OBAMA

As the Yazidis were lying on the pavement in front of the White House, President Obama and African leaders met for the final sessions of the summit. The morning was dedicated to exploring issues of common interest such as sustainable development and economic growth. A working lunch focused on solutions to regional conflict and peacekeeping challenges. The afternoon session, Governing for the Next Generation, brought the discussions to a close on an optimistic note. The president concluded his day with a press conference at the State Department. Newspaper and network reporters asked about the Ebola outbreak in Africa, Russian meddling in Ukraine, corporate inversions for tax avoidance, and the Gaza Strip, but, even as Obama's administration was debating whether to re-enter the Iraq conflict, there was not one question about Iraq.

Twelve hours later American F/A-18s bombed Islamic State positions in Iraq.

ATROCITY PREVENTION

In August 2011, President Obama stood beside Holocaust survivor Elie Wiesel and addressed an audience at the United States Holocaust

Museum and Memorial. The world, Obama said, would be "haunted by the atrocities we did not stop." He asserted that "preventing mass atrocities and genocide is a core national security interest and a core moral responsibility of the United States of America," a statement that placed the issue at the center of his administration's foreign policy.

Shortly after the speech, he issued Presidential Study Directive 10 that instructed the National Security Council to determine how the Washington bureaucracy could be managed to achieve the goals he had laid out. A few months later, Obama announced the establishment of the Atrocity Prevention Board (APB), an interagency policy committee whose mandate was to bring together US officials from the National Security Council, the Departments of State, Defense, Justice, and Treasury, the US Agency for International Development, and all the various members of the intelligence community to assess the risks of atrocities around the world and to coordinate the US government response.

Unfortunately, as with most unfunded mandates, the effectiveness of the board depended solely on the goodwill and cooperative spirit of its participants since, without a budget, its power was nonexistent. Its interloper status often caused it to be viewed with skepticism in some parts of the national security establishment. And like all bureaucrats who live in fear of budget reductions, it is often easier for personnel in agencies, departments, and internal bureaus to pursue and impose their own policies without waiting for the coordination or cooperation of sister organizations.

The APB quickly devolved into a nonessential, monthly meeting of information-sharing and note-taking, but, nonetheless, it forced high-level intelligence and foreign policy officials to sit together, acknowledge each other, and forge relationships.

In February 2014, newly confirmed State Department under secretary Sarah Sewall joined the APB. The fifty-three-year-old Sewall, a former professor at Harvard's Kennedy School of Government, had been an early foreign policy advisor to presidential candidate Barack Obama and later collaborated with Gen. David Petraeus on his revision of the US counterinsurgency doctrine in 2011. She specialized in the field of civilian security in conflict regions and was tapped to run one of Secretary of State Hillary Clinton's "Super Offices," bureaucratically known as "J," the office for Civilian Security, Democracy and Human Rights. With an annual budget of $5 billion, she was tasked with restructuring a team of two thousand employees, many posted outside the United States.

By August 2014, the board, chaired by National Security Council advisor Stephen Pomper, had come under harsh criticism from members of Congress who complained the group was shrouded in secrecy and was not responsive.

As reports of the atrocities in Sinjar began to trickle out to the media, Virginia's Republican congressman Frank Wolf addressed a letter to Obama questioning the efficacy of the board.

"Tragically, mass atrocities are happening again today—and on your watch. Genocide is taking place today in northern Iraq, where the Christian and Yazidi populations are being exterminated by the Islamic State of Iraq and Syria (ISIS). There is no question that systematic and targeted brutality is occurring. Yet, as I said on the House floor last week, the silence from you and your administration is deafening. Why have you not spoken up, and why has the Atrocities Prevention Board not taken action? Just today, the editorial page of the *Washington Post* described your administration's response to this emergency as 'listless.'

"Over the weekend, approximately 200,000 Yazidis were forced to flee their homes. Your own administration has reported that anywhere from 35,000 to 60,000 of these Yazidis took refuge in the Sinjar Mountains without any protection from the elements and little access to food and water. Children and the elderly are dying of thirst, families are being separated and women and young girls are being raped and sold into slavery.

"It is now clear to the nation and the world that your words were hollow; your 'presidential directive' apparently was nothing more than a token gesture. You will come to sincerely regret your failure to take action to stop the genocide in Iraq. Your conscience will haunt you long after you leave office. Mr. President, say something; do something."

The Obama Administration's commitment to preventing atrocities, a key component of its foreign policy, was fast losing credibility.

OBAMA

That evening when President Obama left the Africa Summit and stepped into his limousine to return to the White House, he was greeted by the eighteenth Chairman of the Joint Chiefs of Staff, US Army general Martin Dempsey. According to the *New York Times*, Dempsey told the president that Erbil was in the path of Islamic State and that American consulate personnel were at risk. After arriving at the White House, they were joined by Chief of Staff Denis McDonough, National Security Advisor Susan Rice, and several other officials to discuss military options. President Obama had already decided to airlift humanitarian aid to the Yazidis trapped on Mount Sinjar, and felt he had few choices other than pursuing a military intervention.

As it had many times before, the discussion of intervention focused on the specter of another Benghazi, something the *New York Times* called "a potent symbol of weakness for critics of the President." A little after 8:00 p.m., the president left the meeting and took his wife along with his friend and senior advisor, Valerie Jarrett, to dinner at Fiola Mare, the Georgetown waterfront's newly opened Italian seafood restaurant where, according to press reports, he claimed he had a "very good meal."

PANIC

As the city of Erbil woke on the morning of Thursday, August 7, terror roiled its inhabitants. Television news showed crowds of westerners and wealthy Kurds at the Erbil airport, shoving each other as they crowded the airline counters for tickets out to Amman or to anywhere in Europe. Oil companies were sending their expatriate staff out of the country if they could find tickets, but few were available.

Meanwhile in Baghdad, lawmakers exchanged insults in Parliament after a Sunni member accused the Maliki government of using barrel bombs against Sunni civilians in Anbar Province. The session spiralled into chaos. Excluded from the chamber in a nearby cafeteria, Iraqi journalists heard "coward" and "traitor" flung with hatred. It seemed impossible that Shia and Sunni lawmakers could reach a deal on a new prime minister.

Maliki was still clinging to his position. American officials had implied that more military aid would become available to both the Iraqi army and Kurdistan Peshmerga if the parliament were only to name a new prime minister, so political leaders met late into the night in the fortified Green Zone to choose his replacement.

"Everyone is saying no to Maliki now," an anonymous member of Parliament told the *New York Times*. "He's rejected by all parties."

But Maliki stalled, demanding immunity from prosecution for himself, his family, and his inner circle. He also called for a large twenty-four-hour security detail paid for by the state. Maliki was aware that his time in power had brought his enemies to an almost fanatical hatred of him and members of his family. He feared arrest or assassination.

The Obama Administration continued to state publicly that Maliki had to leave before the United States would act to stop Islamic State's advance.

THE TRANSLATORS

In one of Washington's older residential neighborhoods that feels like a suburb, in a prewar townhouse close to the road where the trolley once ran, William "Spence" Spencer has headed the Institute for International Law and Human Rights for twenty-five years. A former State Department Foreign Service officer and an expert in international diplomacy, Spencer had been advising the government of Iraq on a wide range of constitutional and parliamentary issues since its formation after the American invasion. Over the years he had reached out to American Iraqis, both Arabs and Kurds, and maintained a large network of contacts.

When Hadi Pir of the Lincoln, Nebraska, Yazidis set out for Washington, he and former translator friends telephoned Spencer, the only person they knew in the city. Spencer instantly agreed to set up meetings for them at the State Department and the Pentagon. Pir had faith that his adopted country would not allow his culture to be extinguished. He just needed the opportunity to make the case.

Spencer contacted State Department under secretary Sarah Sewall, head of Department "J," the office for Civilian Security, Democracy and

Human Rights. By the time the Lincoln contingent met up with the Houston contingent at a small hotel in suburban Maryland's inexpensive Silver Spring neighborhood, Sewall had scheduled the meeting for 3:00 p.m. and asked Spencer to escort the former translators to her office.

Hadi Pir, Haider Elias, and Khalaf Smoqi all spoke fluent English, Arabic, and Kurdish and were experts in all facets of technology. They had honed these skills while working for the US Army in northern Iraq, often risking their lives in the early years of the war to accompany American soldiers into hostile Sunni territory. By far their greatest asset, however, was their learned ability to convey information in a precise, linear manner.

"I spoke US Army as my fourth language," Pir said. "I knew all the slang and all the acronyms. I also knew that you tell them facts, not speculation. You don't tell them speculation until they ask for it."

Spencer escorted these three former translators and other Yazidis to the same meeting room where Dakhil Shammo and Hussein Khalaf had shed such bitter tears four days earlier. They were introduced to Doug Padgett and Leanne Cannon, Tom Melia, and, finally, Sarah Sewall.

As Sewall listened to Hadi Pir outline what he knew of the situation in northern Iraq, she grasped right away that this was an extraordinary opportunity to see if the mandate of the Obama Administration, the United States's "core moral responsibility" to prevent atrocities, could be upheld.

President Obama had created credibility problems in 2013 when he backed away from a statement that the use of chemical weapons by Syria's president Bashar al-Assad was a "red line." When Assad killed nearly fifteen hundred people in a sarin gas attack on a rebel-held area of Damascus, Obama got cold feet and brokered a deal with Russia whereby Assad agreed to destroy his arsenal of chemical weapons. Assad, not surprisingly, lied. In April of 2017, he dropped bombs containing nerve agents on a small town in northwestern Syria, killing eighty-nine people.

"So often that when one meets with people who are telling stories of outrage and victimhood, it is after the fact, and it is too late, and all you can do is empathize," Sewall said. "I think what was unique or different in this case was the sense that we could galvanize and act in a way that was meaningful."

The conversation moved from the state of the Yazidis on Mount Sinjar to the brutal murders of hundreds if not thousands of Yazidis on the day Islamic State invaded. Haider Elias began to recount the story of his brother's death, but he broke down several times in grief and exhaustion.

"The fact that the narrative that we had built and feared about ISIS in that region juxtaposed with the isolation and uniqueness protectiveness of the Yazidi community," Sewall said. "That narrative, the unfamiliar narrative of the Yazidis, was so stark. There was something that was urgent, seemingly on the cusp. You had a community that was the kind with which one could be particularly empathetic and which felt very as though it had been in a bubble and this bubble was about to be burst by demons, the bad guys, the people we had already come to hate. They were about to intrude on this community that seemed very vulnerable."

That afternoon Sewall attended a regularly scheduled meeting of the Atrocity Prevention Board. She asked all interagency participants to agree to share information via email chains.

THE SITUATION ROOM

On May 1, 2011, President Obama addressed the nation on television to announce the death of Osama bin Laden following a successful raid on his compound in Abbottabad, Pakistan. The mission, carried out by members of SEAL Team Six, the Night Stalkers, a US Army unit that provides helicopter support for military forces, and the CIA's Special Activities Division, ended a ten-year search for the mastermind of the 9/11 attacks.

Several hours before his announcement, White House photographer Peter Souza snapped what was to become an iconic photo of the president, along with Vice President Joe Biden, Secretary of State Hillary Clinton, Secretary of Defense Bob Gates, Brig. Gen. Marshall "Brad" Webb, the assistant commanding general of the Joint Special Operations Command, and Denis McDonough, the deputy national security advisor, seated at a conference table in the West Wing basement area referred to as the White House Situation Room. Standing behind them were, among others, Admiral Mike Mullen, Chairman of the Joint Chiefs of Staff, and James Clapper, the director of national intelligence.

In the photo, all but Webb are staring straight ahead at a drone feed of the operation to kill bin Laden. It had been live but the screen had suddenly gone dark. (Webb is looking at his computer screen.) Obama is pitched forward, wearing a dark blue windbreaker jacket and a white polo shirt. His jowls are loose, but his eyes appear to contain a controlled fury. Clinton's right hand loosely covers her mouth. Her head is tilted and her blue eyes appear slightly unfocused. The others seem somber and tense.

The photograph graced the front page of just about every American newspaper and the homepage of every news website as soon as it was released by the White House. It seemed to capture the exact second when the powerful are consumed by the horror of responsibility: If a young American soldier dies, it is they who sent him to his death. In the Situation Room, the president and other leaders face the consequences of their decisions in real time and either take the blame or rejoice in the victory.

For forty minutes, they listened to the voices of Americans engaged in a gunfight on the other side of the world until bin Laden was killed at approximately 3:00 p.m. "We got him," said the president before returning to the Oval Office.

The White House Situation Room was created by President John F. Kennedy after it was decided that the Bay of Pigs invasion failed due to a lack of real-time information. Today, the room's secure communications systems are constantly updated and are operated on a twenty-four-hour basis, monitoring world events for White House intelligence. It functions as the gathering point for all information, classified and nonclassified, that will be passed to the president. Most importantly, however, it allows the president to maintain command and control of US military forces around the world.

On Thursday morning, Doug Padgett and his superior, Tom Melia, entered the White House grounds to attend an Interagency Policy Meeting to discuss humanitarian needs in northern Iraq via a secure video teleconference system. Sitting in the Situation Room, the two men were joined by several national security advisors, including Ben Rhodes. Surrounding them were giant television screens that brought live participants from American government representatives on the ground in Baghdad and Erbil.

Most of the discussion centered on the wildly varying estimates of the number of Yazidis actually on the mountain. Some NGOs were reporting more than two hundred thousand while others seemed to imply that the number was much smaller and dropping.

General Bednarek, participating from his office in Baghdad, was prepared for the main question: How many people are actually on Mount Sinjar?

"How the hell many people were really there? How many families? How many men? How many YPG? How many other tribal elements that just wanted to protect their families because it's all about honor as an Arab man, or any ethnic group for that matter, particularly in the Middle East. So, we were trying to figure out exactly what those numbers were. UNHCR wants to help. So does the World Food Programme and all these other NGOs. What do we tell them? It was challenging. The best planners, and we are the best planners in the world, plan worst cases. We had everything from there are eight thousand that are really at risk to up to thirty thousand or more that are scattered from east to west all over the mountain . . . It was uniquely frustrating—no complicated—in the sense of everybody and their half-brother was asking 'How many people are there?' 'Well, we're not really sure. Here's what we think we know,'" Bednarek told the assembled agency participants.

Discussion moved on to usable and confirmable intelligence on the ground.

"This was the day before the first humanitarian drop in the beginning of the campaign against Islamic State fighters," Melia said. "The senior person on screen from the CIA said 'There is no communication with Mount Sinjar.' And it was me that said Doug and Leanne are in hourly communication with people. They are within a mile of where we are sitting here who are on the phone with their relatives on Mount Sinjar and they know what's going on, so we have real-time communication with them."

Melia, a man who will shyly let a certain pride steal over his poker face, took down the email addresses of several meeting participants to add their names to a growing list of recipients of emails from Doug Padgett and Leanne Cannon. (Melia had instructed them to set up a "real time" email chain a few days earlier.) He was now certain that his staff had the most reliable primary source information.

"The CIA was relying on the Peshmerga and the Iraqi government to tell us what was going on on Mount Sinjar, and they had a conflict of interest in this," Melia continued. "The Peshmerga, well, the Yazidis didn't feel that the Kurds are their friends. But the US feels that the Peshmerga of the Kurdish region is the best military we have in the Middle East, other than the Israelis. They trust them implicitly. So when the Peshmerga told the United States 'We can't find anybody. We don't know where they went. There's no communication,' Our government took it literally. The CIA thought 'Well they can't be there or the Peshmerga would know.' They didn't understand that the Yazidis wouldn't talk to the Peshmerga because they fled in the face of ISIL in the previous weeks."

"They are both correct, State and the CIA," said Bednarek. "From the CIA view, they don't have vetted intelligence operatives up on the mountain that gives them A1 source information that is credible, reliable and actionable. Period. That is CIA-think. From the State Department, the lower level Foreign Service officer, this VOIP talking to a Yazidi man on the ground with a cellphone who is providing information from his location near a thick outcropping with [a] group of about nine hundred people that need food and water. Well, what about the other ten thousand spread all over the mountain? So is that a credible, reliable source of information? It certainly is from that guy on the cellphone calling VOIP. You're darn right for him that is saying 'I am in dire straits and I need XYZ, but that may not be the case for somebody a mile away.' You have to understand the nuance."

Yet the most important piece of nuance was ignored not only by the CIA, the State Department, and the White House, but also by the Pentagon. No one noted a single Reuters report quoting a spokesman for the United Nations Office for the Coordination of Humanitarian Affairs, who said "We've just heard that people over the last 24 hours have been extracted [from Mount Sinjar]. We've received reports that thousands may have fled across the border into Syria and are waiting to cross back."

The Syrian Kurds, the YPG, had begun their rescue operation.

When the meeting adjourned, Tom Melia was certain military action was inevitable to save the Yazidis and stop the advance of Islamic State, but he had to wait for confirmation to come from the White House. Several hours later, at a Washington dinner party, his BlackBerry chimed. "It's a go."

At 9:05 p.m. in Washington, two F/A-18s took off from the aircraft carrier *George H. W. Bush* in the Persian Gulf to escort one C-17 and two C-130 cargo aircraft loaded with emergency supplies to airdrop to desperate Yazidis on Mount Sinjar. They held seventy-two pallets that contained fifty-three hundred gallons of fresh drinking water and eight thousand meals ready-to-eat. By 9:20 p.m., they had made the drop and cleared the airspace over Islamic State–held territory. News of the successful mission was passed to the White House, and President Obama prepared to address the nation.

PRESIDENTIAL ADDRESS

The Virginia home of Dakhil Shammo was unusually quiet. For the past five days, friends and family had walked in and out of this house exchanging information, comforting each other, and following social media. Now he sat alone with his wife and sons, waiting for President Obama to announce his plan to save the Yazidis.

At 9:30 p.m. in Washington, not quite dawn in Iraq, the White House cut into US network programming. President Obama, standing at a podium in the State Dining Room, announced he had authorized two operations in Iraq—targeted airstrikes to protect American personnel and a humanitarian effort to aid the Yazidis. American aircraft had already begun conducting humanitarian airdrops of food and water.

"ISIL forces have called for a systematic destruction of the entire Yazidi people, which would constitute genocide. So these innocent families are faced with a horrible choice: descend the mountain and be slaughtered, or stay and slowly die of thirst and hunger," he said.

Responding to the now viral appeal of Vian Dakhil, he said, "Earlier this week, one Iraqi in the area cried to the world, 'There is no one coming to help.' Well today, America is coming to help."

Aware of the country's war fatigue after more than a decade of sending American soldiers to fight in Iraq and Afghanistan, Obama reassured viewers that combat troops, the infamous "boots on the ground," would not be deployed, but he acknowledged his actions were bound to cause concern.

"As commander-in-chief, I will not allow the United States to be dragged into fighting another war in Iraq. And so even as we support Iraqis as they take the fight to these terrorists, American combat troops will not be returning to fight in Iraq, because there's no American military solution to the larger crisis in Iraq," he said.

Obama cast the mission to save the Yazidis as part of America's unique responsibility to prevent massacres, and he used the morally loaded word *genocide*.

"We can act carefully and responsibly to prevent a potential act of genocide," he said.

Only ABC, NBC, and CNN opted to cut into East Coast programming for the eight-minute speech. CBS News in New York stayed with a Jets vs. Colts preseason football game. Fox News also chose to stay with primetime programming.

Dakhil Shammo immediately called his mother and brother.

"The Americans are going to save us," he told them.

CHAPTER SEVEN

America Responds

Friday, August 8, Saturday, August 9

THE FIRST AMERICAN AIRSTRIKE OCCURRED FRIDAY AT 6:45 A.M. Washington time, 1:45 p.m. in Erbil. Two US Navy McDonnell Douglas F/A-18 Hornet fighters dropped five-hundred-pound laser-guided bombs on an Islamic State convoy that included a truck towing a mobile artillery gun. Islamic State had been using artillery to shell the far outskirts of Erbil. In an odd and unexplained decision, Pentagon spokesman Rear Adm. John Kirby announced news of America's first military offensive in Iraq since its withdrawal in 2011 through his Twitter account. Kirby was famously called "an idiot" by Senator John McCain after failing to agree with the esteemed senator's poor appraisal of the Obama Administration's fight against Islamic State.

Dakhil Shammo had risen early. As he drove along Virginia's I-66 highway toward Washington, listening to National Public Radio, he was thilled to hear the first reports of the airstrikes and excerpts from the previous evening's presidential address. He learned that the Kurdistan government was joyous when the United States assented to its request for an emergency shipment of small arms and ammunition.

His elation, however, ceased immediately upon hearing the report of a startling statement from Iraq's Human Rights Ministry. It said Islamic State held hundreds of Yazidi women under the age of thirty-five in the notorious Badush prison in Mosul, a city they now controlled. The statement said many of the girls, some as young as seven or eight, called their families with cellphones they had hidden from their captors. The statement included the stunning information that the militants had buried alive "tens of older women." There were no more details. A few minutes later, he received a call from an exuberant Doug Padgett.

"The White House wants to talk to you today," Doug said. "They want to hear your stories."

Padgett explained that the president's national security advisor, Ben Rhodes, had requested a meeting with the American Yazidis. He and members of the president's national security team wanted to discuss the humanitarian needs of the Yazidis of Sinjar with a small representative group from the diaspora community. Shammo redirected his attention from the plight of the Yazidi girls toward Padgett and told him he considered it an honor. He asked if the president would attend.

"I doubt it," said Padgett. "He's leaving for his annual vacation."

Shammo was pleased. He knew attention from the White House meant the Yazidi issue would not evaporate from the front pages of the international media, but he was not happy. The events of the past few days weighed heavily on him.

"By this time we knew, we American Yazidis, that our people were destroyed. Thousands of girls gone. Young massacred. Yes, it is good to stop them, but as for the Yazidis of Sinjar—they were gone forever," he said.

A few hours later, in a second airstrike, four F/A-18s destroyed an Islamic State convoy of seven vehicles driving around the base of Mount Sinjar. The vehicles were all American, captured, most likely, in Mosul. An American drone took out a rocket launcher.

White House officials moved quickly to assure the public that the action was a limited engagement, citing the need to protect the American consulate in Erbil.

Ben Rhodes appeared on CNN's *The Situation Room*.

"The threat that they [Islamic State] pose most acutely now is in Iraq and Syria. And what the line the president drew and is enforcing right now is that we're going to protect our people and facilities in Iraq. We saw them get close to Erbil. We take shots to make sure there is a periphery, so that our people are protected and the city of Erbil is protected," he said.

CNN reporter Barbara Starr said, "A US official telling me a short time ago they felt they cannot let Erbil fall to ISIS, the same thing that happened in Mosul where it fell to ISIS. They cannot have Erbil. That is why you are seeing the airstrikes."

That morning's *New York Times* lauded the president's decision to intervene, titling its lead editorial "Preventing a Slaughter in Iraq," but added: "After so many years in Iraq, Americans are justifiably skeptical about what military involvement can accomplish anywhere—and the Middle East is so complicated that even seemingly benign decisions can have unintended consequences."

Times reporter Peter Baker was even more skeptical. "Mr. Obama became the fourth president in a row to order military action in that graveyard of American ambition," he wrote in a news analysis.

THE ROOSEVELT ROOM

Barring an invitation to the Oval Office from the president of the United States, the Roosevelt Room is the closest any individual can get to the heart of the presidency. Directly across the hall from the Oval Office, this room often serves as a staging area for delegations preparing to meet the president to discuss legislative or policy concerns. It is a small, windowless room lit by a false skylight. It holds a large conference table and sixteen faux-Chippendale chairs, a grandfather clock, and a few easy chairs.

Traditional paintings of the twenty-sixth president of the United States, Theodore Roosevelt Jr., and his fifth cousin, the thirty-second president, Franklin Delano Roosevelt, flank the north and south walls. Since President Nixon opened the room in 1969, traditionally, a Republican president had placed Teddy Roosevelt's painting above the main fireplace mantel on the south wall until a Democratic president switched them, giving FDR's painting the place of honor. President Clinton abandoned this little lark and now Teddy stays above the mantel.

At 11:00 a.m., Dakhil Shammo, Hussein Khalaf, Hadi Pir, Haider Elias, and a few other outspoken members of the American-Yazidi community cleared the North Gate of the White House, showing their passports and driver's licenses, and were escorted through the West Wing to the Roosevelt Room. As they passed, White House staffers abruptly broke off conversations to watch the small group, casually dressed in the only clothes they had with them, jeans and T-shirts. Only Shammo wore a suit and tie.

In addition to Leanne Cannon and Tom Melia from the State Department, the Yazidis were accompanied by William Spencer, the former Foreign Service officer, and the executive director of the Institute for International Law and Human Rights, a Washington and European think tank, acting as an informal liaison between the State Department and the Lincoln Yazidis. Thirty-seven-year-old Ben Rhodes, President Obama's deputy national security advisor for strategic communications, had invited the group to the White House to elicit information about the Yazidi community. The story of this ancient community and its mysterious, almost antediluvian faith, appealed to his literary sensibility. The Manhattan-born Rhodes had received a master of fine arts from New York University years earlier and had attempted a literary career before joining the Obama presidential campaign as a speechwriter in 2007. His respect and loyalty to President Obama were legendary in Washington as was his contempt for the established Washington, DC, foreign policy community.

In a fawning 2016 *New York Times Magazine* profile of Rhodes, writer David Samuels described him as "what Holden Caulfield might have looked like if he grew up to work in the West Wing," eliciting both groans and snickers from Washington's longtime political class. The story of the Yazidis trapped on Mount Sinjar, a tale with contemptible villains and innocent victims, enticed Rhodes with its literary simplicity. The hero protagonist, of course, would be the American military, led by the Obama Administration.

Key members of the president's National Security Council, including Shannon Green, the senior director for global engagement on the NSC staff, Laura Abrahams Schulz, the NSC director for global engagement, Steve Pomper, NSC senior director for human rights and head of the Atrocity Prevention Board, and Andy Kim, the twenty-five-year old NSC director of Iraq, sat around the table.

Rhodes welcomed everyone to the White House.

"I hope events of the last 24 hours have signaled the American support for the Yazidi, especially those on Sinjar Mountain," he said, referring to the recent airdrops of humanitarian supplies as well as the morning's airstrikes on Islamic State positions.

He turned to Dakhil Shammo and asked for the latest information the group knew from their contacts in Sinjar. Shammo addressed the room. He recounted the massacres that had occurred during the invasion just six days earlier, describing the murders that took place on the road outside Siba and the execution of the men of Hardan. He repeated conversations he had had with those still trapped on the mountain, and chronicled their sunburn, their thirst, and their hunger. He spoke with the passion of a man whose life bore the scars of having faced bigotry and dodging death. As he laid out the number of kidnapped young women and the odd circumstances in the village of Kocho, every slight he had suffered as a Yazidi added up, building to a rage that seeped into his words and made his body shake. His voice was clipped and accusatory, not the impression he wanted to convey, so he referred to the traumatic phone calls received by Yazidis Haider Elias and Hussein Khalaf, allowing each man to describe the murder of family members. As Hussein spoke, tears ran down his face, stopping at the tips of his white, handlebar mustache. He dabbed at them with the sleeve of his baggy, gray jacket. Then, overcome by emotion, he stopped speaking and sobbed inconsolably. Rhodes's face turned white. The room was quiet. Rhodes firmly assured Hussein the United States would not stand by and watch a genocide.

With a nod, Dakhil thanked Rhodes and the other NSC members for the airdrops. Then he characterized the retreat of the Peshmerga and the abandonment of the Yazidis as "the real issue" and steered the conversation toward the need to airdrop weapons to Yazidi men on the mountain so they could protect themselves.

For the White House, humanitarian issues were the sole item on the agenda for this meeting. But for the Yazidis, the meeting was a critical opportunity to impress upon the White House the long-term vulnerability of the Yazidi people—both to Islamic State and, in their eyes, to a duplicitous Peshmerga.

Rhodes attempted to redirect the meeting.

"The airstrikes are pushing ISIS back. The Peshmerga are on the mountain reinforcing defenses. Humanitarian drops will continue. We will take airstrikes if we can find targets, but the ideal scenario is an open corridor organized by the Peshmerga," he said.

"This is pure fantasy," Spence Spencer thought. He knew the White House hoped the Peshmerga would eventually be able to open a corridor from Sinjar to Dohuk, but the Peshmerga was in disarray and had suffered another defeat fewer than forty-eight hours earlier when Islamic State crossed the Great Zab River.

"There are no Peshmerga on the mountain. We Yazidis kicked them out because of their cowardice," an angry Hadi Pir responded.

"There are Yazidi fighters, but no leadership," said Canadian Yazidi Mirza Ismail, a colleague and acquaintance of Spence Spencer, who believed the Yazidis had a constitutional right to form and defend their own nation-state. "We need to invoke Article 125 of the Iraqi Constitution, which allows decentralization. Please do not bring Peshmerga to protect us."

"The pesh won't fight for us," Dakhil Shammo said quietly, but firmly. "They are just posturing to get American weapons. In truth, they prefer we die."

"It may be that you are right, sir," said Rhodes. Attempting to steer the conversation back to the issue of humanitarian aid, he added, "But our immediate challenge is to get your people to safety. Have they seen the humanitarian supplies?"

"No," said Shammo. In fact, many Yazidis had received the water and food, but Shammo was unaware of that.

Pushing back against Rhodes's desire to avoid military discussions, Hadi Pir interrupted Shammo.

"We need more airstrikes right now to intimidate ISIS. They need to hear from the United States. To feel the power of the United States," he said.

"Strikes will happen as soon as we have targets," Rhodes responded. "So we know we are hitting ISIS and not civilians."

Hadi Pir rose from his chair and straightened the large maps of Iraq and the Sinjar region that lay on the table. He pointed to the roads held by Islamic State.

"They have one hundred trucks at these checkpoints," he said. "Their base is in Tal Afar. They are holding five hundred female hostages there. They have moved five thousand women to the Badush prison in Mosul. They are massing at Khanasour with plans to move toward Erbil."

As he described the locations of Islamic State checkpoints around Mount Sinjar, two uniformed men with clipboards and pens rose from the back of the room and started taking notes. Pir then realized they desperately needed basic information—the type of intelligence he knew how to get after years of working with the American army.

"What about American Forces?" Shammo asked. This, of course, was the issue on the minds of all the participants: To what extent would the Obama Administration risk American lives to save the Yazidis?

"This is the White House view: We are not going to commit US forces as proxy for the Peshmerga," Rhodes answered. The room was quiet.

"Look," said Andy Kim, Iraq director for the NSC. "Whatever your history with the Peshmerga, they are preferable to ISIS. We are in contact with the Peshmerga and they are on the mountain." This was true, but most of the Peshmerga on the mountains were Yazidis, not full Kurdish Peshmerga units, and they were mostly on the north side of the mountain helping the YPG open the corridor, not on the south side where the refugees were cowering.

"They are not there," said Shammo. "If you don't believe us, you will believe your own satellites. The Peshmerga is not there. This genocide is happening. There is no time for questions. It is time to act."

"We will take action," said Rhodes, "and this genocide will be stopped."

As the meeting wound down, the Yazidis and their advocates knew they had made an impression on Rhodes and the NSC staff.

"We knew they would do something. We knew they were taking us seriously," Spencer said.

"You could see he was committed and affected by the real life aspect of the meeting," said Cannon.

Rhodes detested playing in the political arena with those who pushed their own agendas before the needs of people. In this meeting, he felt, the mandate of democratic government had been carried out: to hear and respond to the needs of its citizens.

"Fascinating, here they are sitting ten feet from the Oval Office—they don't have on suits, just ordinary clothes, this is the remarkable thing about America. I will never forget their point, their community existed for thousands of years and now only the United States can save it. To hear that, put so starkly, is that kind of thing you don't forget," he recalled. "This was a unique event with a unique people whose advocacy really mattered. It really made a difference. There are a number of things competing for the attention of the United States government officials at one time and they brought theirs to the forefront of the government."

He went immediately to the Oval Office to brief President Obama.

"I saw it as a part of my job to give him the texture of that meeting," said Rhodes. "The emotion of it. Also, their message. They felt the entire community was at risk. This was a real genocide and that added to the momentum to take action. Their advocacy was extremely effective. They reinforced what we were hearing from others about Sinjar, so we took the genocide possibility very seriously. We very rarely use that word, but we did because there was intel to support it. There was reporting on both the fact that Yazidis were being killed as well as the motivation to carry out a genocide. That intel led us to use the word genocide. That word is very specific. There are atrocities that take place, but don't often rise to that level of genocide, but in this case there was the evidence. It was very unusual for the president to use that word as he did in his speech, but we felt confident."

As the group walked off the grounds of the White House, past the guardhouse and onto tourist-filled Pennsylvania Avenue, their spirits lifted. In the five days since the catastrophic invasion of Sinjar had ripped apart their lives, they had found a way to walk into the White House and make their plea to the leaders of the most powerful military machine in the world.

In an uncharacteristically self-important, but probably truthful, moment, Hadi Pir later told his hometown newspaper, the *Lincoln Star*, "Tens of thousands of people have been saved. If it wasn't for what we accomplished here, the world would be hearing about tens of thousands more people being killed by ISIS."

Former Army translators Pir and Smoqi headed back to their hotel room in Maryland alarmed by the realization that the Obama Administration would continue to rely on the advice of the Peshmerga and their shaky intelligence. Politically and militarily, Washington invested deeply in the Peshmerga—it was, perhaps, the only institution in Iraq whose competence and loyalty Washington did not doubt. Both men believed the Peshmerga would continue to feed Washington with inaccurate information tweaked to imply they still held ground at Mount Sinjar.

Pir and Smoqi had trained with American soldiers, fought alongside them, and advised them. While the White House and the State Department saw them as members of a diaspora, a curious people who practiced an exotic faith, they viewed themselves as veterans of the Iraq War. Now they would serve both of their countries, old and new.

An hour later Rhodes tweeted, "I was deeply moved by my meeting with the Yazidi community at the White House. The US stands with the Yazidi people in this tragic time."

What were President Obama's thoughts about saving the Yazidis of Sinjar after Rhodes briefed him on the emotional meeting with the Yazidis? A few hours later, the president gave a rare one-on-one interview with the *New York Times* columnist Thomas Friedman.

"When you have unique circumstances in which genocide is threatened and a country is willing to have us in there, you have a strong international consensus that these people need to be protected and we have a capacity to do so, then we have an obligation to do so," he told Friedman.

President Obama expressed respect for the Kurdish quasi-state.

"I think the Kurds used that time that was given by our troops' sacrifices in Iraq. They used that time well and the Kurdish region is functional the way we would like to see. It is tolerant of other sects and other religions in a way that we would like to see elsewhere. So, we think it is important to make sure that that space is protected," he said.

On the larger issue of the Iraqi State, and the reason for the American pressure on Maliki to step down, Mr. Obama made his message to Baghdad clear.

"We will be your partners, but we are not going to do it for you. We're not sending a bunch of US back on the ground to keep a lid on things. You're going to have to show us that you are willing and ready to try and maintain a unified Iraqi government that is based on compromise. That you are willing to continue to build a non-sectarian, functional security force that is answerable to a civilian government."

WAR POWERS

Article 1 of the Constitution of the United States unequivocally gives Congress, not the president, the power to declare war. Obviously, the framers sought to prevent one man from holding the authority to commit the country to conflict, and they sought broad consensus through Congress instead. Presidents have often found their way around this provision. In fact, despite the multitude of wars and military actions of the past seventy-five years, Congress has not declared war since June 1942 when it authorized the fight against Axis Powers Bulgaria, Romania, and Hungary.

Following the revelation that President Richard Nixon had ordered secret bombings of Cambodia without notifying Congress during the Vietnam War, legislators crafted and passed the War Powers Resolution of 1973. Also known as the War Powers Act, it requires the president to notify Congress within forty-eight hours of committing armed forces to military action.

Realistically, President Obama was unable to seek congressional approval since the body had adjourned August 1, and most lawmakers had left Washington that week for their legislatively mandated five-week summer recess. A recall of Congress, although not unprecedented, would have taken several days, time the Yazidis did not have. Furthermore, Obama maintained he did not have to seek approval since, as president, he had the right to act unilaterally to protect American citizens, like those Americans in the Erbil Consulate.

Probably because most Republicans agreed with his decision to take military action, and because the War Powers Act would prove irrelevant, Obama decided to comply with its tenets and sent his notification Friday afternoon.

TEXT OF A LETTER FROM THE PRESIDENT TO THE SPEAKER OF THE HOUSE OF REPRESENTATIVES AND THE PRESIDENT PRO TEMPORE OF THE SENATE

August 8, 2014
  Dear Mr. Speaker: (Dear Mr. President:)
  As I announced publicly on August 7, 2014, I have authorized the US Armed Forces to conduct targeted airstrikes in Iraq. These

military operations will be limited in their scope and duration as necessary to protect American personnel in Iraq by stopping the current advance on Erbil by the terrorist group Islamic State of Iraq and the Levant and to help forces in Iraq as they fight to break the siege of Mount Sinjar and protect the civilians trapped there.

Pursuant to this authorization, on August 8, 2014, US military forces commenced targeted airstrike operations in Iraq.

In addition, I have authorized US Armed Forces to provide humanitarian assistance in Iraq in an operation that commenced on August 7, 2014. These operations will also be limited to supporting the civilians trapped on Mount Sinjar.

I have directed these actions, which are in the national security and foreign policy interests of the United States, pursuant to my constitutional authority to conduct US foreign relations and as Commander in Chief and Chief Executive. These actions are being undertaken in coordination with the Iraqi government.

I am providing this report as part of my efforts to keep the Congress fully informed, consistent with the War Powers Resolution (Public Law 93-148). I appreciate the support of the Congress in this action.

Sincerely,

BARACK OBAMA

THE TRANSLATORS

At a motel in suburban Maryland, four former translators for the US Army in Iraq deployed their combined quarter-century of US military training into a makeshift command center to gather as much information as they could about the status of the Yazidis on Sinjar. The four Yazidis who now hailed from Lincoln, Nebraska, and Houston, Texas, gave a tactical name to their emergency operation, founded on the spot after their meeting with US officials to address the country's worrisome deficit of reliable intelligence. "I named our group the Sinjar Crisis Management Team," Hadi Pir said. "It was military sounding and blunt."

After calling their wives and bosses to tell them they would not be back at home for at least another week, the men went to work in one of the motel rooms with three laptops, four Samsung smartphones, a tangle of chargers, and long lists of contacts. They taped maps, some drawn by hand, to the walls above the desk. They slept in shifts in a second room. They had one change of clothes.

Khalaf Smoqi, Hadi Pir, Haider Elias and Murad Ismail knew the roads, fields, and villages around Mount Sinjar, and they knew the mountain itself. Importantly, they also understood, from years of working with Army planners, the precision and technical skills required to create effective plans from raw intelligence gathered on the ground.

They began to trace the location of groups of Yazidis who needed water, or those who had serious medical conditions. By talking to the armed Yazidi men who were patrolling the perimeter of the mountain at the halfway point, they located Islamic State convoys as they moved around the mountain. Soon they could pass along not just the location of Islamic State, but the number and type of vehicles they were driving.

The men created Google maps and dropped pins on the exact coordinates of Islamic State checkpoints.

"ISIS checkpoint was a red pin," Smoqi said.

Twenty-five-year old Khalaf Smoqi was the youngest member of the team and the newest arrival to the United States. Just two years earlier, he had received his Special Immigration Visa while working as a translator for the US Army. He relocated from Sinjar to Lincoln where he worked full time in an automotive store while attending the University of Nebraska at night.

"I worked as a translator at the US Army Technical Operations Center in Mosul," Smoqi said. "FOB Marez, next to the US military airfield. I was a translator for an Iraqi commander and every day we sat in front of six large screens that received video from drones watching the city. We would call checkpoints for reports and build coordinate maps. So, I knew what the Americans wanted these maps to look like. I knew how to speak their lingo."

Their idea was remarkably simple: Using WhatsApp, they called relatives, friends, and acquaintances on the mountain. "Where are you?" they asked. "How many Yazidis are with you? What is their medical condition? What can you see from your position? Where did you last see

Islamic State? Who is near you who also saw this? Give me their phone number." Working methodically, they debriefed anyone who still had a working cellphone.

WhatsApp is a free smartphone app that uses the internet or mobile data connection to make voice calls, send text messages, and other communications using standard mobile phone numbers. It is very popular in Iraq and parts of the Middle East because it facilitates inexpensive international phone calls. The Sinjar Crisis Management Team knew that by using WhatsApp they could immediately connect to Yazidis trapped on the mountain.

"Hadi called people whose number he already had," Smoqi said. "They would say 'There's a convoy.' They would give him the number of someone closer and I would call. I knew the mountain and understood the roads."

Some Yazidis on the mountain began to take photographs of Islamic State positions or checkpoints that they could see from the higher ground. Adding specific coordinates they pulled off another smartphone app, they forwarded those photos to Smoqi and the others. After parsing every scrap of information and cross-referencing to avoid duplication, Hadi wrote emails from a newly created Sinjar Crisis Management Team email address detailing the latest intelligence, attaching maps and photographs, and sent them to Doug Padgett and Leanne Cannon in the IRF office.

"We were very cautious. We didn't put anything on our Facebook feeds about what we were doing. We used the precision training we got from the US Army. We only took information from people we knew personally or once removed, someone recommended by someone we knew personally. We tried to confirm everything with more than one source. We knew if we made a mistake they would stop taking our information. Hadi stopped us from sending non-relevant information," Smoqi said.

Working in shifts over the next forty-eight hours, the four men traced the movements of Islamic State at the base of the mountain. From their contacts higher up and closer to the north side of the mountain, they slowly began to piece together an understanding of a small open corridor off the mountain created by the YPG, the Syrian Kurdish fighters who had responded to the call of imprisoned leader Abdullah Öcalan. YPG fighters had defeated Islamic State in fierce combat at the northern base and were pushing their way up Mount Sinjar to establish a safe escape route. Eventually, the team in the motel was able to draw a map of the route to freedom, and they sent it on to IRF.

"What was impressive about what they were trying to do and what they were trying to give us was the specificity of the information," said Padgett. "I've worked with DRL [State Department Office of Democracy, Human Rights, and Labor] for six years. Our whole job is working with civil society and working with community groups who have information to give us. What these guys did is unique. It was remarkable in its specificity and concreteness and in the action oriented way they presented the information. This wasn't vague reports of something bad happening someplace. It was specific and it was important that it got to people who could do something with it."

The four men were also able to provide specific information about the location of large numbers of displaced people that helped the Pentagon avoid civilian casualties.

"We (told) the State Department where exactly people were, how many, when they move, where they move (to)," Pir said. "They told us 'The people at the Department of Defense, they listen to you because they trust you.'"

Doug and Leanne built an email list that included all the members of the APB as well as contacts they had in Iraq. Tom Melia provided the emails of everyone who had attended the interagency meeting a few days earlier. The small IRF office in the Office of Democracy, Human Rights, and Labor was almost instantly besieged by requests to join the email list until hundreds of US government civil servants, officials, military planners, and diplomats were receiving messages from the Sinjar Crisis Management Team.

At their rooms in the motel, soon littered with pizza boxes and cola cans, the men worked with a ferocious intensity. The lives of their loved ones depended on their skill.

"Murad was very emotional. He often had to leave the room to cry," Smoqi said. "Hadi was filled with energy. He bounced around the room, encouraging us, telling us this was the most important event of our lives. Because they were older than me and had more experience, I just followed their orders."

After hearing about their work piecing together reliable information and finding out that it was being forwarded to Washington's government offices, Ben Rhodes asked the staff of the National Security Council to ensure its distribution to Central Command (Centcom), the Defense Department's Tampa-based unified command responsible for American interests in twenty-seven nations from the Horn of Africa through the Arabian Gulf and into Central Asia.

"We worked with NSC staff to get the information from people who were hearing from their loved ones to report to State and feed that to Pentagon as the military campaign ramped up. We wanted reporting from that group. So, we worked to set up reporting mechanics with DRL. Centcom said they took all that information and it added to the picture. Was there a direct correlation between some information and a specific airstrike? No, but we got the reports. If they matched our own intelligence, well, that's one more factor," said Rhodes.

Rhodes found Centcom was already aware of the remarkable information the Yazidis were supplying.

"The J2, the intelligence operations center at Centcom, had called and said they were getting the information in forwarded emails, but they wanted to be on the distribution list," Cannon said. "I said yes absolutely. I told them I would forward actionable items immediately, not wait for a summary, if they wanted. 'Oh yeah, great,' they said. So, they created an email for us to send the real time information to them as fast as we could get it."

As the emails dropped into Sarah Sewall's inbox, she understood that this "game changer," as she called it, could become a crucial paradigm for interacting with immigrant communities during international crisis.

"What I recognized immediately was the ability of the diaspora community to connect us in real time with the victims themselves. This was something that would be invaluable for the evaluation if not the catalyzation of the military action. So, that was the clear value. By making it [the information] as public as was practical, it was a way of putting pressure for action in the system. And that was probably more effective than anything the Atrocities Prevention Board could have done. It made transparent that (a) we knew what was going on and it is always harder to not act when you know what is going on because there is not deniability and (b) we had the tactical information that one would need to shape military action so it was no longer possible to argue that it was not feasible to act," she said.

"We learned about the corridor from their reporting," said Rhodes. "We learned some people didn't want to leave Sinjar from their reporting, and so we kept up the supply airdrops. I hope going forward the United States government continues to develop that capacity—to use the diaspora community for information."

In the ensuing days, Pir and Smoqi began to hear references to a small village far south of the mountain. The entire village was being held hostage and no one understood why. What, they asked, was Islamic State planning to do in Kocho?

Saturday, August 9

Midmorning on a warm August Saturday, President Obama, along with his wife, Michelle, his older daughter Malia, and their two dogs, Bo and Sunny, walked from the White House onto the South Lawn. Obama peeled away from his family and approached a press podium set up by the network pool for a quick news conference. Reporters stood a few yards in front of him. With *Marine One*, a helicopter from Marine Helicopter Squadron One, posed on the lush lawn behind him, a casually dressed Obama justified the actions in Iraq by reiterating the two main objectives of the mission: to protect American diplomats and property, and to prevent a genocide. Then he gave Prime Minister Maliki another good shove toward the door, saying "What we don't yet have is a prime minister and a cabinet that is formed that can go ahead and move forward."

The bulk of his statement, however, prepared the country for what the White House assumed would be a complex and dramatic multiday military operation to remove the Yazidis from Mount Sinjar.

"The next step, which is going to be complicated logistically, is how do we give safe passage for people down from the mountain, and where can we ultimately relocate them so that they are safe . . . how do we potentially create a safe corridor or some other mechanism so that these people can move. That may take some time—because there are varying estimates of how many people are up there, but they're in the thousands, and moving them is not simple in this kind of security environment."

White House and Pentagon officials continued to believe that breaking the siege of Mount Sinjar and removing the Yazidis would take weeks longer, requiring a virtual ground campaign of combined Kurdish, Iraqi, and possibly American Special Forces. While they acknowledged the escape of Yazidis into Syria with the help of the YPG, they did not see this as a significant part of the solution.

Fearing the worst, Obama attempted to prepare Americans for an extended military presence in northern Iraq, saying airstrikes could go on for months. "This is going to be a long-term project," he said, before striding toward the helicopter. Within minutes of his departure, however, aides told The Associated Press he had not committed to years of airstrikes, but merely wanted his comments to reflect the acute uncertainty surrounding the flow of events. The decision to engage with Iraq was difficult for a president who had campaigned against the war, often referring to it as "dumb."

The nature of the president's remarks about Iraq had changed markedly since Thursday evening when they took on the tone of an immediate crisis. These new remarks demonstrated American resolve and commitment to pushing Islamic State out of northern Iraq. The United States was in it for the long term. As the president boarded the helicopter and waved to onlookers, US Central Command announced another set of airstrikes.

At 11:00 a.m. Washington time, US fighter jets and drones conducted the first of four airstrikes that day designed to push Islamic State away from Mount Sinjar. Earlier that morning, Islamic State fighters had begun to advance along the main road up the mountain and Washington feared that a new attack on the Yazidis was being staged. That first American airstrike destroyed several armored personnel carriers and killed sixteen Islamic State fighters who had been firing indiscriminately as they patrolled the base of the mountain. In follow-up airstrikes,

American aircraft hit three more Islamic State armored personnel carriers and a Ford truck filled with weapons.

Republican senator John McCain, a vociferous critic of the president, told The Associated Press that Obama's vision for military operations was too narrow. He bemoaned the president's lack of policy strategy, calling the airstrikes a "pinprick," "meaningless," and "almost worse than nothing."

Later in the day, McCain appeared on CNN's *State of the Union with Candy Crowley* live from Jakarta, Indonesia. The senator was in Indonesia as guest of President Susilo Bambang Yudhoyono, who had invited McCain to thank him for his support to help modernize the Indonesian military's weapons systems. McCain said there was a "vacuum of American leadership." Islamic State presented "the possibility of a cataclysmic scenario," he opined, and said the group was a direct threat to the security of the United States.

In fact, the US airstrikes had an almost immediate effect. After the hits on Islamic State positions around Makhmour and Gwer, the jihadists appeared paralyzed. By afternoon, a regrouped Peshmerga had counterattacked and battled to push Islamic State out of those cities and back across the Great Zab River. At Mount Sinjar, Islamic State's chokehold on the southern perimeter of the mountain was broken. Most importantly, the airstrikes buoyed the spirits of the Peshmerga, the Kurdistan Regional Government, and the Kurdish population in general, who all knew that the United States once entered in the fight, would stay until Islamic State was contained or defeated.

MARTHA'S VINEYARD

The tiny Martha's Vineyard town of Chilmark was first settled in 1660 by, among others, Lt. Josiah Standish, the son of Capt. Myles Standish, the English military officer hired by the pilgrims to accompany them on the *Mayflower*'s sail to the New World. The nineteen-square mile residential community incorporated the small fishing village of Menemsha, famously used as the backdrop for the film *Jaws*. Between its several nature preserves and animal sanctuaries, lie vast estate homes, including the ten-acre manor of Joanne Hubschman, the widow of a former GE executive, and a Democratic fundraiser.

The Obamas rented Hubschman's seven-bedroom house for their traditional two-week summer vacation in Martha's Vineyard. Residents greeted them Saturday morning the way they did all presidential visitors, by crowding on the side of the road to watch the motorcade speed past. Small, family-owned businesses sported "Welcome Obamas" placards. Shortly after landing, the president headed to Oak Bluffs to play at Farm Neck Golf Club, one of the top-ranked courses in the Northeast.

CHAPTER EIGHT

The Prime Minister

Sunday, August 10, Monday,
August 11, Tuesday, August 12

On Sunday, the political deadlock in Baghdad began to show movement. Faced with a serious threat from Islamic State, Iraqi parliamentarians knew they had to find a solution, fast. The American government's public statements outlining the mission in Kurdistan pointedly omitted any mention of the preservation of the Iraqi nation. At every press conference and briefing, Washington used the same language, repeating: We will save the Yazidis, and we will protect Erbil. We will not commit combat troops. Maliki must go. Yet parliamentarians sprang into action because of what was left unsaid: If Maliki stays, we will not prevent Islamic State from moving toward the capital and threatening Baghdad.

So they scrambled to find a consensus candidate who would placate the Americans' unhappiness with Maliki's divisiveness and disgust at his graft, and who would win a measure of approbation from Iraq's Sunni community. Haider Jawad Kadhim al-Abadi, the deputy parliamentary speaker, a well-respected political moderate, emerged as the perfect choice.

The Americans considered him an honest and effective politician who would fight corruption within the government. Equally important, Abadi belonged to DAWA, the party that had won the April election and had the legal right to form a government. Abadi's nomination would take the wind out of Maliki's insistence that naming a new prime minister was unconstitutional.

Throughout the day, Parliamentary President Fouad Massoum conferred with members of Parliament to determine the level of support they would show for an Abadi government.

The unknown, of course, was how embattled prime minister Nouri Maliki would react to the decision. But Maliki, with spies in all facets of the government, was already aware of the plot.

As Sunday came to a close, just a few minutes before midnight, Maliki popped up on Iraqi State broadcasting. In a strident and defiant television address, he challenged those who were urging him to step down, implying he would use the army to "defend the constitution." As he spoke, the tanks of Shia militias who were personally loyal to Maliki moved into strategic areas of Baghdad and fears of a quasi-military take-over swirled around the city. In Washington, where it was late afternoon, State Department officials who work on Iraq policy interrupted their weekend to race to their offices in Foggy Bottom.

Maliki was warned against making political arrests. One Iraqi par-liamentary official said, "Maliki has gone out of his mind, and lives on a different planet—he doesn't appreciate the mess he has created."

American officials contacted high-ranking parliamentarians and religious leaders, demanding or pleading with them to support the new candidate, a man they believed would unite the various parties in the government and the three factions, Sunni, Shia, and Kurd, of Iraq.

In Kurdistan, the third day of airstrikes had begun early that morning when US forces launched a wave of attacks on Islamic State–armed vehi-cles and mortar positions that had been assaulting the outskirts of Erbil.

The American strikes were showing clear effects. The Peshmerga, using American air cover, reversed the Islamic State's forward thrust with a successful counterattack in the nearby towns of Makhmour and Gwer.

The Peshmerga pushed to the center of Gwer and then slowly spread east and west to locate booby traps and identify the positions of snipers. In a farmhouse and a barn near the highway, they found the jihadists had hidden three captured Iraqi army trucks with mounted machine guns. American fighter jets streaked in and blew them up.

Local media showed video of truckloads of cheering Peshmerga soldiers cruising the highways in the Gwer region. With Islamic State retreating and the Peshmerga rejuvenated after their disastrous perfor-mance in Ninewah, Kurdish president Masoud Barzani politely pleaded with the United States to sell arms directly to the Kurdish Peshmerga.

"We are the United States' staunch allies in the region, and we have the only force in the area with the means and will to protect thousands of lives from the horrors that these terrorists bring. But we cannot do it alone. We are thankful to our friends on Capitol Hill and in the White House for the support that they have given us over the years. Only because the situation is absolutely urgent do we humbly ask our friends to help us again," he told The Associated Press.

Since the beginning of the war with Islamic State, there had been steady traffic of American high-level military and civilian delegations to the Kurdistan Region. Now the relationship between the United States and the Kurdistan Regional Government began to enter a new strategic phase.

Despite this strengthening alliance, the White House and the Pentagon constantly reassured the American public that the nation was not getting back into a war in Iraq.

"This is a focused effort, not a wider air campaign," said Col. Ed Thomas, spokesman for the Chairman of the Joint Chiefs of Staff, Gen. Martin E. Dempsey. "Our military objectives are limited in purpose."

In Washington, Lt. Gen. William Mayville, the director of operations for the Joint Chiefs of Staff, told reporters that the airstrikes had slowed Islamic State's advance but had done little to degrade their capacity as a fighting force.

"In the immediate areas where we've focused our strikes, we've had a temporary effect. I in no way want to suggest that we have effectively contained [Islamic State]," Mayville added.

NEW PRIME MINISTER

At the age of fifteen, Haider Jawad Kadhim Al-Abadi joined DAWA, a pro-Iran, anti–Saddam Hussein Islamist political party. Abadi's father was director of the Baghdad Neurosurgery Hospital and, later, inspector general of the Iraqi Ministry of Health under Hussein, but Saddam's cohorts accused him of disloyalty, eventually forcing him to retire in 1979. As a result of his father's unfair treatment at the hands of the Ba'ath regime, Abadi joined the Islamic DAWA party that in the 1970s waged an armed insurgency against Ba'athists. With his brother, he worked clandestinely and ultimately unsuccessfully to destroy the party. Two of his brothers were murdered. The third languished in prison for ten years.

In the late 70s, Haider Abadi went into voluntary exile in the UK, studying electrical engineering and receiving a PhD at the University of

Manchester. A few years later, the Ba'athist party sentenced to death all members of DAWA, past and present. Those who were affiliated, and many who were falsely accused of belonging to the party, disappeared into Hussein's torture chambers. The Hussein regime nullified Abadi's passport, and he resigned himself to a life in exile, building a career in London as a transportation expert.

Following the US invasion of Iraq in 2003, Abadi returned to Iraq determined to work for the nation's sovereignty and hasten the departure of American troops. He was named to the interim Governing Council, but clashed with Coalition Provisional Authority head Paul Bremer, who decided to ignore, not only Abadi, but the entire council. Bremer built a government beholden to the United States that Iraqis considered little more than a puppet of the Americans, adding to the anger of a growing insurgency. Following Iraq's first democratic election in 2005, Abadi worked in several government positions, including as minister of communications and later as a Member of Parliament representing Baghdad. In 2014, he was the deputy parliamentary speaker.

MONDAY, AUGUST 11

Parliamentary President Fouad Massoum announced he was inviting Deputy Parliamentary Speaker Haider al-Abadi to form a new government and become prime minister. Abadi called for unity against a Sunni insurgency led by the Islamic State group. Megalomaniac Nouri al-Maliki, who had encouraged sectarian friction in his country to the point where it fueled the rise of Islamic State, made a last-ditch attempt to hold onto power. In the predawn hours, additional tanks and extra units of troops loyal to Maliki moved into the Green Zone to reinforce those he had already deployed. As a counterpoint, police and elite armed units loyal to the anti-Maliki parliamentarians locked down major streets and other strategic areas. While rumors of a Maliki coup continued to swirl around the capital city, citizens braced for street battles between Maliki's followers and those of his rivals. At 9:00 a.m. hundreds of Maliki supporters, most on his payroll, marched through Baghdad to the parliament with massive signs, calling their man "the one true Prime Minister."

Traveling in Australia, US secretary of state John Kerry hastily called a news conference and warned Maliki that a grab for power would result in the cutoff of international support.

"There should be no use of force, no introduction of troops or militias into this moment of democracy for Iraq," he said. "We believe that the government-formation process is critical in terms of sustaining the stability and calm in Iraq, and our hope is that Mr. Maliki will not stir those waters."

In a bold move calculated to halt Maliki's momentum, Iraqi president Fouad Massoum appeared on television with Abadi to congratulate him alongside Sunni and Shia parliamentarians. "The country is in your hands. May God help you," each said to their new head of state as they ceremoniously shook his hand on television.

Abadi called for unity against the Sunni insurgency led by the Islamic State group, saying "I have confidence that, with the people and political blocs, we would be able to overcome this barbaric and savage attack on the Iraqi people and provide a good environment for the Iraqi people to live in."

The United States responded to the new candidate immediately and without hesitation. Brett McGurk, the deputy assistant secretary of state for near eastern affairs, and the Obama Administration's point man on Iraq, released a statement.

"The United States stands ready to fully support a new and inclusive Iraqi government," it said.

Maliki remained quiet, but no one in Baghdad believed he would accept the decision to ask Deputy Speaker Abadi to form a government. The city awaited Maliki's next move.

OBAMA

On a brutally humid early Monday evening on Martha's Vineyard, President Obama stood outside his rented vacation house at a podium on a gentle slope flanked by trees and framed by stunning water views. Reporters stood just a few feet away. Speaking for less than four minutes, he told reporters that he and Vice President Biden had spoken to Abadi to congratulate him.

"This new Iraqi leadership has a difficult task. It has to regain the confidence of its citizens by governing inclusively and by taking steps to demonstrate its resolve. The United States stands ready to support a government that addresses the needs and grievances of all Iraqi people. We are also ready to work with other countries in the region to deal with the humanitarian crisis and counterterrorism challenge in Iraq. Mobilizing that support will be easier once this new government is in place."

The president was signaling to Abadi that the United States would fully support the new Iraqi government in its fight against Islamic State if Abadi could forge a coalition that gave meaningful roles to other factions, including Sunnis and Kurds. He was also sending a clear message to Maliki: You're gone.

"We stand ready to partner with Iraq in its fight against these terrorist forces. Without question, that effort will be advanced if Iraqis continue to build on today's progress, and come together to support a new and inclusive government."

A few hours later, the president left his vacation house to attend a fundraising event hosted by Berklee College of Music president Roger Brown. Tickets to the event ranged from $15,000 to $32,000 and guests included senators Ed Markey of Massachusetts and Michael Bennett of Colorado.

In brief remarks to the political power brokers who gather each summer on Martha's Vineyard, Obama listed the accomplishments of his administration, including his signature healthcare initiative. Pivoting to international affairs, he said:

"I do want to point out, though, at a time when the news seems filled with news of Ukraine and Gaza and Ebola and you name it, that in every instance people are constantly interested in finding out how can America help solve these problems. And there's a reason for that. Because despite the complaints and the second-guessing, and the anti-American sentiment that you hear sometimes on television around the globe, when there's an actual problem they all recognize we're the one indispensable nation. They all recognize that our leadership is absolutely critical."

Point Man

That night on *PBS NewsHour*, anchor and co-host Gwen Ifill interviewed Deputy Assistant Secretary of State for Near Eastern Affairs Brett McGurk, who joined her at the anchor desk. Ifill quickly got to the point.

Ifill: What role did the US have in forcing Maliki's hand? There are reports that you personally may have had a role in that."

McGurk: I can assure you, Gwen, that those reports are not true. In 2010 . . . it was said that we somehow maneuvered Maliki into power. Now it's being said we're somehow maneuvering him out of power. The political dynamics in Iraq have really their own dynamic, which the Iraqis sort through on their own . . . We served as neutral brokers when useful. When we can provide an idea to bridge two different ideas or proposals, we certainly do that. But it's not our job to pick who should be in power or who shouldn't be in power."

Whip-smart Gwen Ifill, who died unexpectedly of endometrial cancer in 2016, maintained an impassive face.

Maliki

For the second night in a row, Nouri al-Maliki popped up on late night television to make a defiant speech. Unable to resist casting himself in the operatic role of a benevolent leader betrayed by those close to him, he railed at the country's president, accusing him of violating the constitution by nominating Abadi. He blamed the United States, saying "The US supports those who violate the constitution, and no one has the right to do so." He wanted a third term. But, even his closest allies, yielding to the inevitable, were now calling for his resignation.

In Washington, just hours later, the State Department issued a statement saying it "fully supports" Abadi's efforts to form a new government.

Kurds

As Islamic State rampaged through Ninewah, massacring Yazidi men and elderly women, kidnapping young girls for sexual purposes and taking young boys to serve as child soldiers, they terrorized their victims and fought their resistors with state-of the-art American weapons they had captured when the Iraqi army fled Mosul.

No one, not even the Pentagon, has estimated how much firepower Islamic State gained when Mosul fell in June 2014, but when the fifteen hundred Islamic State fighters took the city, more than sixty thousand Iraqi soldiers or federal police dropped their weapons, abandoned their vehicles, shed their uniforms, and ran. The Iraqi government said in 2015 that it had lost at least twenty-three hundred Humvees in one day.

Among the numerous ironies that define conflict in the Middle East, it must be added that during the August fight to save the Yazidis and defend Erbil, Islamic State fought with the latest American weaponry while the Peshmerga, America's allies, fought with outdated and jury-rigged Soviet weapons that had been scrounged over the years from Iran and other back-channel providers.

Despite the enormous economic growth of Kurdistan and its relative stability, the United States had long refused to sell arms directly to the Kurdish government, instead mandating that Baghdad share with the Kurds all US military aid, something Baghdad was loath to do.

Despite years of pleas from Kurdistan's government, the United States clung to its "One Iraq" policy, recognizing Baghdad as the primary governmental authority in Iraq. President Obama continued the policy implemented by President George W. Bush even as sectarian divides split the country into the three distinct factions of Shia, Sunni, and Kurd. In Washington, it was believed that a well-armed Kurdistan would eventually declare independence from Iraq and pull the first thread of the nation's unraveling.

Now, as the humiliated Peshmerga regrouped to face Islamic State, the issue of whether or not to sell arms directly to Kurdistan appeared on the front pages of America's newspapers. The Associated Press reported Kurdish government officials said that Washington had promised to begin sending arms to Kurdistan, but the Pentagon denied it, standing firmly behind the administration's One Iraq policy. The *New York Times* reported that the CIA had begun to deliver weapons to the Peshmerga, quoting unnamed administration officials. The Kurds asked for armor-piercing munitions to penetrate fortified tanks, and for long-range missiles. They also requested sniper rifles, heavy machine guns, rocket-propelled grenades, Humvees, tanks, helicopters, and body armor.

Retired general Michael Barbero, who had spent nearly four years in Iraq over three separate tours, told The Associated Press: "This policy of One Iraq, everything goes through Baghdad, ignores the reality on the ground."

During his final tour, Barbero had overseen the training, equipping, and developing of all Iraqi security forces while serving simultaneously as the commander of the Multi-National Security Transition Command—Iraq and the commander of the NATO Training Mission—Iraq. The Americans, he explained, had sold hundreds of millions of dollars of military hardware to Maliki, who promised to deliver $200 million worth to the Kurds. Maliki kept it all.

Immediately after the August 3 invasion, American officials in Iraq tried to force the transfer of weapons from Baghdad to the Kurds, but that process failed, bogged down by excessive Iraqi bureaucracy and corruption. Eventually, the CIA began delivering arms to Kurdistan covertly.

But it was not just the One Iraq policy, and the Bush and Obama Administrations' blindness to Maliki's divisiveness that left Kurdistan vulnerable to Islamic State. General Bednarek believes the Peshmerga shared at least some of the responsibility.

"At the time, I got this question from a lot of our congressional people who asked 'Why are we not selling arms directly to the Kurds, the country of Kurdistan?' Well, there is no country of Kurdistan. One Iraq means—right, wrong or indifferent—that those foreign military sales, foreign military financing, excess defense articles, whatever program from the United States you want to call it, needs to go through the government of Iraq. It was my job to ensure that there was at least a fair and equitable distribution of capability. So, OK, some would say 'Why are we not arming the Kurds directly?' and I say 'Well, let's dissect this to be specific.' What is it that we think their requirements are?

"ISIS came and stole everything in Mosul. They are driving up-armor Humvees. They have all the weapons, and huge amounts of cash because when they destroyed the bank (in Mosul) they took all the currency . . . And the Kurds (would say) 'General we need help; we're fighting . . . with old Soviet stuff and we need tanks.' And I say 'OK, well that's not accurate. Cause I know what you have. I have been around all your camps. I've talked to all your people. I know all your leaders. I'm with you. I'm not saying what you have is not old, because it is, but you've got fifty-four tanks there. So, what are you doing with them?' There is the classic mindset as you are aware, not to hoard stuff, but to keep massive supplies of stuff because the perspective is that they are not going to get anything else and that is historically accurate. (I would ask) 'You've got a million and a half rounds of X, so how come you're not issuing this to your frontline troops?' 'Well, we've got to make sure we are getting more stuff.' 'Will you take this out of the warehouse and issue it?'" he said, shaking his head as he recalled his frustration.

Writing in the *New Yorker*, George Packer wondered how it was possible the Obama Administration could have believed, however briefly, that the One Iraq policy could serve the north of the country.

"It seems delusional to imagine that there is such a thing as an Iraqi central government that should be given priority over stopping ISIS and preventing a massacre. That dream of the American project in Iraq is gone. But perhaps the Obama Administration is being more realistic. Yesterday, I also learned that the US is, in fact, sending arms to the Kurds—just not openly."

To facilitate the movement of weapons, the Americans established a base on the north side of Erbil's brand new civilian airport where the runways connected, and a Marine Brigadier general began preparations to receive arms that would be distributed to Kurds. Support military forces for weapons distribution flew in from Germany, Kuwait, and Jordan.

Obama Administration officials admitted they had begun providing weapons to Kurdish forces. Three planeloads of ammunition had already been airdropped to the Peshmerga, and much more was en route.

The immediacy of the situation required weapons, particularly ammunition that could be used instantly. There was no time to train Peshmerga fighters on the advanced American systems. While Russian-made equipment is less prestigious, most of it is easier to operate and less fragile in a hostile climate. US C-130 cargo planes parachuted crates of Russian-made guns and ammo to Peshmerga units.

Col. Chuck Freeman, the military liaison officer at the US Consulate in Kurdistan, was the point man on this operation.

"The majority of Peshmerga have old Soviet equipment," he said. "They got a lot from Iran in previous years, so ammunition for that is a big problem. We reached out to former eastern bloc countries and asked 'What do you have?' Albania helped first with ammo for Kalashnikovs. They had tons of this stuff stashed in mountains—just warehouses of it. It was not great quality, but OK. Central Command went out and negotiated purchase and sent it to Erbil."

Between 1960 and 1983 the communist government of Albania, led by Enver Hoxha, who also suffered from Lord Acton's diagnosis of the powerful, built hundreds of thousands of turreted concrete bunkers throughout the country as defensive lookouts for his "people's army." Larger bunkers, built into the side of mountains, were stuffed with Soviet weapons and ammunition. In addition to suffering from megalomania, Hoxha was fueled by paranoia and would not allow his government to make records of the locations of all the bunkers. For years after the fall of the Hoxha regime, the larger bunkers were excavated, one by one, and tens of thousands of containers filled with AK-47 ammunition were removed and warehoused.

Albania, NATO member since 2009, sent twenty-two million rounds of AK-47 7.62-millimeter bullets, fifteen thousand hand grenades, and thirty-two thousand artillery shells to the Kurdish forces. The Czech Republic, a NATO member since 1999, provided ten million rounds for AK-47s, eight million rounds for machine guns, five thousand warheads for RPGs, and five thousand hand grenades.

"Why didn't we want to give them American arms? Because the more different types you have, the more difficult it is to procure ammo. Stick with one system. We Americans dug in on this—not getting any new weapons. One system makes it easy to resupply," Freeman explained.

The Peshmerga leaders also asked that the Iraqi army transfer some equipment to them, but the request did not sit well with General Bednarek.

"So, I say 'I will help you, but what are your requirements?'" Bednarek recalled. "And you understand the mindset is, let's ask for the kitchen sink. If the government of Iraq provides you ten M1 battle tanks, what about the drivers, what about the gunners, what about the maintenance, what about the class nine repair parts, what about the ammunition? Where is all this going to go? Where will you maintain it? It's the gift that keeps on giving. You have to be cautious and make sure you think through. Nobody's saying that they don't need it, but let's be prudent and logical and thoughtful in our discussion of how you are going to employ whatever it is that you say you asked for."

A few weeks later, Freeman called a meeting at the US Consulate of all the American allies in the Iraq Combined Joint Task Force.

"I told them 'I am not here to tell you what to do, but to ask for your help and work together,'" Freeman said. "The Europeans came up with a lot. The French gave six anti-aircraft guns, a brute of a gun with 20-25-30–millimeter ammunition to be mounted on vehicles. Germany, and the Netherlands offered training and military supplies. The Belgians gave loads of rifles and Germany gave G3s."

On October 5, 2015, the Combined Joint Task Force—Operation Inherent Resolve, the new name of the operation, announced on its Facebook page that it had given fifty thousand rifles and machine guns, fifty-six million rounds of small arms ammunition, 677–plus mortars, seventy-three thousand–plus mortar rounds, five thousand–plus anti-tank weapons, fifty-six thousand–plus anti-tank rounds, and 150–plus vehicles to the Iraqi Kurdish forces.

TUESDAY, AUGUST 12

As the fifth day of airstrikes got underway, Maliki, now rendered ridiculous by his delusional demands to retain power, issued a statement on his official website ordering all army, police, and security forces to stay out of the political crisis and focus on defending the country. That effectively canceled his threatened coup.

Defense Secretary Chuck Hagel announced that the United States had sent a 130-member military assessment team, including Delta Force soldiers, to Erbil to determine what further assistance the United States could provide to ease the humanitarian crisis of thousands of Yazidis trapped at Mount Sinjar.

That morning, Helene Cooper of the *New York Times* reported the United States was considering sending in "large ground forces," the dreaded boots on the ground, for the rescue operation. If Islamic State engaged those troops during the operation, it could easily draw the United States into a new combat role in Iraq, something the Obama Administration promised would not occur.

"United States officials said they believed that some type of ground force would be necessary to secure the passage of the stranded members of the Yazidis. The military is drawing up a plan for consideration by Obama that could include American ground troops in what is expected to be an international effort to rescue the refugees. American officials say they are convinced that a humanitarian corridor will have to be established soon, with troops on the ground to assure safe passage," she wrote.

Washington worried that Islamic State would climb up the mountain, mingle with refugees, and make it impossible to continue the airstrikes. The pressure to resolve the humanitarian crisis was mounting.

SPECIAL FORCES
1st Special Forces Operational Detachment-Delta (1st SFOD-D) are the most highly trained elite forces in the US military. Along with Navy SEALs, they are the only special operators whose direct engagement with the enemy is a guarantee upon acceptance, whether or not the United States is at war. The Delta Force, its unofficial name, perform clandestine and classified missions around the world, primarily in the areas of hostage rescue and counterterrorism as well as direct action against high-value targets, such as killing, capturing, or rendition.

Col. Charles Alvin "Chargin' Charlie" Beckwith created the Delta Force in the 1970s, after a series of highly publicized international terrorist incidents. Beckwith, a soldier of extraordinary bravery and tenacity, was a Green Beret officer and a Vietnam veteran who was twice triaged in battle as too far gone for treatment and set aside to die before making a full recovery. He had served as an exchange officer with the British Army Special Air Service and advocated strongly for an asymmetrical warfare force, the proverbial "thinking outside the box."

Colonel Beckwith led Delta Force's first mission, Operation Eagle Claw, the attempt to free the American hostages held in the captured American embassy in Tehran, Iran, early in 1980. Unfortunately, the mission was a devastating failure. Dubbed the Debacle in the Desert, it most likely doomed the presidency of Jimmy Carter and stained Beckwith's legacy, but Delta Force was unaffected.

Delta Force members are multilingual, magnificently fit, and experts with firearms. Their selection comes after a series of grueling exercises that test the soldier's physical fitness, stamina, and mental determination. Delta operators, as they are often referred to, are granted an enormous amount of autonomy. They rarely wear uniforms and they sport civilian hairstyles, making it easier to avoid recognition as military personnel. They are tough, smart, single-minded, and prepared to look horror in the face. A team of about fifteen embarked for Mount Sinjar.

VIAN DAKHIL

Seven days after her emotional appeal to her fellow Iraqis, Vian Dakhil was at a Kurdish military base in northern Iraq to thank Iraqi relief workers when she impetuously decided to board an Iraqi aid helicopter leaving for Mount Sinjar. The Russian-made Mi-17, with a four-person crew from Iraqi Kurdistan's Peshmerga militia force, was headed to drop supplies in an area where the pilot had spotted a large group of refugees. In addition, they hoped to rescue as many of the elderly and young among the stranded as possible. In the chopper were a few aid workers, fifty-six-year old Alissa Rubin, a *New York Times* war correspondent and Paris bureau chief, and freelance photographer Adam Ferguson, who was on assignment with Rubin.

It was late on Tuesday afternoon when they boarded. Dakhil sat directly behind the pilot, Maj. Gen. Majid Ahmed Saadi, a veteran Iraqi Arab officer who had taken a leave of absence from his job to assist in the aid mission. Dakhil wanted the pilot to explain the route to her as they flew across the desert plain to Mount Sinjar. Rubin, according to the account she wrote in the *Times* a few days later, sat on a large container of bread behind one of the gunners in the open doorway. Cases of bullets for the Peshmerga lined the sides of the aircraft.

Rubin recalled the pilot's confidence and dedication.

"Adam Ferguson, our photographer, and I were waiting all day at the Kurdish military base in Fishkilbur, Iraq, for a helicopter to take us to Mount Sinjar. General Majid came in from his first run up the mountain with a full load of Yazidi refugees, and a British television journalist said to him, "Why are you taking such risks overloading your helicopter like that?"

He just said, "I checked my numbers, I checked the weight, and it was possible to do it," she wrote.

As they approached the mountaintop, Dakhil and Rubin saw below them children and men running across the rocky terrain, waving their shirts in the air to attract the pilot's attention. Dakhil was low enough to note the sunburned faces of the children and the swollen limbs of the elderly who were barefoot since their shoes no longer fit.

The aid workers tossed oranges to the refugees as the pilot circled, eventually landing near a site secured by Peshmerga soldiers.

Dakhil looked out at her fellow Yazidis. They were desperate, starving, nearly insane with fear and desperation as they approached her. She attempted to alight and greet them, but watched in horror as the hundreds of people racing toward the helicopter became a chaotic, riotous mob, shoving each other away as they tried to scramble aboard. She retook her seat and leaned her body against the side of the aircraft. The Mi-17 is built with a passenger capacity of no more than twenty-four, and at least thirty-five refugees were cramming themselves up the rear landing ramp and onto the carriage, squeezing the aid workers and journalists hard against the metal frame. The crew couldn't get the rear ramp to close because young men clung to the door, trying to force it to stay open so they could enter. Major General Majid signaled to Dakhil for assistance and she beseeched people to get out.

"There will be more helicopters. We will come back. Please, you must get out," she cried. Aid workers pushed a young mother and her two baby daughters down the ramp.

"Please take my two daughters, then I will get off," said the young mother, holding her arms toward Dakhil.

"No," said Dakhil, "I will get out. You stay in with your children."

At that moment, the pilot attempted to lift off, but the load was too heavy. The chopper listed to the left and then the right until the main rotor struck the side of a cliff jetting out from the mountain. Then the nose of the craft pitched down onto the south side of the mountain. The pilot struggled to pull the helicopter up, but within seconds it crashed, nose first, into the hard rocks of Mount Sinjar.

"I was sitting behind the pilot. About forty people fell on me in addition to the other things we had with us. I thought I was dead. In a matter of seconds I saw in front of my eyes a quick videotape of my life," Dakhil said.

She lay face-to-face with the dead pilot, crushed under bodies and the undelivered relief supplies. She realized she was suffocating.

"My breathing stopped, but a little bit of air was coming to me every now and then. I took as much of it in as I could. I knew very well my leg was broken. I could feel it. As I opened my eyes I could see a little hole of light; slowly it became bigger and bigger. I knew by then there are people removing things on top of me. Twice I took out my hand, someone tried to pull me out but couldn't. Here, I lost the little hope that I had. Then I began to hear people calling Vian, Vian, Vian. Then I knew they were looking for me.

"A young man tried to grab my hand, but he couldn't pull me up. My leg and my ribs were broken. Then three more young men came and helped me to get out of the helicopter. I needed to hold my leg with my hands.

"I asked about people—who survived and who didn't, I was told the pilot didn't make it and died immediately. The aircraft landed upside down and survivors had to crawl out of the wreckage. If we had been another fifty meters higher, we'd all be dead," she added.

Adam Ferguson, the *New York Times* freelance photographer, dragged Rubin from the helicopter and tied a scarf around a wound on her head to allay the bleeding. Both of her wrists were broken.

The helicopter passengers lay on the ground. There was no screaming, but a constant low groan rose from the crash site. Stranded Yazidis sat beside the wounded, sharing what little water they had, soothing them. Several hours later two rescue helicopters flew in and evacuated the survivors to a Peshmerga base. They were transferred to a hospital in the small Iraqi city of Zakho, near the Turkish border, to be stabilized before being airlifted to Istanbul.

In her account of the accident, Rubin wrote movingly about the death of Maj. Gen. Majid Ahmed Saadi:

"The pilot really made a big impression. You know, the Yazidis feel so betrayed by the Arab neighbors they had lived among for so many years; they all turned on the Yazidis when ISIS came. Many of the atrocities were carried out not by the militants but by their own neighbors. Yet here was General Majid, an Iraqi Arab himself, who was taking off from his own job—he was in charge of training for the Iraqi air force—to help these people. He told me it was the most important thing he had done in his life, the most significant thing he had done in his 35 years of flying. It was as if it gave his whole life meaning."

Within a few more hours, the soldiers from the YPG made their way to the site and evacuated from the mountain the Yazidis who Vian Dakhil and General Majid had tried to help. They were the final large group of refugees to be brought down the mountain.

USAID

Fifty-four-year-old Alan Dwyer was awoken from a deep sleep in his Seoul hotel room when his boss called from Washington, DC. Dwyer was not surprised. Before turning out the light, he had seen a CNN International report describing the Yazidi crisis in Iraq. After years of working in the disaster relief field, he knew the impact of a 24/7 media frenzy such as the Sinjar coverage.

Based in Bangkok, Dwyer was the senior regional advisor for the Office of Foreign Disaster Assistance for the United States Agency for International Development (USAID). He functioned as the Disaster Assistance Response Team (DART) Team Leader for his region. DART units are designed to be self-sufficient in order to be as flexible as possible when assisting other nations to cope with humanitarian disasters.

Dwyer had done several tours of Iraq for his agency in the years after the US invasion. He was familiar with the people and the terrain and he knew how to get things done. So, when his supervisor said "Get to Erbil," he was on a plane less than five hours later.

"Find out what the hell is going on on that mountain, was my mandate," Dwyer said.

In Erbil, Dwyer met up with the team of US military advisors President Obama had ordered to the country the previous day. The advisors were to supply communications and logistical support for a fifteen-man team of Delta Force soldiers, who, along with Dwyer, were headed for Mount Sinjar to assess the situation.

Their task was to assess the numbers of Yazidis trapped on the mountain needing evacuation in order to make a plan for how to do so. US military estimates ran as high as thirty-five thousand and media estimates up to one hundred thousand. If either of those numbers reflected the situation on the mountain, an airlift would take days and be a logistical nightmare. But it was clearly preferable, in Dwyer's experience, than the vague "ground operation" that was being alluded to by some in Erbil.

Within twelve hours of Dwyer's arrival in country, he and fifteen Delta Force operators flew to Mount Sinjar in Osprey aircraft that have the ability to take off and land on short runways or vertically, the way helicopters do. Mount Sinjar has a seven-thousand-foot elevation and is cool at night. They arrived at 3:00 a.m. under cover of darkness and dressed warmly.

"It was like Vermont in June," said Dwyer. "The mountain is shaped like a tilted dish that catches the sun. It is beautiful. But we expected the worst."

As the sun came up, they started their assessment. They had a vehicle, probably arranged with YPG by the CIA, and they went all over the twenty-one-mile ridge to determine the level of need and an accurate number of stranded Yazidis.

They did not find what they were expecting. They did not see tens of thousands of starving, dehydrated, and desperate refugees; instead they encountered four thousand to five thousand Yazidis, mostly armed men, who either lived on the mountain or who fought with the newly formed Yazidi resistance. They also came across a handful of British SAS soldiers who were in the area to gather intelligence, and the two units exchanged logistical notes about the locations of the few Yazidi militia strongholds on the mountain. The crisis, they realized, was over.

"No doubt there had been 50-K, but by the time we went up to see what was going on, everyone who wanted to get off had gotten off," Dwyer said.

The team determined that the airdrops had been successful and had helped to alleviate the crisis on the mountain. With most of the non-combatant Yazidis gone, the team found dozens of airdropped pallets unopened.

Before boarding an Osprey back to Erbil, both Dwyer and the Delta Forces operators made verbal reports of their initial impressions and recommendations through encrypted means. The mountain was clean. No evacuation necessary.

They returned to Erbil, bringing with them a few injured Yazidi fighters who needed medical care.

EVACUATION PLANS

Two months later, long after the crisis left the American headlines, and as several hundred thousand Yazidis began to adjust to daily life in the mud-strewn IDP camps of Kurdistan, a *USA Today* article outlined the Obama Administration's shelved plan to remove the stranded from Mount Sinjar. Reporter Jim Michaels quoted Gen. James Amos, commandant of the Marine Corps, as he outlined the detailed rescue plan.

"The plan was to pick everyone off the mountain. It was going to be a 'round the clock operation," Amos said.

In a rapid response mission, a Marine-led force planned to use about two dozen V-22 Ospreys. A dozen aircraft flew from Afghanistan to Kuwait to be on standby for the operation.

"It would have been the largest evacuation that I can think of," Amos said. "It could have been very dangerous as well."

The war-adverse administration was aware, of course, that Islamic State militants might attack the Ospreys and cause American casualties. Both Iraqi and Kurdish helicopters had taken enemy fire while ferrying refugees to safety over the past week.

The Marines would have to secure an area on the mountain, then haul and drop large plinths to establish a landing area. The plinths, about eight feet tall, were designed to prevent desperate refugees from storming the aircraft and weighing them down.

CHAPTER NINE

The Mountain Is Empty

Wednesday, August 13, Thursday, August 14

Kocho Part II

Ali Smail rose before dawn Wednesday, August 13, with dread. He peered out his window into the darkness.

"I felt a loneliness so deep, I wanted to weep. It was as if I was among the last people on earth," he said.

Just after sunrise, Khatuni returned to Kocho village with three high-ranking religious leaders from Islamic State. These men were different from their predecessors in the first delegations who had tried to be disarming and calm. Dressed in black with long beards and filthy hands, this assemblage was grim, almost hostile. Khatuni called the village elders, including Mayor Jaso, to the town center. Behind them, the other villagers, about eleven hundred Yazidi men, women, and children, huddled with foreboding. After introducing his cohorts and explaining their religious credentials, Khatuni announced that the Yazidis of Kocho must renounce their faith and convert to Islam or die. They had four days, until Sunday at noon, to decide their fate.

"He said convert or we will kill you. That is a direct quote," Smail said.

Jaso immediately disputed the pronouncements of Khatuni and other members of the delegation. A well-known figure in the area, Jaso had longtime friendships with many of the local Arab tribal leaders. He knew Khatuni and Khatuni's uncles. In the past, he had maintained a strong relationship with Saddam Hussein and had rescued hundreds of young Yazidi men from execution for evading conscription during the Iran/Iraq War.

Many survivors, debating why the Kocho tragedy happened, later said that Jaso may have overestimated the bargaining power of his relationship with neighboring Arabs, particularly with Khatuni. Several of his friendships were decades old, and perhaps he thought they were more meaningful than they actually were, or perhaps he was incapable of imagining that people he had known would betray him. Or, it is possible that he failed to grasp the inherent danger in the situation.

After some back and forth, all agreed that Jaso and a few other elders would travel to the nearby Hatimiyah, a mixed village of Arabs and Yazidis, to confer with Yazidi religious leaders and to discuss the situation with an Islamic State mullah in the town. At Hatimiyah, Jaso's deliberations with the mullah led to the organization of a committee of twelve Arab tribal men who agreed to ask for a pardon for the Yazidis.

"The next day, Thursday, they went to the custodian of Daesh in Mosul to meet with Abu Laith al-Hamdani. He refused to see them, so they met with his brother instead," Smail said. Abu Laith al-Hamdani, a jihadist, was the first designated governor of Mosul after Islamic State occupied the city. A coalition airstrike killed him in November of 2015.

The committee returned in the evening with a message from Hamdani's brother that did not hearten the Yazidis. "Be assured of good. God willing, it will conclude in good. In ten days we will give you a statement regarding the decision."

Jaso tried to convince the villagers of Kocho that negotiation was possible with Khatuni and the religious leaders who had threatened them. But panic had spread in Hatimiyah, and it spurred the Yazidis there into action. Between 3:00 and 4:00 a.m., they stole out of town in groups of four and five. Most stayed off the main road and many completed the journey to Mount Sinjar.

"The following day al-Khatuni came to our village and asked Jaso where the villagers of Hatimiyah went," explained Smail. "Jaso said, 'By God I don't know anything.' And of course he didn't know that Hatmiyah villagers had left. Al-Khatuni left very angrily and said he will pay us another visit. He also said we would not get passes, and we were confined to the village."

As ordered, a few minutes before noon on Sunday, the Yazidis of Kocho gathered in their town square awaiting the arrival of Khatuni. When he failed to appear, most assumed there was no longer a deadline because the message from Hamdani's brother had referred to "ten days." They ambled back to their homes, believing the immediate threat had passed.

Mrs. Clinton

On an overcast day during the height of the tourist season on Martha's Vineyard, a cold, sideways rain pelted the island. That afternoon, former secretary of state Hillary Clinton arrived, along with a small entourage, to hawk her latest book *Hard Choices* at the independent bookstore dear to the islanders, Bunch of Grapes. The bookstore had sold nearly one thousand copies of Mrs. Clinton's book in anticipation of her arrival. Huddled under umbrellas, a long line of well-wishers, clutching their volumes to be signed, snaked out the front door and along the sidewalk.

Before meeting her fans, Mrs. Clinton, wearing a soft pink jacket, took a few questions from the national media who had also gathered at the small store. One reporter asked her if she would "hug it out" with the president.

"Absolutely," she responded in a cheery tone.

The hugging question came on the heels of Mrs. Clinton's public criticism of President Obama's foreign policy in an interview with Jeffrey Goldberg of *The Atlantic* published a few days earlier. In the article, Mrs. Clinton seemed to imply that the Obama Administration's foreign policy, which she had spent years implementing as secretary of state, lacked intellectual heft, saying, "Great nations need organizing principles, and 'Don't do stupid stuff' is not an organizing principle." She was referring to the oft-repeated phrase treasured by Obama's staff describing several Bush Administration actions, including the decision to invade Iraq in 2003. Clinton said Obama's failure to support "moderate" rebels in Syria led to the surge of the violent Islamic extremism now spreading across northern Syria and Iraq.

In Washington, House Majority Leader Nancy Pelosi reacted to the Clinton article with icy anger. "Now is not the time to second guess the commander-in-chief, particularly when you're a former member of his cabinet and national security team," Ms. Pelosi said.

Obama's senior advisor David Axelrod responded with a masterful tweet that hit Mrs. Clinton in her most vulnerable spot.

"Just to clarify: 'Don't do stupid stuff' means stuff like occupying Iraq in the first place, which was a tragically bad decision," he tweeted, referring to then-Senator Clinton's decision in October 2002 to cross party lines and vote to give President Bush the authority to use military force in Iraq. It took Clinton years to acknowledge her decision was misguided.

At the end of the book signing, one woman asked Clinton to take on the amyotrophic lateral sclerosis challenge, a publicity stunt that had gone viral on YouTube, in which a supporter of finding a cure for the disease dumps a bucket of ice water on their head and posts the video on Facebook. Clinton was noncommittal.

"It will be fun to watch Hillary dump a bucket of ice water on her head," the woman told the local press. "Hopefully she does it."

Just a few hours before Clinton's arrival, Principal Deputy Press Secretary Eric Schultz and Deputy National Security Advisor Ben Rhodes ran through the chilly downpour into the press filing center at the Edgartown School for their daily briefing.

As the assembled journalists quieted down, Schultz turned over the briefing to Rhodes for the "nitty-gritty" of foreign policy. Rhodes explained that President Obama was waiting for actionable intelligence that would come from the Delta Forces deployed on Mount Sinjar. The administration wanted a definitive answer: How many people were on the mountain?

"There needs to be a lasting solution that gets that population to a safe space where they can receive more permanent assistance. So, what the president has done is authorized the deployment of 130, roughly, US military personnel who will assess the situation on Sinjar Mountain and in northern Iraq. They then, again, will make recommendations about how to follow through on an effort to get the people off that mountain into a safe place."

Rhodes said he expected a recommendation for the president would be made in a matter of days.

"We're going to rely on what the teams report back in terms of their assessment. But you look at corridors, you look at airlifts, you look at different ways to move people who are in a very dangerous place on that mountain to a safer position. And that's exactly what our team is doing on the ground now in Iraq."

Almost all the questions circled around the issue of the reintroduction of combat forces to Iraq and the potential danger to American military personnel on the ground.

"I think the principle holds that we're not putting ground forces in a combat role in Iraq," Rhodes said.

Rhodes turned the briefing over to Schultz, who faced a barrage of questions about the relationship between the president and Mrs. Clinton.

"They have a close and resilient relationship," Mr. Schultz said, noting that despite their rivalry on the 2008 presidential campaign trail, Mr. Obama appointed her his secretary of state. He added that the president looked forward to seeing Mrs. Clinton at a private party they both planned to attend that evening. Acknowledging there would not be media access at the social gathering, he declined to answer whether the two might embrace each other at the event.

"I believe the president and Secretary Clinton have had many hugs over the past two years," he said. "Many of them have been caught on camera."

DAKHIL

Viewing CNN at his cubicle in the Kurdish Service at the Voice of America building, Dakhil Shammo watched presidential advisor Ben Rhodes brief the national press about the plight of the Yazidis. It was noon, and his broadcast of Kurd Connection had just ended. Like most of his colleagues, he believed the situation on Mount Sinjar was still dire. Reports on the state of the trapped Yazidis grew even more alarming. The United Nations had given the situation its highest humanitarian crisis rating. The Kurdish press reported upward of one hundred thousand Yazidis were near death on the mountain. While the American and Iraqi aid airdrops continued, Shammo knew that the unforgiving climate, the relentless sun and chilly nights, would cause the death toll to rise higher.

While there were stories in the western press about Yazidis escaping, the numbers of those still trapped on the mountain differed wildly.

While the daily media saturation coverage focused on the Yazidis on Mount Sinjar, Shammo was particularly worried about the people of Kocho. He had a nagging feeling about Kocho. No one seemed to understand what Islamic State was doing there. Their actions did not fit the pattern established in other Yazidi towns and villages. Deadlines the jihadists themselves had set passed without any comment, and Kocho residents seemed to believe they would be treated as Christians, as People of the Book, something the jihadists had refused to do in other Yazidi towns. The son of his good friend, Hussein Khalaf, had received several text messages from Kocho villagers who, obviously terrified, wrote as if they had been lulled into resignation, or, perhaps, self-delusion, he thought.

"They simply needed to believe they would not be killed, despite what was obvious," Shammo said. "How would we behave in that situation? It is unknowable."

On Shammo's television monitor, Rhodes stated with vigor "The president has ruled out reintroducing US ground forces into combat on the ground in Iraq." He also said "We believe that some number of thousands of people have been able to escape from the mountain, but not in a safe enough way and to a safe enough space that we're confident that the remaining people who are trapped can get off."

Shammo despaired hearing these two statements. Without American ground troops to fight back against Islamic State and keep a corridor to safety open, he saw nothing but death for the thousands that were still trapped on the mountain. Rhodes added that the president was waiting for recommendations about ways to mount a rescue operation. He clarified these statements by explaining that any operation could involve ground troops, but not combat troops.

From his sources, Shammo knew the White House was considering two plans. One option was to rescue the Yazidis with a combination of ground troops, Peshmerga, Iraqi army, American Special Forces, and Marine contingents. Shammo thought this would be disastrous. The Peshmerga would betray the Yazidis once again, he believed, and the Iraqi army was feckless. Furthermore, an escape route would have to lead through Syria, and the United States would not send their own troops onto Syrian soil. If there was anything Obama was determined not to do, it was to involve his country in the quagmire in Syria.

The second plan involved a multiday helicopter airlift. Obviously, if Ospreys could only carry at most thirty Yazidis at a time, it could take more than a week for a full evacuation of the mountain. Shammo thought the stranded could not hold out much longer. Those who were not rescued immediately would die.

"Meeting Upended"

A few hours after Obama advisor Ben Rhodes told reporters on Martha's Vineyard that an operation to free the Yazidis trapped on Mount Sinjar might include American ground troops, the president's National Security Council convened a videoconference from the White House to evaluate recommendations for a full-scale rescue mission, possibly including the creation of a humanitarian corridor.

The council's members were scattered. Susan Rice was with the president on Martha's Vineyard. Secretary of State John Kerry and his aides were in Hawaii, returning from an Asia tour, and Defense Secretary Chuck Hagel was in the air somewhere over the United States, flying home from a trip to Germany, India, and Australia.

As they debated the effectiveness of an airlift operation, Gen. Lloyd J. Austin III, the head of US Central Comman (Centcom), interrupted the discussion with the stunning findings of the Special Forces Team: There were no Yazidi refugees on the mountain, only a few thousand Yazidis who wanted to stay. Untouched pallets of food and water lay strewn about.

The *New York Times* reported "The meeting was upended" and the participants were "surprised."

"The *New York Times* perhaps overdramatized events," Rhodes said with a chuckle.

"But I was surprised by that Centcom report too, but I also took it with a grain of salt. After years with the administration, I knew, and we all knew that you never accept just one piece of intel. You can't take any one report as gospel. This is just an example of how divergent the reporting was. There is always a limit to what you can know with precision. But it was shocking, I mean, people fleeing into Syria?"

While accepting the findings of the Delta Team report—there were no stranded Yazidis dying on Mount Sinjar—National Security Council members asked, "Had there ever been any stranded Yazidis? If so, where did they go? Where did the original numbers come from? How could we have gotten it so wrong?"

"After the Centcom report meeting we started getting more reporting about the corridor and dedicated more resources—ISR overheat imagery—that did establish the corridor was happening," said Rhodes.

A few hours later Pentagon press secretary Rear Adm. John Kirby released a statement:

"As part of the ongoing humanitarian efforts ordered by President Obama, today a team of US military personnel, accompanied by USAID, conducted an assessment of the situation on Mount Sinjar and the impact of US military actions to date. The team, which consisted of less than twenty personnel, did not engage in combat operations and all personnel have returned safely to Irbil [sic] by military air. The team has assessed that there are far fewer Yazidis on Mount Sinjar than previously feared, in part because of the success of humanitarian airdrops, air strikes on ISIL targets, the efforts of the Peshmerga, and the ability of thousands of Yazidis to evacuate from the mountain each night over the last several days. The Yazidis who remain are in better condition than previously believed and continue to have access to the food and water that we have dropped. Based on this assessment the interagency has determined that an evacuation mission is far less likely. Additionally, we will continue to provide humanitarian assistance as needed and will protect US personnel and facilities."

Despite Kirby's assertion, the Peshmerga played almost no role at all. Syrian Kurds, the YPG, part of an organization the United States designates as a terrorist group, fought their way up the mountain and, in many cases, physically carried the Yazidis on their backs down to safety.

Kirby later appeared on CNN's *The Situation Room* with Wolf Blitzer, most likely with the mission to explain the weeklong discrepancy, which made the administration look feckless.

BLITZER: Because there are limits as to what photo reconnaissance, satellite imagery can do. You had to send people, US military personnel, Special Operations forces on top of the mountain to get a clear assessment of what's going on. I assume you're going to have to do that in a lot of places throughout Iraq right now if there's such great fear of genocide.

KIRBY: Well, it would depend. I mean, you can have a better picture in some places than others. But overhead ISR has its limits. It's a terrific asset but it's not going to tell you everything.

BLITZER: You've got to really check on the ground to see what's going on.

BLITZER: Recapping today's breaking news, President Obama says the United States broke the siege on Mount Sinjar, saving many innocent lives.

The US deputy assistant secretary of state for Iraq and Iran, Brett McGurk, also appeared on CNN. He said the number of Yazidis remaining on the mountain was in the low thousands thanks to US airstrikes that had succeeded in creating an escape corridor.

"The president said when he spoke to the American people that we're going to break the siege of this mountain and we broke the siege of the mountain," McGurk said. "So, the SO [special operations] formations that were there and checkpoints and other columns, they're no longer there. They've been killed, and ISIL columns have not come back. This has opened up a corridor which has allowed thousands of people to escape. [That is] from the reports that I've seen from the assessment team, which is just back. We had seen indications of that happening. We had to get eyes on the mountain to see what was happening, and that is why the president ordered this team, US military assessment team together accompanied by our colleagues in USAID, to go to the mountain with a firsthand look. They linked up with Peshmerga forces on the mountain; they saw the situation, the entire mountain. They went from north to south and discussed the situation with people there, determined that vehicles are able from the north side to get onto the mountain and get off, and so the siege has been broken but we are going to remain vigilant."

It is unclear whether the administration indeed had no knowledge of the extraordinary rescue efforts of the YPG. However, in later statements they referred to the rescuers as "Kurdish forces" or "Kurdish troops," a term that is technically correct, but also potentially deliberately vague. They pointedly avoided crediting the Peshmerga.

After returning from his appraisal of conditions on the mountain, Alan Dwyer worked at the Erbil Consulate on the growing need for humanitarian aid for hundreds of thousands of Internally Displaced

People consisting of not only Yazidis, but Kurds of every faith who had lived in the region.

Every Yazidi village was razed, the roads around Ninewah were littered with booby traps, and throughout the region, bodies lay rotting in the sun. Dwyer coordinated the work of various aid organizations, going out daily on assessments with Consul General Joe Pennington or Col. Chuck Freeman, the Consulate's military liaison. Meanwhile, weapons were arriving in large shipments at the Erbil civilian airport.

PARTY

That evening, the rain subsided on Martha's Vineyard but the air remained cool. The president and first lady greeted former president Bill Clinton and former secretary of state Hillary Clinton at the Farm Neck Golf Club, where both couples were guests at the eightieth birthday party of Ann Biddle Jordan, wife of Democratic Party luminary Vernon Jordan. The four were longtime friends of the Jordans and shared the same round table, with the president and Mrs. Clinton flanking the guest of honor.

The 150 guests included Attorney General Eric Holder, White House Senior Advisor Valerie Jarrett, National Security Advisor Susan Rice, Ambassador to Japan Caroline Kennedy, and American Express head Ken Chenault, who all dined on surf and turf. A DJ spun contemporary tunes and, according to press reports, the Obamas and the Clintons danced to just about every song. Using the ubiquitous church picnic phrase, the White House reported "a good time was had by all" and refused to confirm whether there had been a hug.

THURSDAY, AUGUST 14

Early Thursday afternoon President Obama made a statement to the press that was carried live by all the US networks. The unusual timing of the media event—midday—added to the unease in the press filing center at the Edgartown School cafeteria. More than fifty members of the press waited, uncertain if the topic was the crisis in Iraq or a domestic issue.

The country had been on edge since the fatal shooting of Michael Brown, an eighteen-year-old black man, by Darren Wilson, a white Ferguson, Missouri, police officer on August 9, 2014. The shooting sparked unrest in the northern suburb of St. Louis. The protests, some peaceful and others violent, continued for a week. The incident focused attention on the militarized response adopted by some police forces in the wake of the 9/11 attacks.

But Obama's announcement was about the rescue operation on Mount Sinjar. "Yesterday, a small team of Americans—military and civilian—completed their review of the conditions on the mountain. They found that food and water have been reaching those in need, and that thousands of people have been evacuated safely each and every night. The civilians who remain continue to leave, aided by Kurdish forces and Yazidis who are helping to facilitate the safe passage of their families. So, the bottom line is, is that the situation on the mountain has greatly improved, and Americans should be very proud of our efforts.

"Because of the skill and professionalism of our military—and the generosity of our people—we broke the ISIL siege of Mount Sinjar; we helped vulnerable people reach safety; and we helped save many innocent lives. Because of these efforts, we do not expect there to be an additional operation to evacuate people off the mountain, and it's unlikely that we're going to need to continue humanitarian airdrops on the mountain. The majority of the military personnel who conducted the assessment will be leaving Iraq in the coming days.

"As commander-in-chief, I could not be prouder of our men and women who carried out this operation almost flawlessly," Mr. Obama said.

After the statement, the president returned to Farm Neck for his fourth day of golf. Defense officials announced the airdrops would cease.

REACTION

Dakhil Shammo was stunned. Unaware of the extraordinary efforts of the YPG and the efficiency of their operation, he, like others, believed tens of thousands of Yazidis were under siege by Islamic State on Mount Sinjar. In a rage, he called the State Department IRF office.

It is easy to understand Shammo's confusion and outrage. Just that morning, the United Nations announced that Mount Sinjar met its highest level for a humanitarian crisis. While it acknowledged that some people had escaped, their northern Iraq spokesman David Swanson said

"There are still people up there under conditions of extreme heat, dehydration and imminent threat of attack. The situation is far from solved." He later admitted he had no firsthand knowledge of how many people had come down from Mount Sinjar.

"Our Yazidi friends had a different story, so there are two competing narratives that emerge: the mountain is empty or the Special Forces landed at some place, probably the top, and didn't see the people that were still there. So, it became a point of contention in our internal discussions," recalled Tom Melia.

Yazidi leaders and emergency workers in Iraq were adamant that the American Special Forces could not possibly have visited the entire mountain and insisted that tens of thousands more Yazidis were trapped on the southern side near Sinjar City.

From her hospital bed in Turkey where she was recovering from her helicopter crash wounds, Vian Dakhil refuted the American claims.

"It's just not true that all of them are safe," she said. She estimated there were seventy thousand Yazidis still trapped. She was wrong.

"Over the last few years, I have reflected on this," Padgett recalled. "We were not aware of how quickly folks started to come off the mountain. It did not take more than a day or two before (they) came down. While we had information, I think collectively we were a couple of days behind understanding how quickly it was happening."

He added, "We had an essential victory. The Yazidi community was somehow protected and we worked this as hard as we have ever worked anything for the next two years. We still are. There were many mistakes. There were missed opportunities. There were many things we could have done better. I am agnostic about how many lives were saved, but I am proud of the collective effort and the collective political will that characterizes our actions."

Camp Nowruz

In November 2013, the International Rescue Committee, founded in 1933 by Albert Einstein, among others, to assist Germans suffering under Hitler, built a makeshift camp in northeastern Syria. Sitting several miles from the border with Iraq, it housed twenty internally displaced Syrian families, about one hundred people. Despite the vicious civil war in Syria, the Kurdish portion of the country where the camp was built was relatively calm since neither Islamic State nor Assad's men wanted to make trouble with the YPG.

The absence of violence, however, did nothing to alleviate the scorching heat of the plain. Dry wind blew through the settlement, coating every surface with dust and sand. Looking out on this desolate patch of land, nothing could be seen but sand, a cloudless sky, and the pulsating sun. From afar in this unforgiving desert, Camp Nowruz seemed a mirage. It was little more than five white tents, two latrines, and a few showers. The United Nations delivered water and food to the Syrian families who lived a dreary, isolated life of resignation and hopelessness.

The YPG arrived at Camp Nowruz on August 4. They erected massive tents for a staging area and alerted the Red Cross that extraordinary amounts of help might soon be needed. The next day, hundreds of well-trained, loyal YPG militiamen began digging fighting positions on both sides of a half-mile-wide passageway that extended from the Syrian camp across the border into Iraq and up onto Mount Sinjar. By August 9, the safety corridor was opened, the YPG often battling Islamic State in hand-to-hand combat. Additional YPG soldiers climbed the mountain and pushed east. They combed the summit of Mount Sinjar on foot looking for pockets of Yazidis, carrying older women and children on their backs down to the highest plateau their vehicles could reach.

Word spread on the mountain that the YPG had established an escape route. Soon, thousands of Yazidis began to descend, arriving at a small watering hole established by the YPG at the mountain's edge. With a tenderness that makes Yazidis tear up when they try to describe it, the soldiers helped the refugees into vehicles, covering the sick and elderly with blankets and reassuring the crying children.

"We used everything that could drive," said Syrian Kurdish soldier Alvar Khalil, one of the camp's leaders and an organizer of the rescue operation.

Their SUVs and pickup trucks struggled in the sand. As they bounced along, large posters attached to the sides of their vehicles bearing the face of Abdullah Öcalan flapped with each jolt. Smoking incessantly and singing YPG anthems, the YPG kept their guns pointed out toward the endless sand at an unseen enemy.

Within twenty-four hours, tiny Camp Nowruz held twelve thousand people.

"That escape corridor was like Washington's I-66 highway. It was completely full of refugees. Friday and Saturday they poured off the mountain, but State and most of the US government didn't understand how quickly things were moving," Doug Padgett said.

Five days earlier on Saturday morning, The Associated Press reported that twenty thousand "starving" Yazidis were coming down from Mount Sinjar via a tenuous "safe passage" that was protected by Syrian Kurdish troops—YPG. Described as "being under constant fire as they descend," the Yazidis either walked or were driven in YPG vehicles to Camp Nowruz near the Syrian city of Qamishli. The report said ten thousand, mostly the sick and elderly, descended the first day, aided by YPG fighters who brought trucks, tractors, and cars along makeshift pathways onto the mountain. A YPG spokesman told The Associated Press that they had engaged in "brutal" combat with Islamic State jihadists along the base of the mountain and left dozens of them dead or wounded.

When queried, a senior Obama Administration official told The Associated Press that this was an ad hoc effort and, the official said, it was not a significant part of the solution. The administration, he told the wire service, was working on its plan.

Most of the arrivals needed immediate medical care for dehydration, starvation, sunstroke, high blood pressure, emotional exhaustion, and shock. By Sunday the International Red Cross had asked for two hundred additional doctors, and local authorities scrambled to find medicine, food, water, and hygiene supplies. Diarrhea was rampant, especially among the younger children. There were also multiple cases of extreme allergic reactions following the consumption of shrubbery and weeds.

Supplies were trucked in hourly from a distribution point in the nearby town of Derik where international aid organizations—the World Food Program, Save the Children, and UNICEF—had set up to assist displaced Syrians. Hundreds of large white cotton tents were erected, and health workers dug trenches to contain human waste.

Most Yazidis remained at the camp just long enough to regain the strength to continue their journey home. To contain the chaos and avoid a health catastrophe, YPG soldiers helped the refugees locate family members in Dohuk or Erbil. Once they had made contact and arranged a place to meet, the YPG drove the refugees north to Fishkilbur where a small wooden footbridge spanned the border between Syria and the Kurdistan area of Iraq.

The YPG drove the seriously ill directly to Fishkilbur and transferred them to ambulances or cars that brought them to the hospital in Dohuk.

Over the next three days, the convoys from Mount Sinjar to Camp Nowruz were unceasing. During the daytime, new arrivals emerged from the vehicles and were quickly triaged and processed. At nighttime, a lookout followed rows of white headlights as they bounced eerily across the desert plain until their approach neared, and a medical team was alerted.

Many Yazidis who were in good enough health bypassed the camp. The YPG drove truckloads of Yazidis from the mountain through Syrian land directly north to the Fishkilbur border crossing. From there, the Yazidis walked over the bridge into Iraq where local Kurds had emergency medical stations, food, and water. Doctors and nurses distributed rehydration tablets and warned the refugees not to drink too much water until their bodies had recovered from the shock of their ordeal. Family members stood on the Iraqi side of the border waiting, scanning the crowds for their husbands, wives, children, brothers, and sisters.

At Camp Nowruz, huge numbers of people flowed in just as equal numbers were departed. No one kept an official count, but based on the amount of supplies used during the one-week operation, the International Rescue Committee estimated it served nearly fifty thousand Yazidi refugees who fled to Syria from Iraq.

The corridor remained open from August 9 until August 16, by which time Mount Sinjar was empty except for those who wished to stay. Roughly thirty YPG fighters died fighting Islamic State during the operation.

The YPG, Syrian military wing of the Turkish PKK, were hailed as heroes by the Yazidis, the Kurds, and, within weeks, by the Obama Administration.

KOCHO PART III

Like the Yazidis on Mount Sinjar during the first week of the invasion, the Yazidis of Kocho were also trapped.

Perhaps the villagers of Kocho talked themselves into believing they had been pardoned by Islamic State or perhaps they just desperately needed to believe it. Even if they could sneak past the few Islamic State guards lingering around Kocho, it would be impossible for them to slip out of town, as the residents of Hatimiyah had, because small Arab villages that house Islamic State sympathizers surrounded Hatimiyah.

Friends and relatives called on cellphones with the latest news, telling them of the massacres in Hardan and outside Siba. To call attention to their plight, they began to send text messages to friends in Europe and the United States, begging someone, anyone, to come free them. Those messages, written in the Kurdish dialect, were translated by American Yazidis in Virginia and Lincoln, and forwarded to Douglas Padgett and Leanne Cannon at the State Department, as well as to international human rights organization and the United Nations.

"I would get a text that said 'I am on the phone with someone from Kocho right now.' And we would get more information," said Padgett. "In the days leading up to Kocho, we had multiple scares where we were told there are 'people' there and that's a bad sign. One group (of Islamic State) moving here or there. These were reasonable panic attacks. Everyone knew that Islamic State was capable of doing something terrible in Kocho. But, they kept pushing the date back. Were they serious? We had several conversations about what could be done, but you are faced with an existential problem."

"At some point the Yazidis started asking for targeted bombings of the places, like Kocho, where hostages were being held—to kill them before they could be raped or murdered by ISIS," Melia said. "I mean there were some pretty horrific discussions and requests. They were talking about how parents were ready to shoot their own children rather than let them fall into the hands of (Islamic State)."

On Monday, the day after the deadline, Khatuni returned to Kocho mid-morning. He and two armed jihadists went directly to see Mayor

Jaso and informed him the villagers would not be forced to convert to Islam. On Tuesday, he returned, telling Jaso that an agreement had been reached with Islamic State religious leaders in Mosul. The Yazidis of Kocho would be treated like Christians, he explained. If they agreed to abandon their property and belongings, they would be driven to Sinjar Mountain and released. Before leaving, he said it would take a day to determine the safest route to the mountain.

While the residents of Kocho were as good as under house arrest waiting for Khatuni's return, Hadi Pir, Khalaf Smoqi, and the other members of the Sinjar Crisis Management Team at the motel were piecing together information about Islamic State. On Wednesday, they received a series of calls, more than six, from men in Kocho who identified the location of all the Islamic State checkpoints around the Kocho area. Based on that informaton, the team sent Padgett and Cannon new maps with red pins to show the exact locations of the jihadists.

"We begged them. Just strike these points. There is a siege at Kocho," Smoqi said. "I don't think they believed us. That's why they didn't help."

"We requested air force flyovers. We had conversations about Kocho being bombed," Leanne Cannon said. "We were looking at cutting off ISIS. Anything."

"One of the things I know from working on the question of civilian harm is that force is a double-edged sword," explained Sarah Sewall. "Even if particular political and military leaders are emboldened to want to act. They need to be confident that in the ways they act will not have secondary or third consequences that mitigate the effects or undermine the strategic intent of the use of military force."

Airstrikes are not undertaken haphazardly. Each strike location is the result of hundreds of tiny bits of collated intelligence. The information coming out of Kocho was too nebulous to justify an airstrike in an area with unarmed civilians.

MALIKI

On Iraq's state broadcast late Thursday night, a defeated Nouri al-Maliki finally acknowledged the end of his term of office. Standing at a podium,

Abadi beside him and surrounded by more than thirty of his fiercest supporters, the grim-faced and slump-shouldered Maliki read from a prepared statement.

Relinquishing his post to his fellow DAWA party member Haider al-Abadi, Maliki said he would not be the cause of bloodshed in his country, basing his decision on a desire to "safeguard the high interests of the country." He added, somewhat ominously, "I will stay a combat soldier to defend Iraq and its people."

The crisis had passed. Iraq had its first peaceful transition of power.

CHAPTER TEN

Kocho

Friday, August 15

IN THE REGION OF KOCHO VILLAGE ON FRIDAY, AUGUST 15, DARK, ANGRY clouds monopolized the sky. Billowing like a cowl over the village, they hung low and blocked the sun, creating an ominous chill that made the villagers shiver.

Just before midday, Islamic State fighters, armed with heavy weapons, drove into Kocho from every direction. Two white Land Cruisers led each line of cars that rumbled into the village, and four trucks followed. The trucks held rocket launchers shrouded in blankets. A backhoe entered last.

"When I saw the loader entering the village, I knew something bad was awaiting us," Ali Smail said. "But the men around me said 'Friend, rely on God. Perhaps it has come to block a road or open another.' I said 'The whole region is under Daesh. They will open or close a road for what?'"

A black GMC truck headed straight for the house of Ahmed Jaso. Khatuni jumped from the vehicle and strode into the small dwelling. Islamic State fighters dispersed around Kocho, telling everyone to gather at the high school.

"Take your vehicles and drive them to the high school. Leave the keys in the ignition. Then we will drive you out of here as if you are Christians, they told us. By God, I went to my father right away and found him sleeping. I woke him up and told him that Daesh members were here to let us go like Christians. He told me, 'Calm down. Let's wait until other people go and we will join them.' Eventually we all went to the school," said Smail.

As the Yazidis gathered in the gymnasium of the school, lightning shot through the clouds and a powerful storm broke. Heavy rain poured onto the rattling windows and obstructed the view to the outside. Between the claps of thunder, the villagers heard the angry wind howling.

Islamic State leader Abu Hamza Khatuni, surrounded by black-clad fighters, some wearing balaclavas, and all holding AK-47s, addressed the assembled community. Khatuni demanded their money and cellphones. He ordered the women to remove their jewelry and place it in a pile on the floor. A fighter walked through the crowd collecting car keys. They would behead anyone who resisted, Khatuni said.

The fighters separated the women and girls from the men and boys over seven years old.

"My wife and two daughters were pulled away from me," Smail said. "They put them on the second floor of the school and kept the men and boys on the first floor."

The nearly three hundred terrified men grasped each other's arms tightly. Standing before them, Khatuni delivered a brief speech.

"For me is my religion, and for you is yours," he began. "On August 3, we came to liberate you from ignorance. We put you from darkness to light. We told you to become Muslims and stay on your properties in your village. But you refused to become Muslims. Now we have come back to give you two options: the first option is again to convert to Islam and stay on your property. The second option is that we will let you out like Christians on the condition you leave your property behind. Do not worry. We will not harm you."

Citing a well-known verse from the Koran, he added "There is no compulsion in religion.

"Whether you're a Christian, Jew, Yazidi, and I am a Muslim, I don't mind. I will give you a chance now."

"Every one of us holds his and her religion dear to heart. We want you to let us go like Christians," Mayor Jaso said.

"I will let you leave like Christians," Khatuni said solemnly and respectfully.

He told the men to organize into groups for the drive to Mount Sinjar.

"They took three groups before us to outside of the village and killed them without us knowing," Smail said. "They took a group to an area called Tal Aatfal southeast of Kocho and killed them there. They took the second group to the same place and killed them there in a grave. There were two graves in that site. They also had dug a grave in Abbas Qasim's farm where they took the third group and killed them there.

"Then it was our turn. The storm ended and the sun came out. The heat returned quickly, and I was sweating. The groups were not divided equally. Some groups had forty-five people—others were fifty or sixty. I was in the fourth group and had thirty men. They put us all into a car. They forced us into the car like a herd of animals. There was another car behind us, but we couldn't know how many people it had. My brother Saeed was in another group.

"Six or seven of Daesh cars were ahead of us, and six or seven more were behind us. They were driving us toward a village called Qapusi some nine to ten kilometers away.

"There was a farm on the way that had a water cistern. A farmer had used it to water his plants, but now it was empty. More than twenty-five Daesh fighters stood all around the cistern. It was twenty yards wide and three yards tall.

"They suddenly dropped us by the cistern. They told us in Arabic, 'Get into the cistern. Put your heads down.' They started chanting to each other, 'God is great. The Islamic State remains. Video record. Shoot.'

"They started shooting us. They fired at the people three times. The first time they opened fire at everyone. The second time, there were shouts and screams in the cistern. They said, 'Some people are still alive. Shoot again.' The third time, they said, 'Aim for their heads.'

"After they thought they had killed everyone, they started chanting, 'God is great. The Islamic State remains and grows.' These people were talking in a local dialect. They were from this region. There were also some who were talking in Kurdish, the Kurmanji dialect of Sinjar among themselves, saying sarcastically, 'You can't become Muslims now because we killed you.'

"After the Daesh fighters left back to the village to kill others, after ten to fifteen minutes, I said out loud 'Anyone of you who is still alive, let's escape and rescue ourselves.' There were two other people who were alive, Dilshan Sleman Qasim and Saeed Murad Psi. With difficulty and covered in blood, we got up. I saw around fifteen dead bodies on my side. That means there were around forty-two men in that grave. I was wounded and wanted water. But Dilshan said, 'Don't drink water. It's bad for you.' One bullet hit my lower back and another my shoulder. My shoulder injury was small, but the lower back wound was very deep. Dilshan walked out immediately to rescue himself. So, he left us there. I don't know why.

"There was another farm some 350 meters away from the farm we were at. Saeed and I went to another farm, called Simo Elias farm, about three hundred yards away. We hid by its power generator until the evening. About an hour and thirty minutes after we were hiding in Simo Elias's farm where the power generator was, we saw some backhoes coming. I do not know whether they were trying to put the rest of the dead bodies into the cistern or not. I do not know what they were doing. We stayed hiding in that place until sunset. During sunset, two more Daesh cars came to the farm and kept searching around. I do not know whether they were looking for wounded people. There were a lot of them searching with flashlights. Later a bulldozer arrived, and they tried to bury all the bodies."

During the night, Smail and Saeed walked to the village of Qapusi where Smail had a trusted friend.

"They secretly brought a nurse from the village to treat our injuries. He came to our help, but couldn't do much besides giving us first aid. He cleaned our wounds, but said to me 'Oh, you will have to be taken somewhere urgently. Your injury is very serious.' After the nurse left, we were staying at that home. They were, by the way, Muslim Kurds. They cried and said according to Sharia law a person is only asked once to convert to Islam and left alone. Sharia does not allow killing. They brought us food and water. But we couldn't eat because of what we had seen. I was thinking about my son, father, daughters, wife, sister, and village. We could not eat anything. But I need to say they brought us food to keep it as a record for history.

"After about two to three hours, the family came to us and told us, 'If you don't mind, we would like to ask you to leave our house.' 'Why?' we asked. They said, 'Daesh has threatened to cut off heads of whoever is giving refuge to Yazidis and Shias.' We got up to leave the house. They told us how to get to Sinjar. We started to walk, but heard the Islamic call to prayer. We knew this meant it is early morning, and there was no way we could make it out. So, we just returned to Qapusi."

The Kurdish Muslim mullah of the town saw them and brought them to his house where they stayed for two days. The mullah, they discovered, was also hiding Dilshan, who had walked away from the same shooting spree they had survived, leaving them at the murder site. For the next few days, they stayed, switching between the families of Qapusi, who hid them in back rooms, basements, and barns until they decided to leave.

The villagers of Qapusi gave them food, water, and a mobile phone. An elderly woman cleaned and bound Smail's wounds, to little avail as they continued to bleed intermittently. The group walked by night, evading Islamic State patrols and checkpoints.

"Anyway, we arrived at a shrine called Rashaka Shrine. We entered the shrine and walked for about one hundred yards. I was physically very exhausted and mentally very sad for my family, son, daughter, father, sister, village, and people. I could not walk anymore. My friends tried to help me. One of them was injured in the arm. The other one said, 'Hold on to my neck.' We continued walking while I was behind my friend and holding his neck as a support. After a moment of walking, I told them, 'I cannot walk anymore. You go and rescue yourself.' They left me and walked towards the north. I was left there alone in Rashaka. I slept on a rock until morning. When I woke up in the morning, I saw cars, trucks, and belongings of people who were displaced.

"I was very thirsty and started searching the trucks and cars. One of the cars had a radiator. I walked towards it with hope, but it did not contain a drop of water. I started feeling dizzy, and I did not find a drop of water anywhere. Then, I found a hose in one of the cars, and I started using it to pump water out of car radiator tanks. I was pumping out the water and using a piece of cloth as a strainer to clean it up for drinking. This helped me survive there for two days.

"On the night of the third day, I started walking towards the north. I continued walking until I could not anymore. When I became too tired, I laid down on a rock and slept until around dawn.

"On the next day, I resumed walking until I arrived at an area called Tapshi or Havshi or something like that. I suddenly heard dogs barking and sheep bleating. I saw a shepherd down in a valley and, from a distance, I shouted, 'Hey, shepherd. I am very thirsty and hungry. I am injured. I hope you can provide me some water and help me.'"

"The shepherd responded, 'Where are you? I can't see you.'"

"I said, 'Just look up towards the north and you will see me.'"

"He tried to come towards me but he could not climb up the valley. I was also not able to go down. So, I walked northwards to the end of the valley and reached Chilmera. When I arrived there, I met some three or four youngsters. They asked me, 'Are you the person who was calling?' I said, 'Yes.'

"They gave me water, some bread, a tomato, and a few pinches of salt. They called their friends to get someone to help me. They said, 'You go up this way. We have our work to do.'

"I walked up that way for a while and found another group of youngsters. They had a donkey with them. They got me on that donkey; two of them were holding me, one on the right and the other on the left, and the third one was walking in the front. They took me to the PKK.

"When I went to the PKK, they gave me first aid. They brought some liquid Dettol to clean up my wound. After totally cleansing the wound, they said, 'Stay here for now until evening. We will take you to a hospital in Syria.'"

"I became very scared and said, 'But Syria is also under Daesh.'"

"'They said, 'No, that hospital is under our control.'

"Before the YPG was able to take me to their hospital in Syria, the security forces of Sinjar (the Peshmerga) found out about me and came to take me. By God, the YPG became very discontent, but the security forces insisted to take me. They said, 'We have sent a car of food supplies to our colleagues. We will take you back with us as soon as the car arrives here.' The security forces of Sinjar cleaned my wound and gave me some food. And when the car arrived, they drove me into Syria and back to Zakho's public hospital on August 24, 2014."

Islamic State took Ali Smail's wife and two daughters to Tal Afar, then to Raqqa, the Islamic State base in Syria, and after that to Aleppo where they were sold as sex slaves, according to Yazidi women who escaped and made their way back to Kurdistan.

Ali Smail lost more than a hundred blood relatives, who were either murdered or kidnapped. He lost his wife, his son, his two daughters, and his father, two sisters, and nieces and nephews.

◆━◆

On the day of the massacre, phone calls from the villagers suddenly stopped. Outsiders knew something terrible had happened, so Yazidi fighters drove into the village to investigate and found it deserted. Islamic State were gone but had left their mark.

"There were corpses everywhere," Yazidi fighter Mohsen Tawwal told Agence France-Presse. "We were too late."

When Islamic State moved the captive women out of Kocho, they stopped briefly and executed those who were not young. In late 2014, in the village of Solagh, just north of Sinjar city, near the grounds of the Sinjar Technical Institute, soldiers discovered human remains lying amid muddy, ripped scarfs, blouses, and skirts. The clothes belonged to the mothers and grandmothers and great-grandmothers of Kocho. Investigators believe there are around seventy-five bodies buried beneath the depression in the ground there.

Murad Ismail, one of the translators who had worked with Hadi Pir and Khalad Smoqi, told the *Washington Post* he believed Islamic State was emboldened to murder the Kocho villagers after President Obama called off the evacuation plan and announced the Yazidis were out of danger. "ISIS," he said, "did not kill people when there was air coverage. They started killing after Obama said the siege was over. They got the message and decided to kill these people."

In the name of the Sinjar Crisis Management Team, the still angry men emailed a press release to various media organizations a few days later.

"Our group has provided the United States government, the Iraqi Government and the Kurdish Regional Government with solid information about the situation in the village. We expressed in numerous calls and reports the urgency of action to free these villagers, but all parties failed to take any action and inaction resulted in this massacre," it said.

While the massacre at Kocho might have been prevented, the successful engagement of the federal bureaucracy and military machinery was sustainable only for a short time. Motivated by human decency, the United States bombed Islamic State positions, forcing them to pull back from the mountain, while the YPG opened the corridor to safety through which thousands of Yazidis walked. Unfortunately, for the people of Kocho, the world exhaled one day too early.

"The fact of the matter is that on the day Kocho happened, we wanted a flyover, buzz those ISIS fighters and scare them . . . , but the fact of the matter is the Pentagon does its thing and State does its thing and the White House does its thing and Homeland Security another thing," Padgett explained. "And they are often extremely hard to bring together. It was simply we had ten days, maybe eight days to get a handle on Kocho, and when it happened, we were surprised. The other thing is that sometimes we are asked to do things that are incredibly hard to do."

The morning of the Kocho massacre, Dakhil Shammo was at his desk in Voice of America's Kurdish Service newsroom when a Yazidi friend called from Germany.

"It's all over," the friend said. "In Kocho, it's happened. The worst thing. The men are dead and the women are gone, taken."

Dakhil asked a few questions to confirm the information. He called sources at the Kurdish Regional Government, and then he called Vian Dakhil. She confirmed the deaths and kidnappings of the Kocho Yazidis. He wrote up his copy and sent it to the Kurdish editor. He turned off his computer, straightened his papers, and went home.

Unlike the translators, Dakhil Shammo feels no bitterness toward the United States about the massacre in Kocho.

"The Americans," he said, "simply didn't understand the nature of Islamic State at that time. Remember this was a few days before the beheadings began and the release of the horrible videos. [On August 20, 2014, Islamic State released a video showing the beheading of American journalist James Foley.] I think the Americans thought ISIS would leave, withdraw like a real army, and not waste time killing people. I mean, particularly the American army, they are trained to be logical and efficient. Who among us can really think like a monster? Or understand the logic of a monster?"

Epilogue

AFTER SEVERAL WEEKS AT THE MOTEL, HADI PIR, KHALAF SMOQI, AND the other former translators wound down their operation and returned home to Nebraska or Texas. Pir was thrilled to reunite with his wife and two young daughters, the second born just a few weeks before he left for Washington.

Politicized and energized by their success, the men founded Yazda, an international nonprofit organization that advocates on behalf of the Yazidi population.

"(It) strives to bring justice, sustenance, healing and rejuvenation to Yazidis who have suffered under or are affected by the genocidal campaign against their people by the so-called Islamic State (IS) as well as the IS campaign against other vulnerable ethno-religious minorities," their website states.

With offices in Dohuk and Baghdad, in Iraq, as well as the United States, United Kingdom, Sweden, Germany, and Australia, Yazda supports humanitarian assistance for the hundreds of thousands of internally displaced Yazidis in Iraq. In October of 2014, Yazda began a documentation project to collect and organize a database of the testimonies of the survivors of the Yazidi genocide. It opened a documentation center in 2016. The organization also opened a small women's center in Dohuk that has provided psychological counseling for more than a thousand Yazidi survivors of sexual assault and abuse.

Just as important as their advocacy work, however, these former translators and new Americans brought to the US government a new paradigm for international crisis intelligence gathering. Due to the extraordinary leaps in communications technology, any American can reach out to relatives or friends at the site of an international catastrophe and provide crucial details to save lives.

In the spring of 2016, Yazda recruited Amal Clooney as its legal counsel. She also acts with Yazda on behalf of United Nations Goodwill Ambassador Nadia Murad, a survivor of the Yazidi Genocide and the author of the recently published book *The Last Girl: My Story of Captivity, and My Fight Against the Islamic State.* The Iraqi government nominated Nadia Murad for the Nobel Peace Prize in 2016.

Speaking to the United Nations Office on Drugs and Crime in the autumn of 2016, Clooney characterized the genocide, rape, and trafficking of women by Islamic State as a "bureaucracy of evil on an industrial scale." She went on to describe a slave market for Yazidi women that exists on Facebook and other websites that is still active today.

Clooney spearheaded a year-long advocacy campaign that led the United Nations Security Council to unanimously adopt Resolution 2370 in September of 2017. The resolution calls for the establishment of a United Nations investigative team to secure evidence of Islamic State crimes against humanity, including genocide, sexual enslavement and trafficking, recruitment of child soldiers, and additional war crimes.

In May of 2017, the Lincoln, Nebraska, Yazidis opened their first Yazidi Cultural Center on North 27th Street amid the Vietnamese and Mexican restaurants that line the multicultural avenue. With the help of Yazda, and a small grant from the US Department of Health and Human Services, the center will provide opportunities for newly arrived Yazidis to learn English, get driver's licenses, and work toward citizenship.

Standing under an American flag, Pir explained the center was not just for Yazidi Americans. "Part of our job will be teaching other people about the Yazidis, where they came from and their background, I think bringing people together is going to be unique," he said.

Vian Dakhil remains in Iraq's parliament. She has been recognized and honored for her efforts to bring the plight of the Yazidi people to the international community. She is the winner of the 2014 Anna Politkovskaya Award for her "courage to become the voice of the Yazidi community and by her determination to campaign for the protection of all Yazidi and other Iraqi women under ISIS, despite the danger she is facing as a Yazidi woman politician opposed to ISIS." She was named Woman of the Year in 2015 with an honorary prize for Arabic achievements in Dubai. She received the Bruno Kreisky Prize for Services to Human Rights in Vienna in June 2015, and in February 2016, Dakhil was awarded the Geneva Summit Prize for Human Rights in Geneva.

In September of 2017, Dakhil told a French reporter she planned to push for the creation of a separate territory for Iraq's minorities in Ninewah alongside Kurdistan. She has been adamant that Yazidis will not leave the IDP camps as long as they must live alongside Iraqi Arabs.

"I don't think that the Arabs will live there after Sinjar will be liberated. Because all the Yazidis know that the Arabs in Sinjar helped ISIS to take over the region. These Arabs have also killed many Yazidi men, children and abducted girls and women. The Yazidis don't trust them anymore. The Yazidis have suffered too much. They cannot live with the Arabs in one village anymore. The pain for those who lost a mother, father, wife, husband or child will be too great. The situation could escalate into Yazidis and Arabs killing each other once ISIS is gone. The Arabs must leave Sinjar," she said.

In February of 2017, Dakhil was invited to the United States to receive the Lantos Human Rights Prize at the US Capitol. The prize is awarded by the foundation named after Holocaust survivor and late senator Tom Lantos, a fierce champion of human rights while serving in the US Congress.

Unfortunately, Dakhil was forbidden to enter the country that wished to honor her due to the Trump Administration's ninety-day ban on travelers from Iraq and six other majority Muslim nations. Her predicament was front page news, a startling example of the unintended consequences of the executive order.

"It adds a deep level of irony that this award is given in the name of my late father, the only Holocaust survivor ever to be elected to Congress," said Katrina Lantos Swett, the president of the foundation. "He exemplified how America is strengthened and enriched by immigrants and refugees. I assure you he is turning in his grave at this."

The State Department, deeply embarrassed, bestowed an exemption, allowing her to fly to the United States the day before she was due at the Capitol Hill ceremony.

"Mr. President Donald Trump, Iraq is not a terrorist," she said as she stood before a crowd of more than one hundred, including politicians and diplomats at the Rayburn House Office Building. "Iraqis are not terrorists. We are friends and allies. And we are looking forward to have exceptional relations with all people, especially with the United States of America."

She drew a standing ovation. The next day, a three-judge panel in the Ninth Circuit Court of Appeals ruled against reinstating the then-blocked travel ban.

Col. Charles "Chuck" Freeman and his family live in Raleigh, North Carolina, where he serves as the senior army advisor to the Army National Guard, First Army East. In the spring of 2017, while stationed at Fort Benning, Georgia, Freeman and I discussed the role the US Army should play in humanitarian crises like Sinjar. In a voice filled with conviction, he said, "If you're going to say 'not my job' shame on you. No one else can do it. For a sense of duty to be truly consistent with our message of democracy and our ability to govern and our way of life, it is only natural to use our resources in this way."

Sarah Sewall is now the Speyer Family Foundation Distinguished Scholar at the Henry A. Kissinger Center for Global Affairs, a Washington, DC, think tank. An expert in international security and civilian protection, Sewall researches systems that will incorporate civilian protection into official institutions and practices. She is the author of *Chasing Success: Air Force Efforts to Reduce Civilian Harm.*

Sewall, a graduate of Oxford and Harvard, submitted her letter of resignation to the Trump Administration on inauguration day as was required for all presidential appointment positions. Unusually, every resignation was accepted.

"All officers understand that the President may choose to replace them at any time. These officers have served admirably and well. Their departure offers a moment to consider their accomplishments and thank them for their service. These are the patterns and rhythms of the career service," said a White House official at the time.

Eleven months later, just ten of the top forty-four political positions in the State Department had been filled, and Secretary of State Rex Tillerson failed to nominate candidates for the remainder.

On March 3, 2017, the State Department released its congressionally mandated annual reports on the state of human rights across the globe. For decades, the release had been accompanied by a televised press briefing from senior officials as well as introductory remarks from the secretary of state. During this release, however, Tillerson chose not to hold the event.

On May 3, 2017, Tillerson addressed his agency's employees to outline the goals of the Trump Administration's America First policy. He explained that American foreign policy should separate values such as freedom and human dignity and "the way people are treated" from its other policies. He cautioned, "If we condition too heavily that others must adopt this value that we've come to over a long history of our own, it really creates obstacles to our ability to advance our national security interests [and] our economic interests."

By December of 2017, the entire senior management level of the State Department had resigned or retired. All were career Foreign Service officers who had served under Republican and Democratic administrations.

"It's the single biggest simultaneous departure of institutional memory that anyone can remember, and that's incredibly difficult to replicate," David Wade, former chief of staff under Secretary of State John Kerry told the *Washington Post*.

Following through on their America First policy, the White House had hosted Egyptian president Abdel Fattah el-Sisi, who, human rights watchers allege, is holding more than forty thousand political prisoners, congratulated Turkey's autocratic president Recep Tayyip Erdoğan on winning a referendum that reversed the course of democracy, and invited Philippine president Rodrigo Duterte to the White House. Duterte explained his brutal war on drugs when he said in 2016, "Hitler massacred three million Jews. Now, there are three million drug addicts. I'd be happy to slaughter them."

Joseph Pennington, a career member of the Senior Foreign Service at the State Department, became deputy assistant secretary for Iraq, in the Bureau of Near Eastern Affairs, in December 2015.

Civil servant Douglas Padgett and Foreign Service officer Leanne Cannon continue their employment at the State Department. Alan Dwyer continues to work for USAID.

Thomas Melia, a political appointee, was among those who submitted their resignations from USAID on inauguration day. It was accepted.

Dakhil Shammo continues to work at the Voice of America.

In June of 2017, the executive director of the Institute for International Law and Human Rights, William "Spence" Spencer, released *Crossroads: The Future of Iraq's Minorities After ISIS*, a report based on his organization's extensive fieldwork in post-conflict Ninewah Province and other parts of Iraq. "With the impending liberation of Iraqi territory from ISIS forces, minority populations continue to diminish," said Spencer. "All indications point to a post-ISIS phase that could be just as—or even more dangerous to minority groups than the ISIS occupation. Many leaders fear that the 'peace' could be more perilous for their survival as communities than the war."

The report made sixty-three specific recommendations to the Iraqi Federal Government, the Kurdistan Regional Government, and the international community to address the concerns of Iraq's minority populations. None of them have been adopted.

Iraqi prime minister Haider Abadi declared the city of Mosul liberated from Islamic State on July 10, 2017, following a military campaign launched by combined Iraqi and Peshmerga forces and supported by American airstrikes. The battle for Mosul killed between nine thousand and eleven thousand civilians, according to an Associated Press estimation.

If Mosul's deliverance back to Iraq marked the beginning of the fall of the barbarous Islamic State, one hopes that the collapse of the Islamic State stronghold of Raqqa, Syria, in October of 2017, marks the end of their claims of a caliphate. Islamic State is not, however, dead. Its adherents are simply scattered.

In September of 2017, the Kurdistan leader Masoud Barzani foolishly insisted on holding an independence referendum despite protestations from the governments of the United States, Turkey, Iran, and, of course, Iraq, who all feared the results would lead to regional destabilization. Approximately 93 percent of Kurdish voters favored independence, but the referendum backfired on Barzani. Prime Minister Abadi angrily sent Iraqi troops into the oil-rich region of Kirkuk, just south of the Kurdistan capital of Erbil, and took the city from Kurdish forces. Turkey and Iran squeezed Kurdistan economically, and the United States condemned the effort.

"The vote and the results lack legitimacy and we continue to support a united, federal, democratic and prosperous Iraq," Secretary of State Rex Tillerson said in a statement.

Seizing the momentum, Prime Minister Abadi sent Iraqi troops into Ninewah and, as part of his offensive to punish the Kurds for the referendum, took back the territory, including the ruins of Sinjar city.

Humiliated by his miscalculation, Masoud Barzani resigned November 1, 2017. His nephew now runs Kurdistan.

Among the stories of suffering and resilience, hubris and heroism, arrogance and naivete that drove the events of August 2014, perhaps the most extraordinary outcome of the Yazidi genocide emerged from a decision by the Baba Sheik, the Yazidi highest spiritual leader, just two weeks after the invasion. The eighty-year-old man, who had devoted his life to maintaining conservative customs, decided to jettison centuries of tradition and issued a religious edict clarifying that women who had been raped by Islamic State men remain Yazidi and should be welcomed back into their faith and community.

In earlier times, Yazidis did not distinguish between rape and consensual sex; sexual contact with a non-Yazidi resulted in immediate expulsion from the faith and life-long ostracization.

The Baba Sheik and other religious leaders developed a new rebirth or baptism ceremony at the Yazidi Temple in Lalish, outside of Dohuk, for women who had been sexually violated. The ceremony, performed at the sacred fountain inside the holy caves of Lalish, can be repeated as many times as the affected woman wishes. The Baba Sheik's decision has been critical for the survivors' attempts to heal as they reintegrate into their society. Yazidi men, both young and old, have also embraced the new ceremony, an extraordinary change in sexual attitudes brought on by the tragedy their mothers, wives, and daughters endured.

Resources

Author Interviews
    Lt. Gen. John Michael Bednarek (ret.)

    Leanne Cannon

    Vian Dakhil

    Alan Dwyer

    Congressman Jeff Fortenberry (R-NE)

    Col. Charles "Chuck" Freeman

    Hussein Khalaf

    Thomas Melia

    Alifa Murad

        Daoud—her older son

        Nadira—Daoud's wife

        Jamil—her younger son

        Haval—her grandson

        Vian—her granddaughter

    Douglas Padgett

    Joseph Pennington

    Hadi Pir

Ben Rhodes

Sarah Sewall

Dakhil Shammo

Hakim Shammo

Morbad Shammo

Abbas Kheder Silo

Andrew Slater

Ali Abbas Smail

Khalaf Smoqi

William "Spence" Spencer

Barakat Sulu

Books

Acikyildiz, Birgul. *The Yazidis: The History of a Community, Culture and Religion*. London: I.B. Taurus & Co. Ltd., 2014.

Chandrasekaran, Rajiv. *Imperial Life in the Emerald City: Inside Iraq's Green Zone*. New York: Alfred A. Knopf, 2006.

Fishman, Brian H. *The Master Plan: ISIS, al-Qaeda, and the Jihadi Strategy for Final Victory*. New Haven: Yale University Press, 2016.

Khalaf, Farida, and Andrea C. Hoffman. *The Girl Who Escaped ISIS: This Is My Story*. New York: Atria Books, 2016.

Layard, Austen Henry. *Nineveh and Its Remains: With an Account of a Visit to the Chaldean Christians of Kurdistan, and the Yezidis, or Devil-Worshippers; and an Enquiry into the Manners and Arts of the Ancient Assyrians*, Vol. II. London: John Murray, Albemarle Street, 1848.

Marr, Phoebe. *The Modern History of Iraq*, Third Edition. Boulder, CO: Westview Press, 2012.

McCants, William. *The ISIS Apocalypse*. New York: St. Martin's Press, 2015.

Murad, Nadia. *The Last Girl: My Story of Captivity, and My Fight Against the Islamic State*. New York: Tim Duggan Books, 2017.

Otten, Cathy. *With Ash on Their Faces*. New York: OR Books, 2017.

Packer, George. *Assassins Gate: America in Iraq*. New York: Farrar, Straus & Giroux, 2005.

Power, Samantha. *"A Problem from Hell": America and the Age of Genocide*. New York: Basic Books, 2002.

Ricks, Thomas E. *Fiasco: The American Military Adventure in Iraq, 2003–2005*. New York: Penguin Group, 2006.

Warrick, Joby. *Black Flags: The Rise of ISIS*. New York: Doubleday, 2015.

Reports

Amnesty International Annual Report 2014/2015.

Battle For Sinjar, Iraq, US Army Threat Action Report, Rick Burns, April 2016.

Between the Milestones: The State of Iraq's Minorities Since the Fall of Mosul, February 2015. Institute for International Law and Human Rights, Minority Rights Group International, No Peace Without Justice, Unrepresented Nations and Peoples Organization.

Children and Armed Conflict, Report of the Secretary-General, General Assembly Security Council 5 June 2015.

Country Reports on Terrorism (Iraq), US Department of State, April 2015.

Crossroads: The Future of Iraq's Minorities After ISIS, June 2017. Institute for International Law and Human Rights, Minority Rights Group International, No Peace Without Justice, Unrepresented Nations and Peoples Organization.

Ethnic Cleansing on a Historic Scale: Islamic State's Systematic Targeting of Minorities in Northern Iraq, Amnesty International, September 2014.

Human Rights Facts and Figures, Amnesty International, 2014.

International Religious Freedom Report 2014, Bureau of Democracy, Human Rights and Labor, US Department of State.

Iraq—Complex Emergency, Fact Sheet #5 Fiscal Year 2014, USAID, September 11, 2014.

No Way Home: Iraq's Minorities on the Verge of Disappearance, July 2016. Institute for International Law and Human Rights, Minority Rights Group International, No Peace Without Justice, Unrepresented Nations and Peoples Organization.

Our Generation Is Gone: The Islamic States Targeting of Iraqi Minorities in Ninewa, Naomi Kikoler, United States Holocaust Memorial Museum, The Simon-Skjodt Center for the Prevention of Genocide, November 2015.

Report on the Protection of Civilians in Armed Conflict in Iraq, 6 July–10 September 2014. United Nations Assistance for Iraq (UNAMI), Office of the United Nations High Commissioner for Human Rights (OHCRC)

Report on the Protection of Civilians in Armed Conflict in Iraq, 11 September–10 December 2014. United Nations Assistance for Iraq (UNAMI), Office of the United Nations High Commissioner for Human Rights (OHCRC)

Report on the Protection of Civilians in Armed Conflict in Iraq, 11 December–30 April 2015. United Nations Assistance for Iraq (UNAMI), Office of the United Nations High Commissioner for Human Rights (OHCRC)

Report on the Protection of Civilians in Armed Conflict in Iraq, 1 May–31 October 2015. United Nations Assistance for Iraq (UNAMI), Office of the United Nations High Commissioner for Human Rights (OHCRC)

"They Came to Destroy": ISIS Crimes Against the Yazidis, United Nations Human Rights Council, June 2016.

Articles

Tim Arango, "Iraq Agrees to Help Kurds Battle Sunni Extremists," *New York Times*, August 4, 2014.

Avi Asher-Schapiro, "Who Are the Yazidis, the Ancient, Persecuted Religious Minority Struggling to Survive in Iraq?" *National Geographic News*, August 11, 2014.

Peter Baker, "Obama, with Reluctance, Returns to Action in Iraq," *New York Times,* August 7, 2014.

Peter J. Boyer, "Downfall," *New Yorker*, August 20, 2006.

St. John Barned-Smith, "Yazidis in U.S. Traumatized by Crisis in Iraq," *Houston Chronicle,* November 27, 2014.

Aaron Bowles, "Tragedy Interrupts Lives of U.S. Yazidis," *Nebraska Mosaic,* November 7, 2014.

Sara Brown, "President Obama Arrives Saturday for Fifth Summer Vacation on the Vineyard," *Vineyard Gazette,* August 7, 2014.

———, "Presidential Vacation Is a Mix of Work and Down Time, *Vineyard Gazette*, August 14, 2014.

Helene Cooper and Michael Shear, "Militants Siege on Mountain in Iraq Is Over, Pentagon Says," *New York Times*, August 13, 2014.

Michael C. Duke, "Houstonians Aid Victims of ISIS Attacks," *Jewish Herald-Voice*, December 18, 2014.

Charlotte Florance, Anthony Kim and Brett Schaeffer, "Setting a Course for Obama's Rudderless Africa Policy," The Heritage Foundation, August 2014.

Susannah George, "Saving Sinjar from a Super 8," *Foreign Policy*, August 19, 2014.

Michael R. Gordon and Alan Cowell, "U.S. Signals Willingness to Help New Iraqi Government," *New York Times,* August 12, 2014.

Beth Griffin, "Iraq's Humanitarian Need Is So Vast It's Shocking, Says Speaker," *Catholic News Service,* May 16, 2016.

Syeda Hasan, "Iraqi Father Shares Experiences as Refugee in Houston," *Houston Public Media*, December 8, 2015.

Abigal Haworth, "'If They Capture Me, They Will Execute Me at Once'": Meet the Iraqi Woman Standing Up to ISIS," *Marie Claire,* January 13, 2015.

Olivia Hull, "In Briefing, White House Details Working Vacation," *Vineyard Gazette*, August 13, 2014.

Ali Khedery, "Why We Stuck with Maliki and Lost Iraq," *Washington Post,* July 3, 2014.

Sheshadri Kunar, "Houstonians Unite to Help the Cause of Yazidis," India-Herald.com, December 7, 2014.

Mark Landler, Alissa J. Rubin, Mark Mazzetti and Helen Cooper, "Fear of 'Another Benghazi' Drove White House to Airstrikes in Iraq," *New York Times,* August 8, 2014.

Tom Miles, "U.N. Says Some Rescued from Iraqi Mountain Siege, 200,000 Flee," Reuters, August 7, 2014.

George Packer, "A Friend Flees the Horror of ISIS," *New Yorker,* August 6, 2014.

———, "In Iraq, That Kind of Phone Call Tells You a Lot," *New Yorker*, August 7, 2014.

———, "Common Enemy," *New Yorker,* August 25, 2014.

————, "ISIS for Us Too," *New Yorker,* October 15, 2014.

Ahmed Rasheed and Isra Al-Rubei'I "Kurds, Islamic State Clash Near Kurdish Regional Capital," Reuters, August 6, 2014.

Amanda J. Rothschild, "ISIS and Genocide: How the United States Talks About Atrocities," *Foreign Affairs*, February 28, 2016.

Alissa Rubin, "On a Helicopter, Going Down: Inside a Lethal Crash in Iraq," *New York Times,* August 16, 2014.

David Samuels, "The Aspiring Novelist Who Became Obama's Foreign Policy Guru," *New York Times Magazine*, May 5, 2016.

Ken Silverstein, "The Stolen War," *New Republic,* August 22, 2016.

Liz Sly, "Islamic State Fighters Kill Dozens of Yazidi Villagers," *Washington Post*, August 16, 2014.

Sade Strehike, "How These Yazidi Girls Are Finding Hope After Escaping ISIS Sex Slavery," *Teen Vogue*, May 24, 2016.

ACKNOWLEDGMENTS

Special thanks to Stephanie Slewka, Leah Spiro, Eric Phillips, Andrew Slater, Ibrahim Elias, Joe Halderman, and Eileen Shand.

INDEX